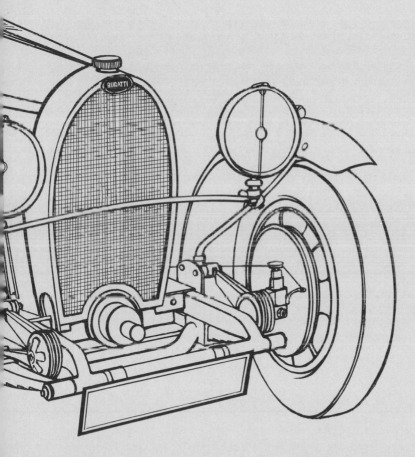

BUGATTI

Distributed in the U.S.A. by
MOTORBOOKS INTERNATIONAL
PUBLISHERS & WHOLESALERS INC.
3501 Hennepin Avenue South
Minneapolis
Minnesota 55408, U.S.A.

G T Foulis & Co Ltd
Sparkford
Yeovil
Somerset

BUGATTI – le pur-sang des automobiles

H. G. Conway

First published 1963
Reprinted October 1964
Reprinted October 1965
Second edition September 1968
Third edition May 1974

© H. G. Conway 1963, 1968, 1974

ISBN 0 85429 158 X

Library of Congress Catalog Card Number 74-80931

PRINTED IN ENGLAND BY J H HAYNES AND COMPANY LIMITED,
SPARKFORD, YEOVIL, SOMERSET.

4

Contents

PART II – HISTORICAL INFORMATION

PART III – BUGATTI MISCELLANY

PART IV – THE BUGATTI CLUBS

APPENDICES

Foreword to the Third Edition

SINCE THIS BOOK WAS WRITTEN IN 1962–3 INTEREST IN Bugatti as a make of car and in Ettore Bugatti as a man has continued to grow; indeed, judging by market values, the Art World has rediscovered the furniture of his father, Carlo, and the animal sculpture of his brother Rembrandt. And if we may object to the cinema and television picturing the death of Isadora Duncan in a Bugatti (it was an Amilcar!), we do not object to our favourite motor-car being used on posters all over Britain, in several press advertisements or in T.V. commercials.

All this has unhappily contributed to the escalation of values of Bugatti cars by a factor of at least ten over the recent ten years or so. A G.P. Bugatti advertised in 1960 for £500 would bring at least £15,000 today. And the chances of finding a Brescia for £250 as the Introduction suggests have long since receded. So today it is very difficult for the young, impecunious enthusiast to acquire a Bugatti which in many ways is a pity, although we are now seeing many of the cars in the hands of the sons of the fathers which helps to keep the cars in use and on the road.

This revised edition now includes reference to new information which research has made available. This has been incorporated into a new edition in such a way as to minimise re-setting the original type which unhappily was destroyed by flood, and by making full use of modern offset-printing techniques.

Publication of the original edition made many friendships which have been rich in sources of further data. M'lle L'Ebé Bugatti and her sister Lidia, the Contesse de Boigne (unhappily

7

no longer with us), have been very helpful. Elizabeth Junek, the most distinguished of all women Bugatti drivers, has provided historical material of the utmost value relating to the origins of the Type 35 Grand Prix Bugatti. And many others too numerous to mention have helped, and in particular have pointed out mistakes or anomalies. Thus if we cannot claim to be fully error-free we can at least say that many people as well as the author have tried to keep this book as accurate and objective as possible.

Foreword to the Original Edition

THE ORIGINAL BUGATTI BOOK, PUBLISHED IN 1954, WAS THE outcome of a great deal of hard work on the text and illustrations by C. W. P. Hampton. Hampton was, at the time, Editor of *Bugantics*, the journal of the Bugatti Owners' Club of England, a weekend labour of love if ever there was one. While the Book, no doubt, had a few editorial faults, it was packed with information and is probably the principal reason for the resurgence of interest in the marque Bugatti. It has been bedside reading all over the world.

In this revised or new Bugatti Book another Author has been roped in with the full support of the previous ones, and some effort has been made to eliminate editorial faults, and to correct a few errors which have come to light. The main change has been to separate information on each model or type, so that data can be found more quickly. The bulk of the text on the various cars is thus new and wherever possible more contemporary comment has been added from appropriate motor journals. Additional historical data have been included on early cars and Bugatti aeroengines, and a selection of extracts from folklore is included for interest, and perhaps enjoyment.

The Register of Bugatti cars, now totalling about 1,100 cars, has been published by the Bugatti Owners' Club and makes an excellent companion to this volume.

Special thanks must be made to a number of people who have contributed: to Mr C. W. P. Hampton for much help with many things; to him and Mr J. Lemon Burton for checking the technical data on each model; to Mr F. Seyfried at Molsheim; Mr Tim Cree; Mr J. de Dobbeleer, Mr S. Falise and Mr E. J. de Flines; Mr O. A. Phillips in Los Angeles; Mr D. Park in Chicago and others in the United States. To Mr W. F. Bradley in Roquebrune who discussed Ettore at length, and to Mr Jules Goux, Dr Espanet and Mr Maurice Phillipe who corresponded freely. And finally Mr T. A. S. O. Mathieson in Portugal has been an unfailing source of historical detail.

Acknowledgements must be gratefully made to the Editors of the *Autocar*, *The Motor* and *Motor Sport* for permission to reproduce text and illustrations from early copies of these two journals. As far as possible the source of illustrations and short extracts has been given, as well as the authorship of various contributions.

Introduction

THE CASUAL READER OR THE IDLY CURIOUS MAY WELL ASK – WHAT is there about a Bugatti that makes so many people dream of owning one, and a surprising number actually succeeding in doing so? There are many cars offering far better performance than a Type 57, many vintage racing cars that can outdo the normal G.P. Bugatti, and perhaps other more sensible playthings than a 1923 Brescia for the impecunious enthusiast; but once 'bitten with the Bug.' the Bugattiste regards his car beyond all others, and even after selling it (usually in a fit of irritation) remains faithful to its memory until the end!

The success of the original Bugatti Book and the appearance of a new one result from the widespread interest in the car, its creator Ettore Bugatti and all aspects of its 'folklore'. Mystique is perhaps the word for the Bugatti atmosphere which Ettore Bugatti managed to create not latterly, not even during his successful racing period in the 1920s, but even before the first world war in his first years at Molsheim, 1910–14. There are keen Bugatti Clubs in England, U.S.A., Germany and Holland and exclusive cliques in Sweden, Switzerland, Belgium and Argentina. There is now a splendid Bugatti Club in France actively promoting the interest in Bugatti and enthusiasts in Canada, Spain, India, Malaya, Brazil, Japan, South Africa and great enthusiasm in Australia and New Zealand.

The reasons for the interest are perhaps not difficult to understand. Many men, and a few women, love cars, particularly sports cars; many would enjoy owning a vintage car in this day and age of Detroit and Coventry and cars built (admittedly well) for driving and not to tinker with. And again many would enjoy searching for, buying, let it be hoped cheaply, and restor-

11

ing more or less completely an old quality car. And a Bugatti is a good choice for a variety of reasons. Almost all models have a good or at least interesting performance – they are enjoyable to drive. Indeed there is a wide variety of models to choose from and a remaining population of at least 1,800 cars. Spare parts can be obtained, either new or second hand, from several sources; advice is freely obtainable from the Works, the Clubs or from other owners; technical data, some in considerable detail, have been published on most models; the construction of the cars while complicated in some respects is surprisingly straightforward in most; accessibility is good. The car was made and finished well when it was new and calls for craftsmanship and care now – it is thus satisfying to work on. And if you think your car is well restored there is always another chap (perhaps with more money to spend than you) with a better one, to keep you humble. And this leads on to what may be the most important point – there is a Bugatti for every pocket, from the one with $10,000 to buy a near-perfect 57SC to the young student's with £250 in it to acquire a Brescia or a tattered Type 30*. And even when you have spent two years rebuilding your car, you can still start to do it again three or four years later when the engine shows signs of wear and usage has taken off some paint and brought a few cracks to the bodywork. And who knows: you may find an unknown, unregistered car to add to the Register or even to buy yourself at a sensible price!

And a final word to the Wives! A Bugatti may keep him occupied at weekends, make him late for meals, even absorb cash you might otherwise have been allowed to get your hands on! But it keeps him out of pubs (except when it's running), he'll never have time for other girls, is fun also for young Jimmy (or will be when he comes along), and you'll be real proud when he, eventually, takes you out in it. So if he's a President of a Bank let him have that brand new 46S in a packing case in Marseilles if he wants to, and if you've only been married six months let him keep his cambox and blower beside the bed in your one room apartment if he says he has to.

* This was correct in 1968!

PART I

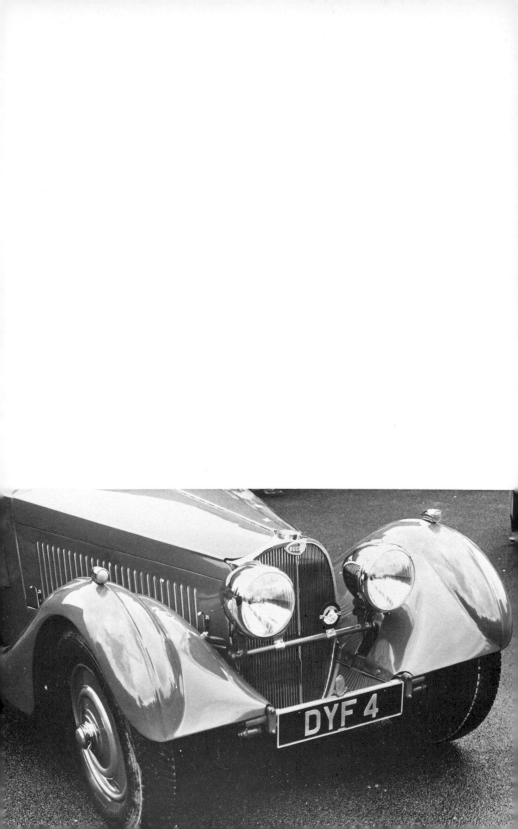

THE BUGATTI CARS

Bugatti types

ETTORE BUGATTI'S LIFE AS AN AUTOMOBILE DESIGNER CAN CON-
veniently be divided into three eras: the period during which he
acted as a consulting designer (1898–1909); the main period at
Molsheim* when he became a manufacturer in his own right
(1910–39), interrupted during the first world war by a period of
activity on aeroengines in Paris, and a final phase during and
after the second world war when a variety of products and a
few unsuccessful cars were produced. In this section we are
concerned mainly with the Molsheim produced cars (Types 13
to 59), but we include some information on the later, twilight
era cars (T.60 to T.102); pre-Molsheim cars and aeroengines are
dealt with later in the book.

The cars are described under type numbers, but a few preliminary remarks are appropriate for the benefit of those who
are not familiar with Bugatti cars or not well versed in the jargon
of the Bugatti enthusiast. All Molsheim cars had either 4, 8 or
16 cylinders; no 6 cylinder Bugatti car was ever sold, if indeed
produced. All Molsheim-sold cars had overhead camshafts, and
from 1912–13 the characteristic reversed quarter-elliptic rear
springs. Although the front suspension of the F.W.D. Type 53
was independent, all other models had conventional fore-and-aft
laminated front springs. Light alloy castings were used extensively in the cars from the earliest model. Even to the
inexperienced eye a similarity between the earliest and the latest
model can be seen, particularly in the detail design of the rear
axle or the gearboxes. Other items such as the steering box or
clutch were used on several models over a period of twenty

---

* Pronounced 'Moltz-heim', rhyming with 'waltz-time'.

17

years. The predominant nut up to about 1924 was 6 mm, thereafter until 1939 (and later) a 7 mm nut with a milled hexagon to give an integral washer, a simple enough detail but one which epitomizes Bugatti's approach to automobile design – quality as he judged it (and he often judged wrongly), uncompromised by manufacturing costs.

The type numbers of Bugatti cars continue to interest many people, particularly as some numbers are missing or their identification is in dispute. The tabulation lists the correct identifications with all the authority that Bugatti Works catalogues and research by the author in the drawing office library at Molsheim can justify.* The existing drawing office records are incomplete, the official records having suffered during the Occupation and memories are faulty, so a few gaps are still present; one thing is clear however, that Bugatti used type numbers as much to identify chassis length as anything else in early days.

Bugatti type numbers

TYPE	BRIEF DESCRIPTION OF MODELS
13	8 or 16 valve, 4 cylinder cars with 2 metre wheelbase, pre- and post-first world war up to 1924 or 1925.
15	8 valve, 4 cylinder cars with 2·4 m wheelbase, 1911–13.
17	8 valve, 4 cylinder cars with 2·55 m wheelbase, 1911–13.
22	8 or 16 valve, 4 cylinder or 8 cylinder cars with wheelbase 2·4 m, 1914 to about 1925 (8 cylinder from about 1923).
23	8 or 16 valve, 4 cylinder or 8 cylinder cars with wheelbase 2·55 m, 1914 to about 1925 (8 cylinder from about 1923).
25	Equivalent to 4 cylinder T.22 with 68 mm × 108 mm engine; believed not made.
26	As Type 25, but equivalent to T.23.
27	1·5 litre, 16 valve 1914 design eventually replaced by Brescia, and not put into production.
28	Prototype 3 litre car, 69 to 70 mm × 100 mm with 2 speed gearbox in rear axle (1921 Paris and Olympia Show model); contemporary press descriptions quote the bore as 69 mm, but a later catalogue quotes 70 mm.

* The factory originally used the designation 607 for the 8 valve cars, 617 for the first series 16 valve and 619 for the early Brescia type, although the usual numbering system was used in catalogues. We also have contemporary evidence that the factory used the prefix 6 on most of the models, e.g. 635, 639 etc. for T.35, T.39. This may mean that 617 and 619 would eventually have been known as Types 17 and 19. It has not been possible to find the reasons for this alternative system.

29	The description may be correct for a short wheelbase Type 30, and might apply to the 2 litre 1922 Strasbourg racer.
30/30A	2 litre, 8 cylinder passenger car; 30A later reinforced frame series.
32	2 litre, 'tank' racer.
33	2 litre prototype with gearbox in rear axle, not put into production (replaced by T.38).
34	2 bank, 16 cylinder geared aeroengine (1923 version).

35   8 cylinder G.P. racers, 2 or 2·3 litre

- 35   2 litre unblown.
- 35A 2 litre unblown imitation.
- 35B 2·3 litre blown.
- 35C 2 litre blown.
- 35T 2·3 litre unblown.

36	8 cylinder, single seat racer.
37	1·5 litre, 4 cylinder G.P. racer; 37 unblown, 37A blown.
38	8 cylinder, 2 litre passenger car; 38 unblown, 38A blown.
39	8 cylinder G.P. racer, 1·5 litre; 39 unblown, 39A blown.
40	4 cylinder, 1·5 litre passenger car.
40A	4 cylinder, 1·65 litre roadster.
41	The Royale, luxury car. 8 cylinder, 24 valve, 12,766 cc.
42	Large marine engine.
43	2·3 litre, 8 cylinder Grand Sport, T.35B engine.
43A	As T.43 with roadster body (but see also page 168).
44	3 litre passenger car.
45	16 cylinder racer, 3·8 litre.
46/46S	5 litre coach; 46 unblown, 46S blown.
47	16 cylinder, 3 litre Grand Sport version of T.45, 4 seat body.
48	Engine only, used on Peugeot 201X.
49	3·3 litre passenger car.
50/50T	4·9 litre supercharged sports passenger car; 50T was Tourisme model.
50B	Racing version of T.50 engine used in various chassis in the 1930s
51	8 cylinder supercharged double ohc racer; 51, 2·3 litre, 51A, 1·5 litre; 2 litre version sometimes known as 51C, but this may be unofficial.
52	Baby electric children's G.P. car.
53	4-wheel drive, 4·9 litre racer.
54	4·9 litre G.P. racer.
55	2·3 litre Super Sport with double ohc T.51 engine.
56	Bugatti's personal electric runabout.

57/57S   3·3 litre double ohc passenger car
57C/57SC

- 57   unblown.
- 57S   dry sump, sports version.
- 57C   supercharged 57.
- 57SC supercharged 57S.

TYPE	BRIEF DESCRIPTION OF MODELS
57S 40 ⎫ 57S 45 ⎭	Grand Sport racer, 57S chassis with T.50B engine; S40, 4 litre probably not made, S45 4·5 litre.
57G	Streamlined 'tank' racer.
58	Diesel engine.
59	3·3 litre G.P. racer.
60	4·1 litre, 4 valve 86 mm × 88 mm aeroengine, not made.
64	1940 version of T.57, prototype only, 4·5 litre.
68	370 cc 1942 baby car, prototype only.
73A/73C	1·5 litre passenger car (1945); 73C G.P. version not produced.
101/101C	1950 version of T.57 or T.64; 101 unblown, 101C blown.
102	1·6 litre supercharged sports car not produced.

This leaves the following early numbers unidentified; 14, 16, 18–21, 24 and 31. Numbers 22 and 23 were definitely allotted in 1913–14; Bugatti may have had plans filling the remaining numbers between 13 and 22. Numbers 12, 18 or 19 could be logical for the 5 litre, 4 cylinder racing cars of the Black Bess or Garros type. Type 10 is believed to be the original 8 valve prototype. Factory part lists quote type numbers: some Brescia engine part numbers still show number 27; Types 29 and 30 are quoted together, no doubt indicating that the T.29 was intended to be a short wheelbase version of the T.30, although for a short while the works catalogue showed 8 cylinder Types 22 and 23 as indicated above – Type 29 presumably being equivalent to the 8 cylinder Type 23.

One Deutz chassis, designed by Bugatti about 1908 was known as Type 21, but it is not known if this is a coincidence. It is out of chronological order if a Bugatti number.

Further note: many French registered 16 valve cars are listed as Type 27, but this has not been noted in any other country. Although the first Type 30 chassis used the normal light Type 22–23 frame, this was soon strengthened and the car then known strictly as Type 30A, but not as such in any catalogue.

NAME PLATES

1a. . . . *earlier type seen as late as 1929 or 30.*

3. *16 valve car number on crankcase boss.*

1b. . . . *later type.*

4. *Chassis number on crankcase.*

2. **Bugatti coachwork plate.**

5. *Typical engine number on crankcase arm.*

MOLSHEIM NUMBERS

21

6. *The original prototype of 'Petit Pur-Sang'. This interesting photograph has been extracted from the personal records of the late Mr Ernest Friderich, and is better than the heavily touched up print showing Ettore in the same car, which has often been published.*

7. *Gaillon 1910.*
Darritchon in the paddock.
　　　(*photo: T. A. S. O. Mathieson*)

Note regarding car serial numbers

With few recorded exceptions, the Molsheim factory made use of a consistent series of chassis numbers, in numerical sequence, for early cars and with the type number followed by the car number from about 1928 onwards.

Eight valve cars were numbered from 361 in 1910 to 843 in 1920 with a few gaps. The 16 valve plain bearing cars were from 900 to 1611 although this last number is in some doubt, since the Crossley-Bugattis were reputed to be 1600 to 1625; the 16 valve ball bearing Brescia cars started at 1612 (or thereabouts) up to about 2900. The engine number in all these cases rarely appears as a separate entry, although invariably found stamped on many engine parts.

Eight cylinder chassis (Types 30, 35 and 39) began at No. 4000 and finished before 5000, but engine numbers were stamped on the crankcase, generally a 1, 2 or 3 figure number. The earliest T.35 is number 4323, and there is a small batch of T.39 cars in the 4800 series. The cars as they left the factory often had the engine number repeated on gearbox and axles or a number close to it.

Types 37, 38, 40 and later have chassis numbers beginning with the type number, e.g. 37204. In the case of rare cars, the numbers do not necessarily start with 100, e.g. 47155 and 47156. These are one or two obscure numbers such as 222570 which cannot be explained, and 27150 which may have been a prototype Type 27 chassis, or even a 'misprint'. After much research work, it can be said that no authentic case of duplicate numbers has been found, most anomalies being explained by restamping for special reasons. Many countries in Europe had been bedevilled during the war with fuel rationing, customs barriers and triptyques; at least several of the number anomalies encountered are known to have resulted from efforts to overcome these difficulties. At least one car entered a country as a Type 43 and left as a Type 44!

Bugatti name plates

Before the first world war, when Molsheim was part of Germany, the car name plate read:

Ettore Bugatti
Molsheim i/Els (for Elsass)
Wagon No., Motor P.S., Gew kg

In the immediate post-war period the name plates read:

Ettore Bugatti
Molsheim Alsace
Chassis, Moteur, Poids

In at least one case the engine power is quoted as 'hp'.

Finally the plates read:

Ettore Bugatti
Molsheim, Bas-Rhin
Chassis, Moteur, Poids,

the motor horsepower being given in the normal French 'cv'.

Radiator Badges

The early pre-1914 badges were attached to the radiators by rivets. Post-war the badge was retained by a brass plate with a flanged edge which was pressed over the edges of the badge. The earliest badges had round dots at the elliptical periphery, but post-war up to about 1928 the dots were square, subsequently reverting to round. The precise reason for, and date of the change have not been discovered. The badge itself is elliptical, 90 mm × 45 mm, and slightly domed; it is enamelled in three colours in Strasbourg by a firm who still supplies them to the Bugatti Owners' Club.

24

8 valve pre-1914 cars

ALTHOUGH CALLED TYPE 13 IN EARLY LITERATURE INCLUDING the Bugatti Book, the 8 valve, 4 cylinder pre-1914 car is correctly known as Type 13, 15, 17, 22 or 23, depending on the wheelbase and other chassis details. As only six or seven cars are known to exist, the precise type number may not be of great consequence, and Type 13 can conveniently be used for all versions.

Bugatti had built the prototype car (page 335) in 1908-9 in his own home while working with the Deutz Company (see page 338). He set up his own Company at Molsheim at Christmas 1909; according to E. Friderich (see page 351) five cars were produced in 1910 and 75 in 1911. Certainly the car was an immediate success and created considerable interest in the various hill-climbs and competitions in which the model was entered. In *The Motor* of 4 October 1910, Mr W. F. Bradley wrote, describing the Gaillon Hill-Climb: 'Second place (in the small Touring Class) went to Darritchon, on a little car known as the Bugatti, its time being 1 min 3⅜ sec. The dainty-looking little vehicle, having more the appearance of a toy than a real motorcar, is a product of Alsace. It is declared to have a motor of 65 mm by 110 mm, nominally rated at 5½ hp. The car only weighs 770 lb.' In fact, the car was 65 mm × 100 mm, at least according to the 1910 catalogue for the car and to *La Vie Automobile* of 10 December 1910. Curiously enough Bradley persisted in this error (if it was an error) in subsequent references in the following month and in his description of the 1911 French Grand Prix where Friderich came in 2nd to Heméry in a Fiat In view of the Works catalogue and Friderich's own story it is only reasonable to assume that 100 mm was correct.

25

On 1 November 1910, *The Motor* carried what must have been the first substantial description of a Molsheim car (by W. F. Bradley); this is worth reproducing in full:

A NEW LIGHT CAR

First Description of Another Light Car having Some Striking and Original Features

Those who estimate motorcar value on seating capacity and superficial area are not likely to become purchasers of the Bugatti. The designer of this little car, indeed, has made no attempt to compete with the low-priced popular models already on the market, the price of the Bugatti being higher than any other car of equal horse-power offered to the public. The reason is that the new production stands in a class by itself. M. Bugatti, an Alsatian designer with a high reputation in German factories, has sought to produce what may be termed the motorcar pony, but a pony that is fit to stand comparison with the most costly product of the best factories, and able, notwithstanding its small size and low power, to hold its own in the matter of speed with any touring car built.

The Bugatti is a two-seater with a wheelbase of 79 in., track 45 in., and weight 660 lb (at the Gaillon hill-climb its official weight with two passengers, full touring equipment, and all tanks filled was 1,168 lb). It is driven by a little four-cylinder monobloc motor, rated by its owner as $5\frac{1}{2}$ hp, the cylinder dimensions of which are 65 mm by 110 mm bore and stroke, bringing it into the three-guineas class under English taxation. The motor is a remarkably fine piece of work and abounds in interesting features. The single bloc of cylinders is mounted on an aluminium crankcase attached direct to the frame members. The crankshaft is carried in two large ball bearings, and the pistons are of steel. The valves are mounted in the cylinder head, with vertical stems, and are operated by a single overhead camshaft, obtaining its motion from the mainshaft by means of a vertical spindle and bevel gearing. All the valve mechanism is enclosed in a bronze housing bolted to the head of the cylinders and carrying the camshaft bearings and the bevel gear of the vertical spindle. On the left-hand side is the exhaust, there being a separate port for each cylinder, the four arms being united to a single exhaust pipe, from whence the gas is passed to the exhaust box. On the opposite side is the carburetter, from which two arms of the inlet pipe are connected up to the manifold cast with the cylinders. The high-tension magneto and water pump are carried across the front of the motor, the two being worked off one shaft. The cooling system comprises a neat honeycomb type of radiator.

26

It is evident that the 5½ hp rating given by the constructor is only nominal, for this motor is designed to run normally at 2,300 rpm, and may be accelerated to 3,000 rpm without danger. Such a high engine speed has only been made possible by the use of the finest and most expensive metals and the greatest care in construction. This explains why the car, which, at first sight, and from an external examination only, might be thought to belong to the £120 class, cannot be put on the market at less than £300.

Lubricating oil and petrol are carried in two tanks built into the dash, the petrol being under pressure from the exhaust, although the flow is assured by gravity, except on hills. For this reason there is no hand pump for getting up pressure. That it is not needed is shown by the fact that, during a trial run, we were able to start up by 'tickling' the carburetter, and opened the tank three times for the Paris octroi examination without a stoppage of the motor.

A multiple disc clutch composed of cast iron and steel plates is used, and the four-speed gearbox is bolted direct to the frame members, the box itself being of such small area that it is difficult to believe that it contains three sets of sliding gears with four speeds and a reverse. If the gearbox is compact, it is difficult to find a suitable expression for the gate, which is of such dimensions that it could, without difficulty, be placed in the waistcoat pocket. The two levers are mounted within the frame, the change-speed lever being on the same transverse tube as the brake lever, and has a total lateral movement of not more than 2 in., and a fore-and-aft motion for the various gear positions of not more than 1½ in. The whole combination occupies less space than on any car we know of, and certainly holds the record in this respect.

From the gearbox the drive is taken to the rear axle by means of a propeller shaft, with a universal joint at each end. The torque stay is a steel stamping of channel section and triangular shape, with its forward end mounted in a spring-fed ball-and-socket joint attached to the gearbox. The chassis is of steel channel section, narrowed in front and raised at the rear. Motor control is by means of an accelerator pedal on the extreme right, and ignition advance fixed on the steering wheel, the column of which is very much inclined.

The claims made by the makers of this little car are that it can hold its own in the matter of speed with any pure touring car on the road. Frankly, we did not think it could, for, notwithstanding a surprising demonstration at the recent Gaillon hill-climb, the impression remained that these small, light cars generally hold the road badly at high speeds. Fully equipped, with mudguards, lamps, horn and all touring accessories, we made a demonstration run in the suburbs of Paris. After being warned twice that speeding was not allowed in the straight avenues of the Bois de Boulogne, we got into the suburbs of Paris, where fate sent us a big Benz Prince Henry car of 105 mm by 165 mm bore and stroke, four passengers, and pure touring body to act as pacemaker. The Prince Henry car was driven by a hot-blooded sportsman in his teens, who went over the most abominable roads between Paris and Saint-Germain at a speed only limited by the ability of his car to hold the road. Yet it was possible with the little Bugatti to keep within 50 yards of his pointed stern all the way, and with less discomfort than is experienced in many cars three times the size and weight. The makers guarantee that the little Bugatti can maintain 60 miles an hour, and, although no opportunity was given of definitely proving this, the claim seems to be well founded.

In city traffic the little car proved as remarkable as on the straight-away stretches, for, being small, it could worm through where larger cars were held up; it was wonderfully quick in acceleration, absolutely silent on low gears, while the changes were made without a click being heard. As a runabout, where one or more large cars are kept, the little Bugatti seems ideal, for, on the open roads, it is as fast as any of the larger mounts, and in traffic it is quicker because of its handiness. Its upkeep is a mere trifle, the tyres being 650 mm by 65 mm, and the fuel consumption works out at 40 miles to the gallon.

It is stated that, for the Paris Salon, another model will be shown with the same motor and a longer chassis, carrying a four-passenger body. This larger chassis will also be fitted with an original body of exceptionally low weight, aluminium construction, and providing four comfortable seats.

The Bugatti is produced at Molsheim, in Alsace, the selling agency being in the hands of M. Huet, 3 Square Saint-Ferdinand, Paris.

It is interesting to note that this description, the article in *La Vie Automobile* and the 1912 Works catalogue all refer to the crankshafts being carried on ball bearings (the 1910 and 1911 catalogues do not mention the point). It seems possible that some of the early engines may have used ball bearings but all known cars have plain bearings. Although Bugatti catalogues are known to contain errors, an error on the crankshaft mounting seems strange. The serial numbers of these early cars have been identified from the original factory record book which has recently turned up, but no details of crank mounting are given. The first car is 361 while car 365 (now in a Prague museum) was delivered to Prince Hohenlohe and later to Patocha in Bohemia. Chassis 366 (now in the Hampton Collection) is recorded as delivered on 13th December, 1910 to the Paris agent Huet as a 'Berline Exposition'.

Friderich quotes the Molsheim output as five cars in 1910, 75 in 1911 and 175 in 1913, total 255. The last serial number recorded in 1914 is 706 making the pre-war total 345. Post-war production of 8 valve cars (serial numbers 760 to 843) resumed in 1919 and finished a year later.

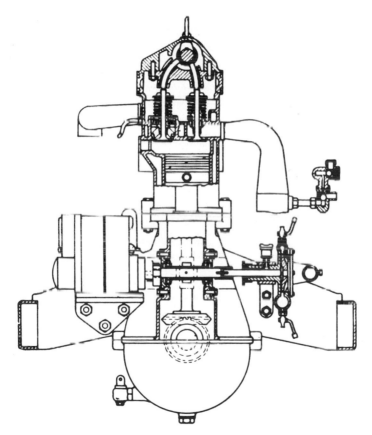

Fig. 1. *The eight valve engine in section.*
(Automobile Engineer)

Precise clarification of the various type numbers which properly apply to 8 valve cars can be obtained by reference to the various contemporary catalogues issued by Bugatti in French and German versions. An unusually complete collection of these early catalogues still survives.

1910 Catalogue. This is undoubtedly the first catalogue issued from Molsheim and contains a statement signed by Ettore and dated 1 December 1910. It quotes from Bradley's article of a few weeks earlier. The catalogue was no doubt issued for the Paris Motor Show held in that month, and where Bugatti had a stand.

1911 Catalogue – Paris Edition. (There is a reference to the Gaillon Hill-Climb which was in October 1910, thus the catalogue was probably printed in early 1911.)

Both catalogues are similar in textual content. No type number is used, but the cars shown are of the 8 valve 65 mm × 100 mm type, with dash mounted oil tank and drip feed lubrication, the oil tank being pressurized from the exhaust. The radiator is of the square-cut type (as on the Hampton car); springs are half-elliptic all round; there is no reference to the crankshaft.

SUMMARIZED DATA

	2 Seater	*4 Seater*
Track – front, metres	1·17	1·17
Track – rear, metres	1·10	1·10
Wheelbase, metres	2·0	2·4
Tyre size – front, mm	650 × 65	700 × 65
Tyre size – rear, mm	650 × 65	700 × 85
Rear springs	Single	Double

BERLINE POUR LA VILLE ET LE TOURISME, 5/15 HP. 4 CYL.
(Trois Places et Strapontin, conduite intérieure)

8. *A 1910 Berline by Gangloff of Colmar, shown at the 1910 Paris Automobile Show. This car is reported to have been used by the Bugatti family. In 1910 it was driven from Strasbourg to Paris at an average speed of 34 mph (The Motor, 20 December 1910). This is now known to be the actual Hampton car; Colonel Dawson, who bought the car from Ettore about 1912, stated in a letter to Mr G. P. Sanders 'when I bought the chassis she had been humping a 4-seater limousine which Ettore built for himself'.*

Exhaust of the Bugatti motor.   *Carburetter side of Bugatti motor.*

9. *The engine of the original series 8 valve type.*

(The Motor, *1 November, 1910*)

10. *Overhead camshaft engine of the Hampton car, 65 mm × 100 mm, 1,327 cc. The camshaft is lubricated by wicks in an oil bath and the crankshaft has three plain bearings, main and big ends being bronze. Splash lubrication comes from a drip feed tank on the dashboard.*

11. *The engine of an early 1912 car 'discovered' in France in 1972, and in the owner's hands since 1927 when he bought it from M. Huet.*

HAMPTON CAR 366   12. . . . *front view, the radiator badge is riveted in place.*
13. . . . *the rear, showing the half-elliptic rear springs, and wooden spoked wheels.*

14. CAR 365. *The oldest known Molsheim Bugatti.*

(*photo: Courtesy Director Prague Technical Museum*)

15. *De Vizcaya senior at Mont Ventoux 6 August 1911. In spite of a puncture and breaking a spring, he finished 1st in the 65 mm Touring class, with a climb in 30 min 55 sec.*

(*photo: T. A. S. O. Mathieson*)

1912 Catalogue. (Contains race results up to July 1912 and thus was probably printed in October 1912.)

Type numbers 13, 15 and 17 are referred to. The engine appears (indeed must have been) identical with the 1911 version (i.e. drip lubricated). The crankshaft in this catalogue is described as being carried on two ball bearings, rear springs are still half-elliptic, the radiator square-cut.

The distinguishing feature between Types 13, 15 and 17 is only in the wheelbase (apart from tyre sizes and number of springs). This system of numbering with respect to chassis length becomes a feature of the catalogues from now on.

SUMMARIZED DATA

	Type 13	Type 15	Type 17
Track, metres	1·15	1·15	1·15
Wheelbase, metres	2·0	2·4	2·55
Tyre size, mm	650 × 65	700 × 85	700 × 85
Rear springs	Single	(not stated but double implied)	Double

The race results in the catalogue start with references to first places in the meeting at La Sarthe, 4 and 5 June 1911. If Bugatti had had earlier wins surely he would have claimed them. The Sarthe Meeting is described briefly by W. F. Bradley in *The Motor* of 13 June 1911, the drivers of the Bugattis being given as Gilbert and de Vizcaya (no doubt the father of the later race driving brothers, and the banker who assisted Ettore to set up at Molsheim). However, in the same publication, 30 May, Bugatti (driver unspecified) had a second place at the Limonest Hill-Climb, and in the earlier issue of 31 January are illustrated two cars which competed in a rally, Paris to Monte Carlo, M. M. Huet, the French Agent, finishing in 51¾ hours.

1913–14 Catalogue (Contains race results up to October 1913 and thus was probably printed in December 1913.) Type numbers 13, 22 and 23 are referred to. The engine of the Type 13 is stated to be as previously supplied, and it continues to have half-elliptic rear springs. There is a reference to a second oil tank on the dash drawing oil from the cambox, with a hand pump to pump it back to the cambox again. The Types 22 and 23 are, however, fitted with an improved 8 valve engine. At the front of the cambox is now a casing containing a suction piston pump and a two-piston delivery pump feeding the crankcase pipes. The catalogue refers to the camshaft being carried on three ball bearings, but this feature is not found in any other description and may not have been put into regular production, although car No. 446 is so equipped. (The 5 litre Black Bess has this mounting however, the cams being separately pinned to a central shaft.) We see now for the first time the Bugatti reversed quarter-

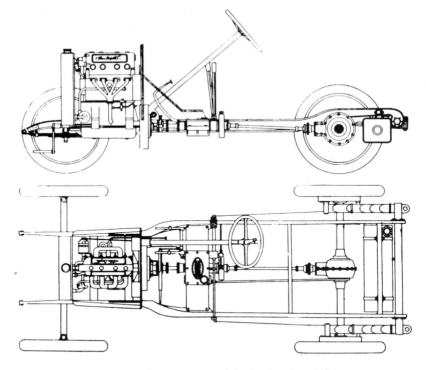

Fig. 2. *General arrangement of the 8 valve 65 × 100 mm chassis of 1913–14.*

(Automobile Engineer)

36

elliptic rear springs and the oval radiator, at this time with an aspect ratio of 6:5 and a curved bottom, and used on all three types. The type numbers 22 and 23 take the place of Types 15 and 17 of the previous year.

SUMMARIZED DATA

	Type 13	Type 22	Type 23
Track, metres	1·15	1·15	1·15
Wheelbase, metres	2·0	2·4	2·55
Tyre size, mm	650 (× 65?)	700 × 85	710 × 90
Rear springs	$\frac{1}{2}$ ell.	Rev. $\frac{1}{4}$ ell.	Rev. $\frac{1}{4}$ ell.

No reference is made in this catalogue to the 16 valve models which were first produced in 1914. Bugatti's practice no doubt would have been to refer to them in the 1914–1915 catalogue had there been one.

There is an excellent description with line drawings of the 8 valve 1913–1914 model in the *Automobile Engineer* of June 1917, some of the text and illustrations being similar to that in the sister journal, the *Autocar*, of 19 May 1917. Details of the construction are worth quoting from the former journal:

The camshaft and valve tappets are arranged in a separate housing or casing, covering the entire cylinder block. The inlet valve is in a detachable seating, but the exhaust valve seats direct in the cylinder head. It will be noticed that it has been made slightly smaller than the inlet in order that it may be assembled or removed through the inlet valve port.

A novel feature of the valve actuation is the employment of curved tappets. These are of oblong section about $\frac{1}{2}$ in. by $\frac{5}{16}$ in., and are so curved as to bring them up to a suitable position under the camshaft for actuation. The manufacturing difficulties involved in this construction have been very simply overcome by arranging the tappets in pairs, each in a bronze casing into which white metal is run with the tappets in position, so that the necessary accurately fitting curved slot is obtained without machining. As the valve tappet guide casings carrying the white metal are cast in pairs and bolted to the main camshaft housing, they are handy for the white metalling process. The tappets themselves are probably machined in the lathe in the form of complete rings and split off into sectors of the required length.

No fan is embodied, but the usual centrifugal pump is used for water circulation, and is driven by a horizontal spindle running across the front of the engine, this spindle being skew gear driven off the vertical camshaft driving spindle. The opposite end of the water pump spindle is employed for the magneto drive, the magneto being bracketed off the front engine foot. The exhaust manifold is arranged on the (left) side of the engine, and has a separate branch from each port direct to the main pipe. A hot air intake is cored completely through the cylinder block, a funnel being fitted on the near side close to the exhaust branch, so that hot air for the carburettor is taken from the exhaust pipe and through the cylinder block to the inlet branch, located on the (right) side of the engine. A simple two-way inlet branch of polished gunmetal is attached by a couple of two-bolt flanges to the cylinder block casting, and a Zenith carburettor is the standard arrangement. At the front of the camshaft housing is what may best be described as the lubrication box. This box is formed in the housing casting, and carries oil pumps that are actuated by a small cross-shaft fitted with a worm wheel and driven thereby from a worm on an extension of the camshaft. Three pumps actually are employed—a main oil suction pump drawing from the oil reservoir tank on the dashboard and delivering into the oil box, and two subsidiary pumps that deliver from the box by separate pipes to the two divisions of the crankcase sump. The oil pumps and their actuation form quite a complicated little piece of mechanism. The main suction pump, in addition to its reciprocating motion, has a partially rotating movement by means of which its inlet and exhaust ports are operated. The movement is effected by arranging a fork at the actuating end of the pump plunger, the fork encircling the main pump actuating cam, and being fitted with pins that engage with cam-shaped grooves on the camface, so giving the double movement to the plunger.

The two subsidiary pumps are located at the other end of the pump driving spindle and are similarly cam-driven. They are, however, separately adjustable as regards the stroke, so that the amount of oil delivered to the crankcase may be regulated. All excess of oil delivered to the lubrication or pump box runs through an overflow port direct into the camshaft housing, so lubricating the bearings and tappets; from the housing it drains back to the oil reservoir on the dashboard.

The lubrication process in itself is fairly simple, as the main bearings and big ends are oiled by splash, the connecting rods being fitted with large dippers for this purpose. On the particular engine

38

we inspected bronze bearings were used throughout, and although we understand that white metal is used on the later models, the bronze bearings were found to be perfectly satisfactory in use. It is stated that the bronze is of some special anti-friction composition [lead bronze].

The crankshaft is of special steel hardened and ground, and the following are a few approximate dimensions: the crankshaft pins and journals are $1\frac{3}{16}$ in. in diameter, while the main central webs between the crankcase are of $1\frac{11}{32}$ in. by $1\frac{3}{8}$ in. section, and the smaller webs near to the bearings are $1\frac{3}{8}$ in. by $\frac{11}{16}$ in. section.

An interesting type of plate clutch is employed in which ten plates are used – five in the clutch casing and five on the shaft; they are alternately cast iron and hardened steel, ground on the working faces. The cast iron plates are those on the clutch body, and the hardened steel those on the shaft. The frictional surfaces are $5\frac{3}{4}$ in. mean diameter and about $\frac{1}{2}$ in. wide. The cast iron plates are $\frac{1}{4}$ in. thick and the hardened steel ones about $\frac{1}{8}$ in.

The clutch housing is solid with the flywheel, and the cast iron plates that it contains are all strung together by bolts running right through the assembly from end to end, and upon these bolts the clutch plates slide and the drive is taken. This arrangement is probably quite permissible in connection with comparatively small powers, and, of course, does away with the costly machining of the clutch body and plates which is unavoidable when the plates are arranged in slots in the usual manner. The plates on the clutch spindle have square holes that are a sliding fit on a square on the spindle.

The clutch spring pressure and actuation is arranged on the usual principle, in which the plates are normally all pressed together, and are moved apart during disengagement. Two actuating pins project into the casing from the outside for this purpose. These pins are actuated by small bell cranks fitted with adjustable screws and pivoted upon the clutch end cover; they are linked together, and are further linked to a rocking cross bar across the chassis that maintains a pressure on the linkage, and thus on the pins by reason of a long coil spring to which one end of the rocking bar is attached. To disengage the clutch the rocking lever is pulled back against the spring. By careful attention to the arrangement of the leverages an extremely soft actuation has been arrived at, little greater pressure being needed to declutch than is necessary for the accelerator on the average car, which is an extremely commendable feature. The clutch pedal is consequently extremely light in design, the pedal pad being a small circular disc about $1\frac{1}{2}$ in. in diameter.

The gear box, which gives four speeds and a reverse, is of very

39

simple design, with short stiff shafts and adequate bearing and oil retaining arrangements. The box is bolted to the main frame by two arms that are the complete width of the box, and consequently of very stiff action. This strength is very necessary by reason of the fact that the gear box forms a frame cross member. The universal joint behind the gear box is a small Spicer joint enclosed by the usual spherical casing, and an open propellor-shaft runs down to a similar joint on the rear axle. The sliding movement of the propellor-shaft is arranged for in the top joint behind the gear box. A pressed steel torque tube reinforced with ash is employed. The usual spring, cup and ball bracket is employed for torque rod anchorage, this being bolted to the rear end of the gear box.

The rear axle casing is built up of steel tubes and aluminium castings. The differential box, which is split vertically, is of aluminium, with flanges at each side that bolt to flanges brazed to the mild steel tube; one of the bolting-up flanges is employed for attaching the torque rod. The axle tubes carry also the shackle brackets for the rear springs; these brackets are in one piece with the brake drum covers, and the brake drum covers are of steel plate, stiff enough to take the brake cam actuating spindles and the pull therefrom. The brake cam bearings are attached by riveting and welding, which is rather daring, but appears to have been satisfactory. The side brakes are the usual solid cam-expanded shoe type, and are of cast iron working on the orthodox mild steel drum of the road wheels.

The front axle is a light stamping, much on the usual lines, and the frame of the car has only one cross member which is located towards the rear, and is employed to carry the petrol tank. At the extreme rear of the chassis there is a cross tube to which is attached the special reversed fixed cantilever springs that form the rear suspension. This system of reversing the cantilever spring formed the subject of one of Ettore Bugatti's patents, and on its introduction it was claimed by him, and hailed by many others, as a momentous discovery. In actual fact it makes no difference whatever to the suspension which way the spring be attached, although it is admitted that superficially it would appear that the Bugatti arrangement gives some advantage over the orthodox scheme. The front suspension consists of the usual semi-elliptic springs.

The side brakes are actuated by cable that runs right through the gear box selector tube. Thus a single length of cable actuates both brakes and also provides the necessary compensation. Although a simple and economical arrangement, the system is open to the various objections associated with the use of cable for such purposes, chief of which is the necessity for continual adjustments owing to stretch. The steering is quite an orthodox worm and sector type, and the steering link and other connections are the usual ball and socket. A spark control is fitted at the steering wheel. The petrol tank, as will be seen from the drawings, is located at the rear of the chassis, and pressure is provided by an exhaust by-pass valve on the exhaust branch.

Road test

An early road test of the 8 valve car was published in the *Automotor Journal* (*The Auto*) of 7 February 1914. Echoing the sentiments of the modern Bugattiste, the article says:

What more can a man want of his car in the way of speed than to be able to hold practically any other car that he may meet outside of Brooklands? And if with it he has what the racing car has not— docility and comfort—he would indeed be hard to please if he were not satisfied.

And these are the qualities that the little 8 hp Bugatti is able to offer him, together with all the refinement in control, steering and suspension that is possessed by the most thoroughbred of modern automobiles—and with the very minimum of charges on his pocket.

We ourselves had heard much of the capabilities of the Bugatti, and fully expected it to be something above the ordinary, but we confess we were quite unprepared for the extraordinary amount of power with which the talented Italian designer had imbued the engine.

And whence comes the surprising power? Certainly not from the cylinder dimensions, which are but 65 by 100 mm bore and stroke, and certainly not from sheer excess of revolutions, for there are many car engines on the market that are capable of turning over at the 2,000 rpm that constitutes the normal rate of the Bugatti. Rather, we should think, is the source to be found in the valves and valve mechanism, the shape of the combustion chambers and the un-restricted flow of the intake and exhaust gases. But whatever the reason may be, the one fact stands out beyond question that the power is there, and this coupled with the efficient transmission and light total weight gives the car a speed which is only comparable with that usually associated with those of at least three times its nominal power.

Power and speed, however, are not the only, nor perhaps the most important, attributes of a car intended for use on the road. To find favour with the *cognoscenti*, it must also possess a sense of liveliness, a delicacy in responding to control movement, as ease of gear change, powerful and smooth brakes – in short, it must possess 'refinement'. It is in the possession of this complex quality that the Bugatti ceases to be a light car. Though light in weight and running expenses, no steps whatever have been taken to simplify the design with the aim of keeping down first cost; in fact, it is an automobile of the highest grade, *en miniature*.

Both the steering and suspension were everything to be desired. In respect to the first of these, we need only say that we have never handled a steering wheel that called for less physical exertion. The rear suspension is somewhat uncommon in form, its peculiar design perhaps accounting for its undoubted excellence.

16. *1913 model. An original illustration of the long wheelbase version.*
(The Light Car, *14 January 1914*)

17. *This 1914 model was bought by Mr (later Sir) Henry Royce during the 1914-18 War when he wanted a car with some 'fizz'. It did not please him much and he sold it to Lord Cholmondeley who took this picture.*

18. *This rare 5 litre model left the factory in 1913 in the possession of the famous aviator Roland Garros. It was the only Molsheim model to have chain drive.*

BLACK BESS

19. *The engine. 5 litre, 100 × 160 mm, 3 bearing crank, single overhead camshaft and 3 valves per cylinder. The magneto timing is varied by a sliding helical keyway arrangement subsequently used on the aeroengine and the G.P. cars. The spare engine still available (No. 471) differs in having a large oil tank cast into the left-hand engine bearers on the crankcase. This feature is also seen in the illustrations of the engine in* The Motor, *1 August 1911, although the caption wrongly describes it as the smaller baby car.*

20. *The rocker gear. Note the rollers on the rockers and the built-up camshaft.*

21. *The young Ettore stands beside one of the 5 litre cars, with his friend the Duke of Bavaria at the wheel. The purpose of the frame in front of the radiator is obscure—surely not for luggage!*

22. *Another version of the 5 litre car, with cowled radiator and curious tail.* (photo: T. A. S. O. Mathieson)

23. *Ettore with Ernest Friderich at the wheel of the shaft-driven 1914 Indianapolis car—a rare photograph from Mr C. Lytle.*

24. *This recently discovered photograph shows a coupé body on what appears to be the Indianapolis shaft-drive chassis.*

BLACK BESS: 4 cylinder 5 litre

IN 1912 BUGATTI BEGAN TO BUILD A BATCH OF 4 CYLINDER, 5 LITRE cars for competition work. Many years later he claimed to have built the first of the model in 1908, which may have been an error (he was working for Deutz at the time —see page 332).* In January 1913 he wrote to his friend Dr Espanet: 'I have under construction several cars of 100 mm bore and 160 stroke. I would wish to have you as a customer for one of these cars if that would interest you and I would make you very special terms. . . . I would like very much to have you visit and I hope that you will profit from the trip of Mr Garros to come with him.'

Roland Garros was a well-known pioneer French aviator who was killed on operations at the end of the first world war. The car that Garros himself b ght has had a remarkable history and seems today as good as ever; in 1935 Ettore wrote to Colonel Giles who had just bought the car, saying 'I only built a few cars of this type, which was one of the best models of the period. The first one was built in 1908 and the first sale was in 1912. The car which you have was delivered 18 September 1913 to my late regretted friend Garros, the airman of whom you have doubtless heard. This car has therefore an historical interest'. The Bugatti family had a chassis (now in the Schlumpf collection), but the Hampton car (No. 474) is otherwise unique. Its full story is told by Mr W. Boddy on pp. 222–6 of *The Bugatti Book*.

The 5 litre car had a bore and stroke of 100 mm × 160 mm, a single overhead camshaft and, unlike the 8 and 16 valve cars (and earlier Deutz designs), had rockers between cams and

---

* The 1910 catalogue illustrates a car similar in general appearance to the 5 litre car, with chain drive and the *oval* radiator. The chassis seems pretty clearly to be Deutz and the car is labelled 'La Bugatti type Prince Henri – 1910'. This may have been the 1908 version.

valves. The general layout however is similar to the smaller engine, with a vertical bevel shaft driving the camshaft and a cross-shaft driving the pump and magneto. Bugatti now introduced the 3 valve arrangement (two inlet valves and one exhaust) which he was to use on the aeroengine and all 8 cylinder designs until Type 50, almost twenty years later. A distinguishing feature on this model (which does not appear to have a type number) was the use of chain drive for the rear wheels. It seems likely that the assemblies used were at least similar to those of the Deutz car, which Bugatti had designed a year or two previously.

Bugatti, as Friderich recounts later in this book, drove one of these cars in various races, winning his class at Mont Ventoux in 1912. Ernest Friderich himself drove one of the cars in the 1914 Indianapolis race, although the car had the chain drive replaced with a normal rear axle and the stroke increased to 180 mm. A bearing failure in this unit eliminated the car, which for a short while is said to have lain second in the race.

Another chain driven car went to the U.S.A. for the 1915 race, entered under the nationality of Germany (America not being at war at that time), and now with a stroke of 150 mm to bring the engine capacity below the 300 cu in. limits specified. The standard dimension 100 × 160 mm would give 306 cu in. (These dimensions are from *Automotive Industries*, 6 May 1915, which quotes 3·9 in. × 5·9 in.; it is assumed that 3·9 was really 3·94 or 100 mm.) The car was entered by C. W. Fuller of Pawtucket, Rhode Island, with B. Oldfield as the nominated driver. He did not like the car, not being able to better 81·5 mph in the timed trials, and threw a rod. Somehow the car seems to have been repaired as Mr J. R. Hill drove in the race, but the car was eliminated after twenty laps. The same car was then in that year driven by Johnny Marquis in the Vanderbilt Cup and the 400 mile Grand Prix of America without success, but managed a 4th place in the Grand Prix of California again in 1915. What happened then to the car is not known.

In 1919, Bugatti announced his intention to market the model alongside the 16 valve car but evidently did not do so.

48

16 valve 4 cylinder car

IF THE 8 VALVE PRE-WAR CARS ESTABLISHED BUGATTI AS AN independent manufacturer of consequence and one to be reckoned with in voiturette racing, it was the improved model with a 16 valve block, originally 66 mm × 100 mm, and then 68 × 100 and finally 69 × 100, which began Bugatti's decade of remarkable success in motor racing. Outstanding early successes were wins in the 1920 Coupe de Voiturettes at Le Mans, and the 1921 Brescia race, good runs in the 1921, 200 mile race at Brooklands and the team prize in the 1922 T.T. Raymond Mays took delivery of his first car in early 1922 (the famous Cordon Rouge) and began an unparalleled succession of seasons of wins at hill-climbs. Many famous drivers used the model.

The way the 16 valve engine could be tuned was astonishing. In touring trim, with plain bearings, it might rotate at 3,000 rpm and do about 70 mph, which coupled with typical Bugatti steering and road holding made it a most attractive sports car by contemporary standards. But the same engine, with plain bearings, was made to rotate at over 5,000 rpm by several drivers – Mays claims 6,700 – and could lap Brooklands at over 100 mph. Mays claims 6,900 rpm for his second ball bearing car (Cordon Bleu)! It is little wonder that various drivers fitted front wheel brakes for hill-climbs!

Not only successful in the sporting world, the 16 valve car created sufficient impression in the motoring world to enable Bugatti to sell licences to Rabag in Germany, Diatto in Italy and Crossley in England immediately after the first world war. None of these licences could have been particularly profitable to Bugatti, except in the short term enabling him to expand his own Molsheim production, since only twenty-five or so cars were, in fact, produced under each licence. But licencing of the

16 valve car in three foreign countries undoubtedly did much to enhance Ettore's prestige abroad and must have helped Molsheim sales considerably. Further details of the licence-produced cars are given on p. 68.

Terminology

In recent years it has become usual to refer to all 16 valve cars as Types 22 or 23. It is more accurate to describe them as Types 13, 22 or 23 depending on the wheelbase which should be respectively 2, 2·4 or 2·55 metres. Type 13 was used exclusively for racing, originally with a plain bearing crankshaft, later with ball bearings (after the 1921 Brescia race success, when the model became known as the Brescia), and sometimes with twin, dash mounted magnetos. The other two cars had proper coachwork, but continued to use the plain bearing crank, until for the last three years or so of production they were fitted with the ball bearing engine (and in 1926 front wheel brakes), and became known as the 'Modified Brescia' model; a 'Brescia' is strictly a short wheelbase car, but sometimes called a 'Full Brescia'.

The model develops

The car shown at the 1919 Olympia Show was 66 mm × 100 mm, fitted with a snappy three-seat clover-leaf body. The cars which won Le Mans 1920 are known to have been built in 1914 and stored. (The Grand Prix des Voitures Légères, usually known as the Coupe de l'Auto, was due to be run on 23 August 1914 on the Circuit des Domes, near Clermont Ferrand in central France. Entries were restricted to cars of up to 2,500 cc engine capacity, but the Bugatti cars would presumably have run in the Voiturette Class.) They were 16 valve, 66 mm × 100 mm models, at least one having 8 plugs, 4 each side (not 8 in line on one side). This is clearly illustrated in the 1921 catalogue. The two-spark single magneto used was at the front, as on the 8 valve engine, not with the double dash mounting used on the later Brescia racing model. A contemporary account states that the other two cars had single ignition.

50

25. *Black Bess with Roland Garros at the wheel.*

26. *The fine front aspect of the 5 litre.*

27. *A pair of cars at Molsheim in 1913 or 1914.*

28. *This model, on the 2 m T.13 chassis, often with twin magnetos, had a long record of race and hill-climb wins and was capable of speeds over 100 mph. Suitably doctored by specialists such as Raymond Mays, it could achieve speeds in excess of 6,500 rpm. The engine was 66 × 100 mm in the 1920 Le Mans race, 68 × 100 mm with a ball bearing and roller crank at Brescia in 1921 (filling the first four places, hence the name) and 69 × 100 mm with a ball bearing crank but plain rods subsequently.*

The authentic 'Full Brescia' as sold had a special crank with short rods and inordinately tall pistons. The ultimate production version retained the ball bearings on the crank and was known as the 'Brescia modifié'.

BRESCIA

30. *The T.22 (7 ft. 10½ in.) and T.23 (8 ft. 4½ in.) 16 valve cars were produced from 1919–26 when they were replaced by T.40. Initially 66 × 100 the engine became 68 × 100 and then 69 × 100 mm. Up to about 1922 (approximately Car No. 1611) the steering box was separate from the crankcase, thereafter integral with it. Only a few of the separate box model remain.*

29. *The pear-drop radiator of the type used in 1920–22.*

31. *Riccordi at the wheel of a 1·4 litre Le Mans type racing car with Jean Bugatti at his side.*

32. *Baccoli and Etien at Molsheim.*

33. *Bought by Henry Segrave and raced at Brooklands, this Le Mans car was slightly lower than standard. The solder on the radiator gives the hint that this was the Baccoli car not in fact the winning Friderich car which turned up in France in 1971.*

34. *Raymond Mays and his famous Brescia 'Cordon Rouge' at Porthcawl Sand Speed Trials in 1923.*

(*photo: Montagu Museum*)

35. (*centre*). *L. Cushman and mechanic Payne in the 1922 200 mile race at Brooklands.*

36. (*below*). *Brescias are still able to give a good account of themselves. Hamish Moffat at Prescott 1960.*
(*photo: Michael E. Ware*)

One of the 1920 Le Mans cars was sent to England and, registered as XE 6132, became the property of H. O. D. Segrave. It was fully described in the *Autocar* of 26 February 1921 in an article entitled 'The Racing Bugatti'. According to this article the car was standard, except that the bore was 65·64 mm, additional main bearing oil feeds were provided, the block had plugs on each side, a weird hot air inlet pipe led from exhaust manifold to carburettor across the back of the engine, and the front axle was up-swept rather more than usual to lower the car. The engine is stated to have developed 29·5 hp at 2,750 rpm.

At Brescia (8 September 1921) however the cars were enlarged to 68 mm × 100 mm, and the crankshaft was mounted on ball bearings. This is an interesting point in this connection which has only recently been resolved. Several experts (for example, Mischall and Friderich's mechanic George Lutz who were both at Molsheim at the time) state categorically that the cranks of the Brescia cars had the later standard twin ball bearing arrangement on the crank, the front bearing and the big ends remaining plain. Commonsense agrees with the first point, because there is no room for a third main bearing in front without a major design change. However, the contemporary description of the race by W. F. Bradley in the *Autocar*, 17 September 1921, states that the 'crankshaft is carried in three ball bearings and as an experiment roller bearings were used in the big ends'. It has now been established with Molsheim and by consulting M. Pierre Marco (who drove in the race) that, in fact, the cranks had one plain bearing in front, but that the connecting rods had rollers, the rod caps being split to allow the crank to be non-detachable.

On test the engines gave no increase in power, and the modification, introduced to avoid the disappointing bearing failure which had been experienced the previous year at Le Mans (see page 355), was removed after the race. Perhaps this accounts for the non-appearance of the team at the 1921 Le Mans race on 18 September although the cars did perform well at Brooklands in the J.C.C. 200 mile race on 22 October. A surprising detail, however, is that the entry at Le Mans and in

55

the 200 mile race showed the cars as 69 mm × 100 mm, not the 68 mm × 100 mm used at Brescia.

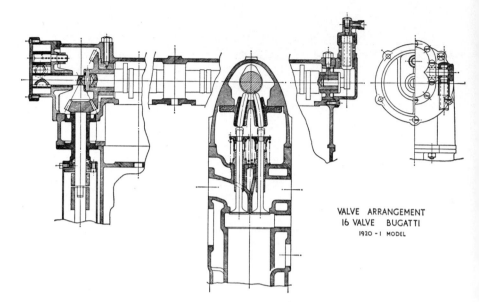

VALVE ARRANGEMENT
16 VALVE BUGATTI
1920 - 1 MODEL

Fig. 3. *Curved valve tappets, made in hardened steel and fitted by casting white metal around them.*

MAX MILLAR DRAWINGS OF THE 16 VALVE CAR

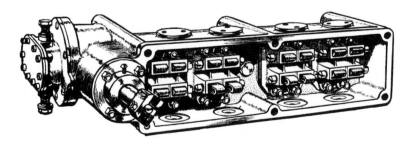

Fig. 4. *Cambox.*

56

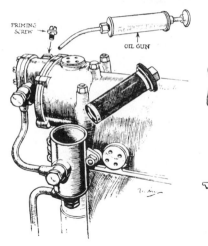

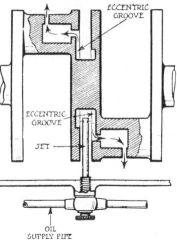

Fig. 5. *Oil pump and filter.*

Fig. 6. *Oil feed to rods through oil jets (ball bearing crank model).*

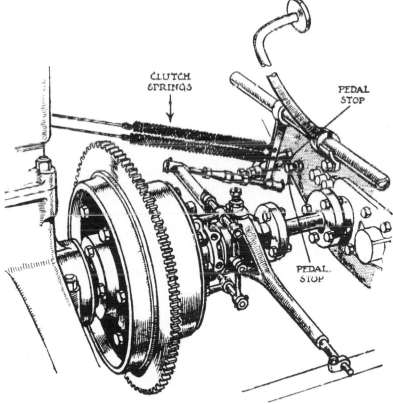

Fig. 7. *Clutch withdrawal mechanism.*

(Autocar, *2 and 9 July 1926*)

57

1921 Catalogue. This makes no mention of a short wheelbase Type 13. Some contemporary race references however give the wheelbase of the Brescia cars as 6 ft 5 in., which is 1·95 metre (see below), and the 1920 Le Mans cars were certainly the same.

SUMMARIZED DATA

	Type 22	Type 23
Engine, mm	68 × 100	68 × 100
Track, metres	1·15	1·15
Wheelbase, metres	2·4	2·55
Tyre size, mm	710 × 90	710 × 90

The 16 valve engine described in the catalogue has plain lead-bronze bearings and the cambox now uses a gear pump for lubrication, an improvement over the 8 valve engine. As compared with the earlier engine the carburettor and exhaust connections are reversed, the inlet being on the left-hand side with the water pump. The steering box is mounted directly on the chassis, and rear wheel brakes plus a transmission brake are used as in 1911. The radiator is now slightly higher with an aspect ratio of 10:7, still with a starting handle cut out at the bottom.

1922–23 Catalogue. This contains the 1922 race results, but not the October Gaillon result, so no doubt was printed in October or November 1922. It states clearly that the 'firm of Bugatti manufactures three types of chassis (13, 22 and 23), that differ only in their "coachworkable" length'. The three main bearings are in lead-bronze as before. Bore and stroke are of 68 mm × 100 mm. The lubrication system consists of a gallery pipe in the crankcase with jets which project oil directly into scoops in the crank webs. Brakes are as before, the rear wheels having cast iron brake shoes, unlined, while the transmission brake is fitted with 'ferrodo'. The radiator seems (but this cannot be stated positively) to be the same as on the previous year. The cars shown at the 1922 Olympia Show conformed to this description.

. *A 1925–6 Tourer. Bore and stroke 69 × 100 mm, 1,496 cc. Plain front and ball bearing centre and ar bearings, and a 2 piece crank; plain big ends fed from jets spraying into the crankwebs. A single gine-mounted magneto. Later type radiator without cut out for starting handle.*

BRESCIA
MODIFIÉ

38. *The treatment of the rear of the body is very effective.*

. *Later Brescias with front wheel brakes were now ready for closed saloon dywork.*

40. *Right-hand, exhaust side. Jets* f *and* g *feed the big ends via the crankwebs,* e *and* h *the front and rear mains. The rear ball bearing housing can be noticed.*

41. *The left-hand, carburettor side of the eng The centre main bearing oil feed is at* I.

THE BRESCIA ENGINE

THE BRESCIA GEAR BOX

42. *The early type with transmission brake and ball joint in the end of the torque rod.*

43. *The later type. This box is very similar in the gear arra ment to the T.35 G.P. box.*

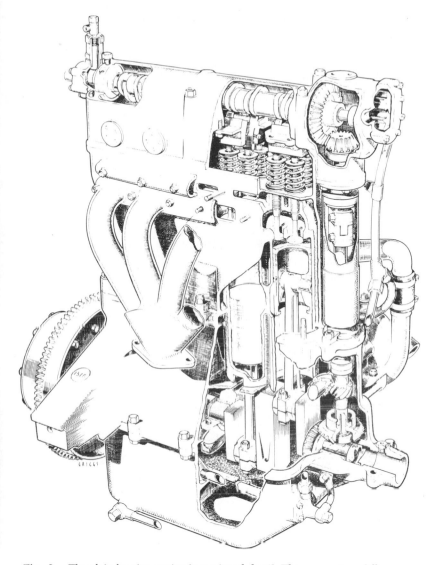

Fig. 8. *The plain bearing engine in sectioned detail. There are minor differences in the lubrication system of the plain bearing engines, the first examples of which had a gallery pipe on the right hand side of the engine with four jets in it, spraying the big ends, the mains collecting splash. From 1922 the main bearings were pressure fed from external pipes and the big ends were fed from troughs in the crankshaft which received oil from two jets in a similarly arranged gallery pipe, as shown in the drawing.*

61

	Type 22	Type 23
Engine, mm	68 × 100	68 × 100
Track, metres	1·15	1·15
Wheelbase, metres	2·4	2·55
Tyre size, mm	710 × 90	710 × 90

There is still no catalogue information on Type 13.

At the Olympia Show in 1923, the 68 × 100 touring model was shown alongside the 69 × 100 'Modified Brescia' car, the latter being more expensive. In the *Automotor Journal* of 15 November, Mr E. Duffield wrote:

The Bugatti exhibit at Olympia was very impressive, in a restrained sort of fashion. To judge by the demeanour of our inscrutable young friend Lefrère, he might have been in charge of a display of Dunkley motor-perambulators. Although he would agree that 'who sells fat oxen should himself be fat', I suppose, he has never allowed himself to betray his enthusiasm in a noticeable manner, and to hear him reeling-off the car-speeds, engine-revolutions, and so forth of the 1924 chassis (received just in time to wheel it into place on his stand), as though he were saying what jolly weather we were having, struck me as most impressive, because of the entire absence of any intention to make an impression!

I gather that the new model is our old friend the Brescia – so nicknamed after its galvanic performance in the Italian Grand Prix of 1921 – minus only the duplicated ignition. It has an engine-starter and dynamo lighting-set in its 1924 development, and is obtainable in two or three lengths of wheelbase. There is still a super-sports model, with duplex ignition, but anybody who wants one of that type stamps himself as a really desperate person.

1923 Instruction Book. Dated September 1923, this describes the 69 mm × 100 mm car and illustrates and describes the ball bearing construction with steering box integral with the crankcase. A works drawing, showing the modification to the crankcase to include the box, is dated April 1923 so it seems certain that this change was made in the autumn of that year. Another change is that the connecting rod bronzes are now white metal lined. This book, however, quotes the wheelbase of the T.13 as 1·95 not 2·0 metres. It thus seems reasonable to conclude that the ball race crank and the integral steering box came in at the same time in 1923, in production cars if perhaps earlier in special race versions. The genuine Brescia racing type of 1921 is known to have had a separate steering box and a small series was made and sold in this ball-bearing construction.

1924–25 Catalogue. The car is now labelled 'Brescia Modifié'; it contains 1924 race results so no doubt was printed in October or November 1924. There is still no reference to Type 13 in the text. The crankshaft, as before, is split and carried on two ball races and a plain front bearing. Lubrication is by jets squirting axially into the crankwebs, where the oil is distributed by centrifugal force, and the steering is now stated to be lubricated from the engine, although it is doubtful if this feature was ever used. Apart from the bore, other relevant data are as quoted in the 1922–23 Catalogue. The radiator is fatter again with an aspect ratio of 4:3, and has no starting handle cut out.

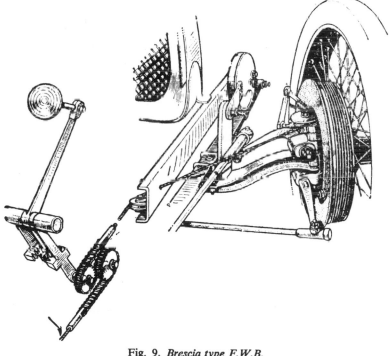

Fig. 9. *Brescia type F.W.B.*
(*drawing:* The Motor)

63

1925 (November) Catalogue. This refers again to the 'Brescia Modifié' and states that three types of chassis (13, 22 and 23) are produced. T.13 was probably produced to special order; its wheelbase is again quoted as 2 metres. The only important change seems to be the addition of four wheel brakes 'as on the Grand Prix cars', but the radiator is now lower and similar to that on T.30 (see below).

1926 (November) Catalogue. This makes no reference to Brescia or Type 30 models. Types 38 touring, 35A 'Course Imitation', 35 G.P., 37 Sport, 39 G.P. and Type 40 are illustrated, all but the Type 35 being mentioned for the first time. Thus the 16 valve car went out of production in mid-1926, although there is some Molsheim evidence that it continued to be produced to special order until early 1928.

Contemporary road test impressions

The following article by 'Omega', E. Duffield, in the *Automotor Journal*, 14 April 1921, entitled '200 miles on the 10 hp Bugatti' is worth reproducing:

The Bugatti, being quite an exceptional car, the Editor of *The Auto* has permitted me to stray over the confines of my usual stamping-ground, in recounting my impressions of a road-test. To come to the kernel of things at once, I regard the Bugatti as a car of a thousand, and the voiturette of the entire world's automotor industry. Unless [Germany] has a super-Bugatti up [their] sleeve – something in the way of possibilities which I doubt, because the Bugatti is an essentially sporting proposition – there is nothing like it. England, France, Italy, America, have nothing to offer which can match it.

Mr W. M. Letts having asked me to try the car, and Major Lefrère, the manager of Chas. Jarrott and Letts, Ltd, having arranged for me to do so, I took over a chassis with a couple of aeroplane seats bolted to it, on the Saturday morning. On the first day I did a matter of 100 miles, by the time I had picked up my moorings; and on the second I again totalled 100 miles by dead reckoning, although no meter was fitted. The mechanical detail of the new Bugatti has been very faithfully described in *The Auto*, but all mention of its behaviour has up to now been of the second-hand, hearsay order.

64

Having been shown the run of its four-speed-and-reverse 'gate', I got aboard, and set forth. In town the Bugatti is decidedly a chassis to know, because of its beautiful responsiveness to the accelerator-pedal, and the surprisingly small difference in gear-ratio between the fourth and third speeds. Once out on *la route libre*, however, one loses the finger-on-lip feeling, and revels in its absolutely galvanic acceleration. Light cars as a class are surprising to those accustomed only to heavier boats; but the Bugatti holds revelations for those even well-accustomed to light cars in general.

The suspension is uncannily perfect. The steering is a delight. The response to the spur makes one forget the lightness of the whole outfit; but the craft embodied in the complete make-up is such that a very tyro could come down off the banking on the forward side of the Members' Bridge at Brooklands well up in the 70s, and yet hit the railway straight without anything in the way of alarm. Tested by a trustworthy chronograph, this Bugatti chassis which I tried lapped Brooklands at 60 odd, which seemed to suggest that the manufacturer's guarantee of 80 mph on the level is quite safely offered. The chassis I had was milk-new, and there was a wicked breeze blowing dead in the radiator of this astonishing baby. I did not time the lower gears, but at a venture I should say that one can get 30 on first, 40 on second, and 60 mph on third gears. The pinions were frankly rough; they were plainly noisy; and if I bought a Bugatti – which, plainly speaking, means if I could afford a Bugatti – I should run it at least 500 miles before handing it to the body-builders. But the suspension, even in front, and still more so aft, is wonderful when running *ventre-à-terre*, and if a round half-dozen of avaricious Brooklands habitués had not already put themselves down for Bugatti chassis this Season I should hypothecate all the assets I have and buy one, looking to the 1921 Season's 'pots' to recoup me, even out of the silversmith's ladle.

On the road, the car is staggering. There was nothing abroad on my two days which it could not 'pip'. Even when hot stuff were sailing uphill, I had only to take a hundred yards of that wonderful 'third' to squeeze comfortably by them, on both Portsmouth and Brighton roads; and a car which will climb Reigate Hill (from the Brighton side, of course) on third speed at 25 mph is one on which the unregenerate could have lots of fun, I should imagine, especially when the same machine will tick along at 5 mph on fourth, as smoothly as any 50 hp 'six'.

Whence the power comes, only M. Ettore Bugatti knows, up to now; but it is there. We know all about the performance of this car in the voiturette Grand Prix last summer, on the Sarthe circuit. Like most other folk, I had imagined that the team of cars used for the job were very, very special, and handled by supermen. I have now satisfied myself that they were not. I have further satisfied myself that, given a day's induction or initiation, the veriest Old Maid of Lee could trundle about on a Bugatti without causing the vicar's eyebrows to arch themselves – unless she happened indiscreetly to depress the accelerator-pedal!

The engine starts easily, decelerates smoothly. The brakes are sweet to astonishment. The suspension is incredibly even. The fore springing is like that of the 1921 Vauxhall. The rear suspension cannot be described so perfect is it. Can you 'corner' at 40 mph on any other car, of twice the weight? I trow not! The steering is excellent, and the chassis as a whole could be improved only by fitting some means of regulating the minimum throttle-setting from the driver's seat, for those meeting the car for the first time. I say this in my search for something to criticize, because I did by failing to keep it primed when I dropped from high speed to a standstill – forgetting that I had only the accelerator-pedal to keep a useful supply of gas going in to the cylinders. This, however, is nothing. The great point, the whole point, is that here is something so light that any fit man can, using both hands, lift the whole rear-half of the car jack-high, and yet is good for 80 mph on the flat, and further yet will tour the British Isles (at a 25 mph average) at over 30 miles per gallon of petrol! The standard tyres, on French Rudge-Whitworths, are 710×90 mm. Those on this chassis were, to my mind, extravagantly inflated. But the wonderful springing (kept in check by the amortisseurs fitted fore and aft) neutralized the effect of this circumstance and I have never completed a couple of days' driving of a strange machine – particularly of a very fast little machine – with less fatigue or more regret.

Modern Road Impressions

Several thousands of miles experience with an early 16-valve car have enabled a modern driver to confirm the charm and performance of this model. Steering and road holding are excellent and if the absence of front brakes requires the car to be manoeuvred rather than stopped – especially as the foot operated transmission brake makes alarming noises when used at any speed – the whole car gives a surprising feeling of safety. Gear noise is considerable and it is difficult to tell the difference in performance between 3rd and 4th gears! Above 60 mph the engine is very rough and 70 mph seems fast!

It is easy today to see why the car evoked such enthusiasm fifty years ago.

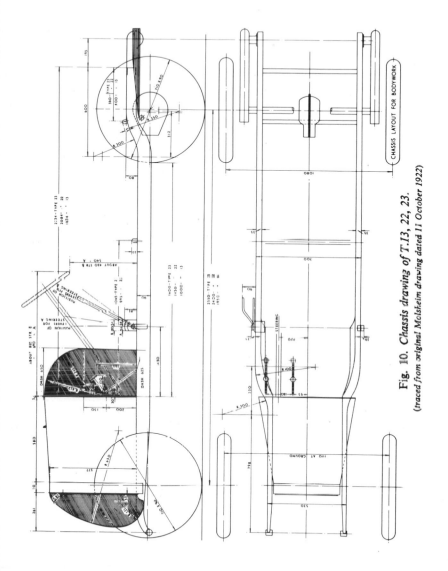

Fig. 10. *Chassis drawing of T.13, 22, 23.*
(traced from original Molsheim drawing dated 11 October 1922)

CHASSIS LAYOUT FOR BODYWORK

16 valve licence cars

THE IMMEDIATE POST-WAR MARKET FOR CARS WAS A HUNGRY ONE
and many new designs sprang up all over the world. Industrial-
ists realized the advantage in manufacturing well-known foreign
cars in their particular country under licence. And the 16 valve
Bugatti car had the unusual distinction of being produced in
three countries other than France, namely Italy, Germany and
England, although probably not more than twenty-five cars
were produced in each country.

Italy

Diatto had had a licence arrangement with Bugatti during the
first world war for his 8 cylinder aeroengine (see page 373). In
1919 at the Paris Automobile Salon, Diatto showed a sample
of their 16 valve chassis fitted with a substantial saloon body
and known as the Diatto model 30. This appears to have been a
Type 23 chassis, although it had a Diatto rather than a Bugatti
radiator. How successful this model was is not known.

Germany

In the *Autocar* of 20 August 1921 was an announcement that
the Rhenian Motor Building Company (Rheinische Automobilbau A.G.) had concluded an agreement with Bugatti to
manufacture the 4 cylinder car at Mannheim and Berlin. This
company (from whose initials derives the adopted name Rabag)
seems to have been more successful than Diatto. The car was
shown at the 1923 Berlin Auto Show, in a specification conforming with the 68 mm × 100 mm, Type 23 (see *Bugantics*
18, 3, 1955); it is not known if any cars were imported into
Britain, but an engine was still running in 1935 (see *Bugantics*
4, 3, 1935).

68

44. *The cover of a Rabag catalogue.*

45. *A Rabag saloon.* (*photo: W. Schmarbeck*)

46. *The Rabag engine was very similar to the original Brescia engine but had a one-piece crankcase with the crank fed in from one end.*
(photo: K. Kiefer)

47. *The three so-called Crossley Bugatti's which did well in the 1922 Isle of Man T.T. were 'Full-Brescias' made in France. Here is L. Cushman in one after the 1922 200-miles race at Brooklands. He had added a radiator cowl and an enlarged fuel tank.*

Mr W. Schmarbeck writes:

The Rheinische Automobil – A.G., Düsseldorf, Deutsche Gesellschaft for the licence Ettore Bugatti, was established by the Funke Brothers on 3 December 1920 with a capital of 13 million marks. The head office was in Düsseldorf and the manager was B. A. Gelderblom. Bodies were made by Bendikt Rock, Nordstrasse, Düsseldorf, using about twenty men. A car was shown at the 1923 Berlin Show. In June 1925 the Firm merged with A.G. für Automobilbau (AGA) in Berlin-Lichtenberg, who already produced Stinnes and Dinos cars. Bankruptcy proceedings, however, began in November 1925.

Rabag-Bugattis were well known in Germany as fast and economical cars and were often seen in rallies and races; a Rabag was a competitor in the Eifelrennen on the Nürburgring in 1930.

England

The *Autocar*, 19 November 1921, contained an announcement to the effect that Crossley Motors Limited would make the 16 valve car under licence at Manchester. This had been arranged by Mr W. M. Letts, Managing Director of Crossley Motors Limited, and also a partner in the British Bugatti Agents, Charles Jarrott & Letts Limited. The model was to be the 68 mm × 100 mm type, no doubt with plain bearings. The story of these cars (two of which are still extant) is best told in the words of Mr Edgar N. Duffield in the *Automotor Journal* of 6 December 1923.

I think it was during the 1920 [in fact 1921] Olympia Show that Sir William Letts, K.B.E., announced his intention of manufacturing in the Manchester Works of Crossley Motors, Ltd, a British edition of the Bugatti. At that date a Bugatti was a rather costly chassis. The price when I bought my first new one was £575, so that a complete car came out at about £700, with anything in the way of bodywork really worthy of such chassis quality. I indicated my interest in Sir William's announcement on the Bugatti Stand at Olympia, by immediately handing a five-pound note (all I had on me) to Mr Arthur Bray, as deposit on the first Manchester-built chassis ready for delivery; but I never got that chassis, because immediately after the announcement Crossley got so very busy upon the famous 19·6 that they could not get down to the Bugatti proposition. Then came

71

the Fourteen Crossley, then the 20–70 sports model, and so the poor little Bugatti was left standing on one leg.

In default of the original programme, Sir William imported a number of sets of Bugatti components from Molsheim, in the rough, so to speak, and set aside a bay or two of his big works at Gorton for machining and assembling them, and I gather that the first batch of Manchester-built Bugattis have only just recently begun to come through.

Hearing of their availability, and having inspected a specimen at Olympia, just after the Show I borrowed one . . ., and am now in a position to speak of its performance. Let it be clear that this chassis is constructed from original, genuine components, but that the machine-shop work is entirely British . . . .

I would not for worlds hurt the feelings of Mr Ettore Bugatti, especially while he is at work on the aircraft motor [Type 34?] to design which the French Government have given him *carte-blanche*, but at the risk of doing so I must say that the Manchester machine-shop work, and erection show quite a useful advance upon those of his own 'model' factory.

Of old the Bugatti was notable for a certain mild whine of gears. One could see nothing wrong, when one examined the transmission, but it was not remarkable for noiselessness, even on fourth speed, and my own little series of Bugattis were alike principally in the fact that their engines were very quiet and their gearboxes very noisy . . . I always felt that if only Mr Bugatti would give us a little less pep, but a little more Englishness of workmanship, as it were, we should get chassis just as good as we wanted, from the point of power and therefore speed, but chassis much smoother in performance, especially as regards noise.

Well, here is the desirability consummated. The 1924 11·4 hp Bugatti built in Crossleys' shops, is a first-rate job selling at a very low price. The chassis is only £350 now. . . .

I must at once say that the British-built Bug. seems to lack some of the sting of the Molsheim production. I should set it at about 8 to 10 miles per hour on fourth speed. That apart, I really regard it as a better car. It is capable of much smoother slow-running. Its gearbox and final drive are almost incredibly less noisy. Its foot-brake is better. Its steering, suspension, clutch and gear-changing mechanism are every bit as good. The facing-up of engine joints, gearbox lid, and so forth, is quite as good. The only thing lacking is just that last ounce of vim – no loss, really, because it is very seldom that one can keep one's foot down for more than a few seconds on British roads. . . .

Mere engine-efficiency was never a fetish of mine, for the reason just stated. I never fell down before motors which would do more than I wanted them to do, just because they were able to do it. My personal affection for the Bugatti was based primarily upon its beauty of suspension, steering and gear-changing. . . .

Gear-noise is apparently unobjectionable to the Frenchman. He does not seem to mind it, in the least. Depending, as he does, very numerously upon a bulb-horn which cost five francs before the War, he may rely upon his gears to give audible warning of his approach! But whatever may underlie the fact, he would seem never to have worried about degrees of silence of gear-pinions, or bevels. . . .

Although, as I have said, the Manchester-built chassis does not seem to have quite the 'fire' of the Molsheim product, it has very wonderful acceleration up to its limits on the various gears. It has, nevertheless, a greatly improved slow-running. Its lubrication seems better, because on a Molsheim Bug, it would be quite notable to do 200 miles without a single suspicion of a misfire, with anything, but Bosch three-pointed plugs, especially in the case of a new car, which any sensible person would be inclined rather to over-lubricate, keeping the level well up to the maximum.

One can get used to anything, and in appreciation of positive virtues can insensibly blind oneself to minor and negative demerits; but I must say that I do not know when I have spent a more pleasant 200 miles on a car other than of my own. . . .

All the old flexibility, all the old charm of suspension and steering, of finger-only gear-changing, all the old acceleration. Not quite all the old genuine stingo, when the throttle is well opened and the spark-lever well forward; but then one could so very seldom get going all-out, or remain all-out for more than a couple of furlongs, that this really does not matter very much.

A very, very pleasant little car, Sir William, at a really wonderful price, and although I would not have you keep Crossley buyers waiting, I hope you will contrive to put-through an occasional batch of 25 or so, especially as nearly all the labour on them will be going into the breeches-pockets of British fitters!

In two respects the improvements on the cars from the Molsheim factory, may have accounted for the qualities noted by Mr Duffield; these were, first, that the width of the gears had been increased, resulting in longer life, and second, that the rear axle shaft was increased in diameter at the outer end and a much larger taper used to secure it to the hub; the latter was a big advantage and overcame the annoyance of losing one's wheels, a mishap which had occasionally happened with the earlier types. A considerable amount of trouble was experienced at first with oiled up plugs, but this was finally cured by fitting split collars to the valve stems with no gap at the split in conjunction with internally skirted valve spring collars and this too without cutting down the oil supply in any way. The performance was improved by milling one-sixteenth inch off the base of the cylinder block, thus raising the compression ratio.

D. B. Madeley, who made these observations, owned one of these cars for nearly eight years, and apart from the defects mentioned above, found it a very satisfactory vehicle. His car is still in existence (No. CM 1614). Threads on this car are BSF rather than metric, and there is a tie bar across the front spring eyes, instead of between the shockabsorbers as on normal Molsheim products.

Crossley Bugattis are reputed to have had chassis numbers 1600 to 1625; the known cars are consistent with this, but car 1612 is a French-built Brescia ball bearing type. On the other hand, the engine of car 1614 is stamped with a prefix CM which is consistent with Crossley.

What appears to have happened is that the works allocated Crossley chassis numbers 1600–1625 at a time when they were well before this in the register, and then forgot to cancel the numbers from their own series. Thus they were eventually allocated by both works.

TYPE 28

the prototype 3 litre car of 1921

A SENSATIONAL NEW 8 CYLINDER CAR WAS SHOWN AT THE PARIS and London Automobile Shows in 1921, the first 8 cylinder passenger car Bugatti designed. The design stemmed in many details from the wartime aeroengine and the chassis as a whole was intended as a high quality product reflecting Ettore's pre-occupation with the fabulous, which ultimately materialized in the Royale or Golden Bugatti. In the *Autocar* of 7 May 1921 W. F. Bradley wrote:

The person responsible for the present revival of the eight-cylinder-in-line is undoubtedly M. Ettore Bugatti. This statement must not be interpreted to mean that Bugatti designed or built the first modern car with an eight-cylinder-in-line engine, but he undoubtedly initiated the present movement. During 1913 Bugatti took up the question of eight-cylinder-in-line engines, and as an experiment built an eight-cylinder of 68 mm × 100 mm, bore and stroke with three overhead valves per cylinder, which was really two of his ordinary engines in tandem. This car was in use at the factory, until the declaration of war, and at the present time is in service in Paris.

It was further pointed out that Monsieur Henry, who had designed the pre-war Peugeot racing cars, was responsible for production of the Bugatti aeroengine during the war; after the war he was engaged by Ballot to design racing models and his Bugatti experience 'doubtless influenced him to adopt 8 cylinders in line'. Further comment added 'in like manner adoption of the straight 8 for the Duesenberg racing cars is doubtless due to experience gained with Bugatti aeroengines'.

The 3 litre Type 28 car, however, never got beyond the prototype stage (the original chassis is still in Alsace), and the considerably altered design which eventually was produced in 1929 (Type 44) is not really related to it, although Bugatti persisted in so claiming in later years. A contemporary account continues:

It is a car bristling with original features and is on that account attracting much attention at the Salon. The engine, which has all the appearance of a monobloc, really has its cylinders in two castings, their dimensions being 69 mm × 100 mm, bore and stroke (2,991 cc). [Strangely enough all contemporary accounts give the bore as 69 mm, but the 1922 Bugatti catalogue quotes 70 mm.] Although it is a most compact group, there is a bearing between each cylinder, and a tenth bearing behind the clutch. A cast aluminium open housing is bolted to the rear face of the engine base chamber, and in the extremity of this is the tenth bearing.

The engine has three valves per cylinder, two inlet and one exhaust, mounted vertically in the head and operated by an overhead camshaft, the enclosed vertical drive shaft of which is in the centre. [The drive to the camshafts was via a pair of bevel-drives differing by one tooth, and held together by a friction clutch, so that the brake drag loaded the teeth and prevented tooth rattle – a device used on the Royale, and incidentally during the recent war on some of the original electronic calculating machines.] A cross shaft at the base of the vertical drive shaft operates the high tension magneto on the right and the water pump on the left.

The magneto is hidden under a square aluminium box, corresponding in shape with the squared cylinder block. At 3,400 rpm the engine develops 90 hp. Plain bearings are used for the crankshaft and the connecting rod end, and the pistons are of aluminium. Lubrication is under pressure throughout. There are two carburettors of Bugatti's own design, bolted up directly to the right-hand side of the cylinder block. In addition to the main throttle control, there are separate hand adjustments for both the petrol and air.

There is not a feature of the car but has been treated in an original and masterly manner. There are only two speeds, and they are accommodated in the rear axle housing, and operated by a hard wood lever. With an engine developing 90 hp and a chassis of exceptionally low weight, two ratios are considered amply sufficient. A central aluminium casing is used for the differential and the change-speed housing, while the axle tubes are machined out of the solid billets. On each side of the differential housing and bolted up to it is a light pressed steel torque member, with hardwood filling

76

in the channel. These two are parallel with the propellor-shaft, and at the forward end attached to the extended crankcase housing in two pairs of compressed fabric links. [The 16 valve cars at that time used a ball and socket, but the flexible coupling was used on all models from then on.] The change-speed and the brake lever are mounted on the front end of the torque member.

The steering column has a ball and socket mounting to the aluminium dashboard, and at its base is connected to the worm shaft in the steering gearbox by a fabric coupling, in the manner usually associated with propellor-shaft drives. This is quite a novel adaptation of the flexible fabric joint, worthy of further study. Above the steering column, and parallel with it, is a second column, also mounted in the dash carrying the carburettor and ignition controls. There are only two spokes on the steering wheel, and these are of such a shape and position that it is possible to pass the hand through the wheel to reach the carburettor controls. Furthermore, the wheel is clamped to the column on a key, and thus adjustable at will by the driver when seated.

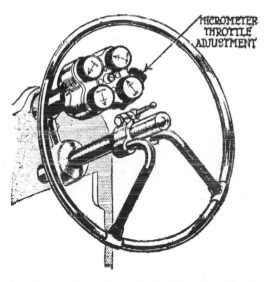

Fig. 11. *The novel steering wheel, with adjustable length, spokes grouped to allow access to the instruments, themselves readily visible.*

(*drawing:* Autocar)

Fig. 12. *'Duplicated stub axle arm, tie rod and steering rod strike an unusual note. The front wheel brake drums are of large size'*, stated the Autocar.

Originality has been displayed in the attempt to obtain rigidity and longevity in the steering gear connections. The fore and aft connecting bar from the main steering lever to the steering arm is double and tubular. There is a star type universal joint to the main steering arm with hardened steel pins working in compressed leather bushings. The transverse tie rod has oval shaped ends formed of compressed fabric held between a top and bottom steel plate. These parts cannot rattle, they are rigid and at the same time absorb shocks, and will require no lubrication. [A Coventry and Detroit novelty of 1963!]

The car is fitted with brakes on all the wheels, these eventually will be hydraulically operated, although at present they are applied manually. Quarter-elliptic springs with the thick ends rearwards are used at the rear and double semi-elliptics at the front, in accordance with Bugatti principles. At the rear a friction type shockabsorber is mounted inside the brake drums. At the front end there is a shockabsorber of the same type, the drum of which is mounted just ahead of the radiator, between the dumb irons. The petrol tank is at the rear, carried by the main frame, and has vacuum supply to the carburettors, whilst a reserve compartment of two gallons is provided in the main fuel tank. (*Autocar*, 15 October 1921)

Friderich in the 8 cylinder experimental car produced in 1913, making use of two 4 cylinder engines ↓pled together.

The Type 28 chassis at a 1922 Automobile show with Mr and Mme Friderich.
TYPE 28

50. *The 8 cylinder engine. Note first use of a flexible coupling on the steering column, the cross mounted centrally placed magneto, twin plugs and twin Bugatti carburettor.*

(*photos:* Autocar)

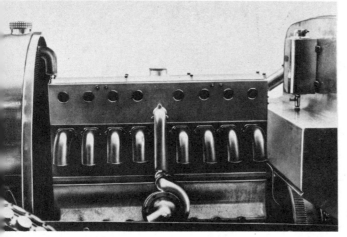

51. *The left-hand side of the T.28 engine, which had nine main bearings and one out-rigger behind the clutch, all of the plain type. The characteristic square cut appearance pioneered in the wartime aeroengines is now seen in the first car design.*

52. *Bugatti rear springs, twin torque arms and a two-speed gearbox in the rear axle; a three-speed bo so located was later used in Types 46 and 50.*

The car caught the eye of the celebrated Mr S. F. Edge who wrote in the *Automotor Journal* of 17 November 1921:

I suppose that the car with more new and striking ideas than any other in the Show was the eight-cylindered Bugatti. Original points obtruded, from whatever aspect one viewed it, and I expect that many of the designer's innovations will be standard practice in a few years from now; but for the time being it was rather 'ahead of the band', and as an exhibit I consider that it suffered greatly from the fact that certain details were not complete, for example, the connections of the front-wheel brakes, the ignition etc. To show such a chassis, absolutely alive with what in vulgar parlance are called 'brain-waves', in any but a perfectly completed state was rather unwise, I should imagine. But the look of what one could see made one wish to have a specimen on the road, so that one could see how much justification Mr Bugatti has for doing so many things in a way quite different from that followed by everybody else. He is a wonderful designer, and those who have met him recently tell me that he has developed a unique personality. But the chassis gave me an idea in my own mind, of being the work of a man who cannot sit in a comfortable armchair, and read a book, for very long. The design was electrical, or rather galvanic. It was one succession of shocks to all our accustomed notions, and although I am all for progress, I must confess that I have also a respect for a certain type of conservatism. We shall see; we must wait to see. But it was quite easy to see that this new model has great capabilities, and no designer looking to the future could afford to miss a most thorough examination of it.

The car was, in fact, ahead of its time, not only in the general sense but in the Molsheim context. Several years were to pass before a luxury car was a practicable proposition from that factory, until the esteem which racing successes brought made sales of such a car possible.

TYPE 30
8 cylinder car

THE FIRST PRODUCTION 8 CYLINDER BUGATTI WAS THE 2 LITRE
Type 30 introduced in 1922 and shown at automobile shows at
the end of that year. No doubt Bugatti felt that the larger 3 litre
Type 28 should be shelved in favour of a smaller, cheaper and
more saleable model. Type 30 consisted of an entirely new
60 mm × 88 mm, 8 cylinder engine mounted in the Type 23
chassis and indeed offered in the short Type 22, 2·4 metre chassis,
although probably only a few racing cars of this length were
produced; later an even longer chassis (2·85 m) was introduced.

The engine was the first production model to use the rectangular slab construction which was to become famous, and had
3 valves per cylinder, along the lines of the 1912, 5 litre racers,
the aeroengines and the Type 28. The valves were small in
diameter to allow them to be removed without disturbing the
valve guides unlike the later T.35 or T.39 blocks. The crankcase
had a detachable sump, the crank being carried on 3 large ball
bearings (plus 1 ball steady bearing) and being fed in from one
end of the case. Big ends were plain with jet-feed from an oil
gallery on the left side of the motor. A cross-shaft at the front
drove a water-pump on the left and initially a gear oil pump at
the right – probably Bugatti was tired of priming troubles with
the high mounted Brescia pump; later the oil pump was lowered
further to a drive off the crankshaft as on the T.35. The blocks
were in units of 4 cylinders with single plugs (a few had 8 plug
blocks) and a cambox as on the later Type 35 design. Early cars
had twin carburettors, but some later ones a single unit. Plug
holes were tapped through to the cylinders, not recessed as
on the later T.35 cars.

The steering box was mounted on the rear engine crankcase bearer, the worm wheel rotating on an eccentric pin to enable backlash to be adjusted. The gearbox was Brescia 'with strengthened gears'. On early cars there was an outrigger bearing behind the clutch and contained in a housing carried off the rear of the crankcase, as on Type 28. The rear axle torque rod used a leather coupling at its forward end, as introduced on T.28 the year previously, but the torque rod was not duplicated as on that model. Front wheel brakes were used for the first time on a production Bugatti and were hydraulically operated by a specially designed master cylinder, the rear brakes being cable operated. Later, cable front brakes as on the last series Brescia and G.P. cars were used.

This model is not one to be enthusiastic about even if Charles Faroux wrote eulogistically to Ettore Bugatti in early 1924:

Whether one considers the engine, the steering, the road-holding qualities, or the suspension (from the point of view of either driver or passenger), you have sold me a motor-car which is absolutely unbeatable, which easily puts in the shade anything else which I have ever driven. I cannot imagine anything which could give me more joy than this experience with my two-litre Bugatti!

I would prefer not to tell you the time in which I drove from Nancy to Paris, but I can tell you candidly, that – well as I know this particular road – I have never on any other chassis, of any power, approached the running-time of my trip of Sunday last. Quite apart from the great pleasure which this car has given me, as one with a reverence for beautiful mechanism, it has also given me profound joy as one of your most faithful admirers.

One feels that he must have bought the car on such favourable terms that he felt bound to be polite about it! The *Autocar*, 8 May 1925, was not so kind, disliking the noise of the engine and the poor brakes. Notwithstanding its faults the car could be made to go: Mr O. A. Phillips wrote in November 1960:

As a matter of fact my first Bugatti, No. 4006 in 1928, was an 8 cylinder bore 60 mm, stroke 88 mm, 2 plugs per cylinder, 2 Scintilla magnetos mounted on a steel firewall on a common aluminium casting, with step-up gearbox to bring the speed of magnetos from camshaft speed up to crankshaft speed.

This car was 95 inch wheelbase [Type 22] and had hydraulic brakes (approx. 11 inches diameter) on front, and mechanical (approx. 16 inches diameter) on the rear. They operated separately – foot on front, hand on rear. The complete car weighed only 1,250 pounds and was, supposedly, the Strasbourg winning car in 1923 [2nd in 1922].

The foot brake master cylinder was simply a direct acting plunger mounted on the firewall. The front axle was an 'I' beam and the ends of the 'tie rod' had leather couplings, similar to the one connecting the front of the torque arm to the gearbox. On the top of the right rear engine leg was mounted the steering box, while on the bottom of the left rear clutch housing was a Robert Bosch starter. There was no generator.

In 1929 I officially recorded 124 mph at Muroc Dry Lake, in full touring trim, but with two downdraft Winfield carburettors, instead of the original Zenith. In 1932 I sold the car to a friend of Eri Richardson in San Francisco, and have since lost all track of it. [The engine still exists.]

Several racing cars were built around Type 30. A team of long tailed models with the exhaust brought out of the point of the tail ran in the 1922 French Grand Prix at Strasbourg and were 2nd and 3rd after Nazarro in a Fiat; these cars were believed to have been fitted with split rods and roller big ends experimentally, but the construction was not perpetuated. Mr W. F. Bradley wrote in *Automotive Industries*, 3 August 1922:

Bugatti came to the start with four cars equipped with a new type eight cylinder engine. Friderich was the fastest of these drivers and succeeded in getting the lead for a few minutes on the third lap. On the 12th lap he went out by reason of the breakage of the gears in one of his two magnetos. These magnetos were mounted side by side on the dash and driven from the overhead camshaft by a universal joint shaft. When the magneto gears went they broke up the intermediaries. The three other Bugattis went to the end, but they were never at any time serious contestants for first place. They were very liberally lubricated and smoked freely throughout the race.

The cars also ran in the 1922 Italian G.P. and next year at Indianapolis, in single seater form. Short wheelbase, tank bodied

TYPE 30

53 and 54. *Mr Peter Hampton's 'toast rack' bodied car. This model originally had hydraulic front and mechanical rear brakes.*

55. *P. de Vizcaya in a T.30 in the Italian Grand Prix at Monza in 1922.*

56. *Pierre Marco changes a wheel during the 1922 French Grand Prix, while Ettore looks on anxiously.*

57. *1922 French Grand Prix at Strasbourg, de Vizcaya at the pits.*

58. *Chiron at the wheel of a T.30 chassis about 1924. Bodies of this type were quite suitable for the Côte d'Azur or Chiron's native Monaco.*

59. *P. de Vizcaya in a single seat T.30 prepared for the Indianapolis race in 1923. Two of the five cars entered had bearing trouble and only one finished.*

60. *The 1923 Indianapolis car which Count Zborowski drove in 1923 at Brooklands. After the Count was killed in a Mercedes at Monza in October of that year the car went to George Duller (the famous jockey) who had many successes with it. The car, rebodied, is still in existence (Car No. 4004).*

versions of strange appearance were built for the 1923 French G.P. at Tours, on a 2 m chassis (strictly known as T.32). All this is recounted in detail on pages, 363–5. The gearbox of these cars was carried in the rear axle, and the front springs were reversed quarter-elliptic as at the rear. The big ends had roller bearings.

In 1924 Pierre de Vizcaya driving one of the 1923 unblown tank cars at the speed trials at Arpajon near Paris broke the 2 litre class world record for the flying kilometre at 117·5 mph and the flying mile at 116 mph – not bad for what was basically a Type 30. At this meeting Eldridge on the monster 300 hp Fiat attained a hazardous 147 mph. 'Eldridge's approach was one of the most appalling sights which the writer has ever witnessed', wrote *The Motor*.

The Indianapolis cars were described in detail by Mr Bradley in *Automotive Industries* of 24 May 1923:

The five Bugatti entries built by Ettore Bugatti, of Molsheim, Alsace, who specializes in a fast, sporting type of 122 cu in. chassis, are said to be stock models with only such detail modifications as are necessary for the special conditions of the Indianapolis track.

The single seater bodies for these cars are in the design of a French aviation engineer, Bechereau, who was responsible during the war for the design of Spad scout planes. As no changes of importance could be made in the chassis, the maximum width of the bodies is appreciably greater than that of the majority of American cars. The driver is placed centrally in the chassis, with his eyes just above the level of the scuttle and the top of his head flush with the top of the tail; this part is streamlined with the pilot's head, as in aviation practice.

The engine has a stroke of 88 mm, and its eight cylinders, cast in two blocks of four, are of 60 mm bore. They are mounted on an aluminium base-chamber which is carried directly on the chassis frame members. The cylinder blocks are rectangular, and the timing gear housing at the forward end is also squared off, giving a box-like appearance to the engine. The detachable cylinder head has a lapped face where it joins the cylinder blocks. [Oh Mr Bradley!] It carries three vertical valves (two admission and one exhaust) operated by a single overhead camshaft mounted in three ball bearings. [Surely wrong?] Light followers are interposed between the cams and the valves, the two shafts carrying these rockers being hollow and forming an oil duct through which lubricant is delivered directly to the

89

cam faces. Maximum engine speed is 4,800 to 5,000 rpm and the power developed is declared to be 104 hp.

A two-piece assembled crankshaft, carried in three ball bearings, is employed. I-section white metal connecting rods and aluminium pistons having four narrow steel compression rings are used. Normally the 122 in. Bugattis are fitted with two Zenith carburettors, but it is probable that they will be run at Indianapolis with four carburettors, and that benzol, or a mixture of benzol and gasoline will be used as fuel. Compression has been raised above normal with a view to the use of benzol. Normally ignition is by a high tension magneto mounted on the aluminium dashboard and driven off the tail end of the overhead camshaft by a fabric universal jointed shaft. In some races, however, use has been made of two magnetos, with external gears, and in others the Marelli combined generator and distributor has been employed. It probably will depend on track tests as to which type is definitely adopted for the race.

Engine lubrication is assured by means of a gear type pump driven off the right end of a cross shaft, the opposite end of which operates the water circulating pump. There is also a direct oil lead to the steering gearbox. All the oil is contained in an aluminium casting bolted to the basechamber and fitted with longitudinal copper tubes, open at both ends for cooling purposes.

There is a rather unusual use in the Bugatti chassis of leather universals and links. Examples are the channel section pressed steel torque member, which is bolted at the rear to the differential housing and at the front end is attached by a double leather link and two pins to the rear face of the gearbox.

There is a somewhat similar use of leather for the transverse tie rod. This connection consists of two steel tubes with flattened ends attached by two bolts to oval-shaped blocks of compressed chrome leather having a top and a bottom plate of steel. A socket is formed in the leather for the usual type of ball, the taper stem of which is mounted in the steering arm in the normal manner.

Contemporary road impressions

Mr E. N. Duffield, after testing the car, wrote in the *Automotor Journal* of 26 March 1925 in his usual style but as a Bugatti fan:

Any little sounds which the engine may develop are lost in air-rush and the murmur of the gears. Bugattis are only relatively silent as to their transmission, but obviously the torque of the eight-cylindered

90

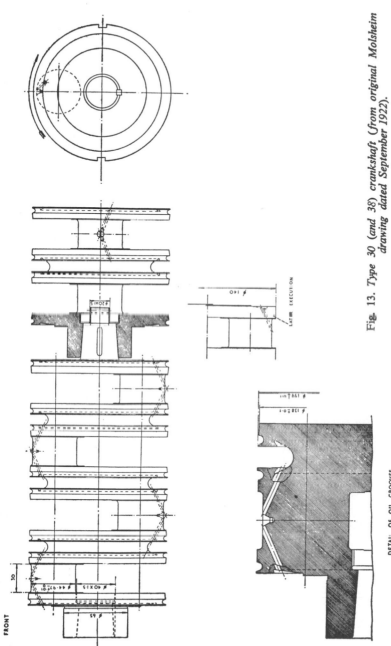

FRONT

DETAIL OF OIL GROOVES

Fig. 13. *Type 30 (and 38) crankshaft (from original Molsheim drawing dated September 1922).*

91

motor tends to demonstrate the transmission at its best, and although it would be futile to speak of this car as dead silent, even on fourth, she is very markedly nearer being so than is any four-cylindered Bugatti which I have driven. She is easily good for 40 mph on second, on the flat, and running well within herself, she will do 65 mph, as registered by an A.T. speed indicator guaranteed dead correct, on fourth. She will probably do more, but that seems enough for two litres, on a very cold, windy day!

Her steering is delightful. I know how much of its charm to attribute to the suspension, but apart from that, the steering itself is wonderfully good. It is very high-geared; it has a gigantic worm-shaft and quite a large worm-wheel; it has the fabric-disc coupling at the base of the pillar to damp-out any little kick what comes through such pretty connections; and additionally it has the assistance of the very thin, very flexible spring-steel spokes of the wheel. Like every other Bugatti, ever since the marque existed, this car can be put around any corner just as rapidly as the driver wishes, in perfect security.

Its gearbox is similarly true to type. In town one gets much practice in gear-changing, especially if one has the Bugatti habit, regarding a spell of third as quite a treat, and a stretch upon fourth as a positive revel; but I fear that I used the change-speed lever much more than I need have done, failing to make proper allowance for the superior torque of the eight-cylindered engine.

This particular car was tuned for power, and so would not run really sweetly upon fourth at less than something between 10 and 12 mph, but the feel of the engine suggested that it could be quite easily de-tuned without going farther than the carburettor, and – anyhow – anybody who buys a Bugatti, of any model, to crawl up and down Bond St and edify its principal or most numerous frequenters is not a really discerning person.

Running freely, at from 25 to 40 mph, the engine is extremely pleasant. Tuned as this car's carburettor was, one had to be careful with one's toe. I should wonder, too, if a Bosch magneto might not give one finer ignition-gradation than could be got with the standard battery-and-coil set; but, again, one does not buy such a car exclusively for shopping.

I made no real use of the front-wheel brakes. They seemed to be there, and in business, but I use the hand-applied brakes of any and every car far more than those actuated by use of the pedal, and I am not a brake-driver, anyway.

The engine is wonderful, in its stream of power. The more one asks, the more one seems to get. The steering and suspension, the

61. *The driving compartment of the T.30. Although Ettore had used a rimmed wheel on the pre-war 5 litre car, the real Bugatti wheel was introduced with the T.30. The accelerator pedal is central.*

The engine from an ...ianapolis car (No. 4006) ...ch stayed in or returned the U.S.A. These early ...s had a high mounted oil ...mp, although the one ...strated is not original.

(photo: O. A. Phillips)

63. *The original 1922 engine on test at Molsheim. Note the twin magneto drive and the knurled nuts on the cambox cover.*

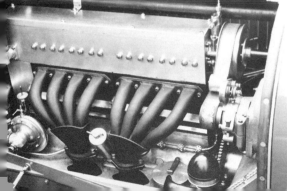

64. *Left-hand side of the engine. Belt driven dynamo, cast aluminium bulkhead and a cast skirt to the one piece crank case.*

TYPE 35

65 and 66. *The original 1924 Type 35 first seen at Lyon in the 1924 French Grand Prix. Narrow horseshoe radiator, one piece hollow front axle, alloy wheels with detachable rim and integr drums were allied to a modified engine with ball and roller bearing crankshaft and connecting ro Note the long tail; to many this was the most aesthetically satisfying racing car ever produce*

gear-changing, are if possible a little better than ever they were, and altogether this is a very wonderful machine. It is an 'outdoor' car, which begins to earn nuts and/or cigars only after Esher, or Staines or Watford. It can and will trickle through Regent's Park very demurely, but to use it for that kind of motoring is rather like using a Grand National winner to haul a cart-full of mangolds. It is a full-blooded, real man's motor-car, by intention and in performance.

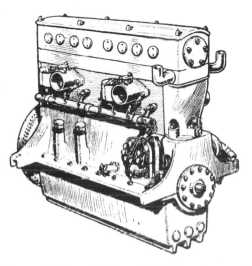

Fig. 14. The Motor, *4 August 1925, published this drawing of the 8 cylinder racing engine, but gives no clue to its origin, although implying that it was the type used in the 1925 French Grand Prix. It is probably an earlier Type 30 (or T.29) racing engine, perhaps of the type used at Strasbourg or Tours. Indeed the artist may have sketched it rapidly, completing his drawing later, so that the detail may not be exact. The drawing was also published in* Svensk Motortidning, *16 August 1925, again without explanation.*

TYPES 35 & 39
famous racing models

IF BUGATTI ESTABLISHED HIMSELF AS A RACING CAR MANU-facturer of consequence with his 4 cylinder 8 and 16 valve cars, it was the introduction of the 8 cylinder Type 35 which began the period of six or seven years when Bugatti dominated motor racing as no maker before nor indeed since has managed to do – although perhaps today Ferrari or Lotus are showing signs of being in the same class. As a racing car the type had almost everything that could be desired in a car of that generation – everything that is except sheer power. It was available to anyone at a price that was within the compass of those who could afford to race. It was a car of considerable beauty – to many it was and is the most aesthetically satisfying car design ever produced – in notable contrast indeed to the ugliness of the earlier tank-on-the-tail designs. It was well finished again in contrast to the earlier cars, making it highly desirable for purely visual reasons. It was small and light, handled superbly and therefore was a pleasure to own and drive to the second rank as well as the top rank of drivers. And above all it won races by the hundreds in the hands of romantic-sounding drivers of all types – capable Italians, titled dilettanti from several countries, mysterious Englishmen and flamboyant Frenchmen.

Bugatti himself claimed in 1927 to have won over 2,000 awards in sporting events. His catalogues of the era sometimes contained as many pages listing his awards of the previous season as on details of the cars he was selling! In one year alone (1926) he won 12 major Grand Prix, including:

G.P. of Rome 1: Maggi.
Targa Florio 1, 2, 3: Costantini, Minoia, Goux.
G.P. of Alsace 1, 2, 3: Dubonnet, Maggi, de Vizcaya.
G.P. of France, *Miramas* 1, 2: Goux, Costantini.

G.P. of Europe, San Sebastian 1: Goux.

G.P. of Spain 1, 2: Costantini, Goux.

G.P. of Boulogne 1: Eyston

G.P. of Italy, Monza 1, 2: 'Sabipa', Costantini.

G.P. of Milan 1, 2, 3: Costantini, Goux, Farinotti.

If any single design is responsible for the interest in the Marque Bugatti which exists today, for the founding of the Bugatti Owners' Club in 1931 and others later, and indeed for the existence of the Bugatti Book, it is the Type 35*.

Evolution of the model

The 1923 Grand Prix had seen the rather unsuccessful tank bodied Type 30, 8 cylinder cars and disastrous entries at Indianapolis. The defects of what was basically a good design were in the engine, which needed more than three crankshaft bearings and a proper means of lubricating the big ends of the connecting rods, in the chassis which needed better brakes, and in the body where a small two-seat layout of low frontal area more like the typical Delage or Talbot of the epoch was obviously (even to the stubborn Ettore!) needed. So Bugatti evidently spent the winter of 1923–24 adding two main roller bearings to the crankshaft and, reluctant as he had shown himself since 1916 to face up to the problems of pressure-fed plain bearings, he designed a complicated, if effective enough roller bearing big end design for the connecting rods; improvements to the chassis and some excellent work on the brakes, and a wholly admirable improvement in the body work resulted in the brilliantly effective Type 35. First produced in 1924 in 2 litre unblown form, for the 1924 French Grand Prix at Lyon (see page 99), it went through several stages of development culminating in the 35B, supercharged 2·3 litre car which continued until superseded by the Type 51, which had a 35B engine fitted with a twin camshaft block. All these models had basically the same 2 metre chassis and body. The various types produced were as follows:

Type 2 litre, unblown 60 mm × 88 mm, small brake drums,
35 cast alloy beaded-edge wheels with detachable rims, small narrow radiator, and first catalogued in the 1924–25 issue.

* The model and its history are described in detail in the Author's book *Grand Prix Bugatti* – G. T. Foulis, 1969.

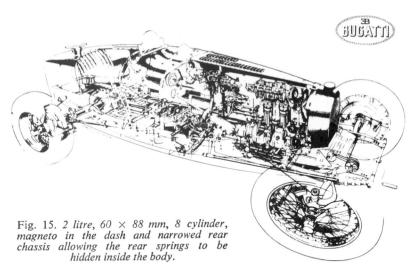

Fig. 15. *2 litre, 60 × 88 mm, 8 cylinder,
magneto in the dash and narrowed rear
chassis allowing the rear springs to be
hidden inside the body.*

(drawing: James Allington)

Type 35 1·5 litre, unblown 52 mm × 88 mm. A few cars were produced for 1925 Grand Prix events, and with blowers added ran in the 1926 French Grand Prix. The T.39 replaced these cars in 1926, as a catalogued model. A few 54 mm × 81 mm cars were also produced in 1927.

Type 35 1,100 cc. Three special supercharged cars were produced for the 1926 Alsatian Grand Prix, the engine being 51·3 mm × 66 mm. This was the first success that Bugatti had with a blown car. The single seat versions are strictly known as Type 36.

Type 35T The 1926 Targa Florio saw the introduction of the unsupercharged 35T (T = Targa) model, an unblown car with longer stroke (100 mm), bringing it to 2,300 cc. Bradley in the *Autocar* of 21 April 1926 quotes the cars as 61 mm × 100 mm (2,350 cc), although 60 mm × 100 mm is normal. The October 1926 works catalogue refers to the T.35 as being available with a 2·3 litre engine and blower on demand.

Type 35B 2·3 litre, 60 mm × 100 mm, at last with a blower; to accommodate the drive for the blower the radiator was moved forward and in fact enlarged. This model, derived from the unblown car first produced for the 1926 Targa Florio,

67. *Lyon 1924—the début of the Type 35.*

68. *Ettore beside the 1924 car at Lyon.*

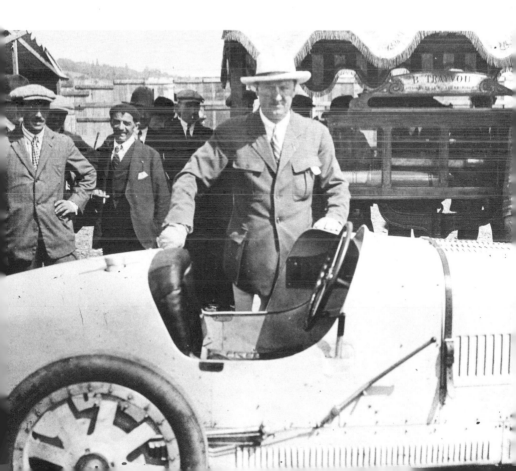

69. *Ferdinand de Vizcaya, brother of Pierre, in the 1925 Targa Florio.*

1925–1926

70. *A superb action photograph of Costantini winning the 1926 Targa Florio.*

71. *Goux winning the 1·5 litre 'touring' French Grand Prix. This model was 60 × 66 mm and these dimensions were adopted for the T39.*

72. *The 1926 Grand Prix of Alsace saw the appearance of two unusual supercharged 1,100 cc cars driven by de Vizcaya and Maggi and a standard-bodied version driven by Dubonnet who won.*

(*photo:* Autocar)

73. *In the main French Grand Prix event in 1925 Costantini and the other Bugatti drivers had cars with the mechanic's seat partially cowled over, much to the dismay of other drivers, and no doubt the mechanics themselves.*

(*photo: T. A. S. O. Mathieson*)

74. *Dubonnet in the 1926 Targa Florio.*

TYPE 39A

75. *Goux, 1926 European Grand Prix winner. Note the large radiator and small brakes.*

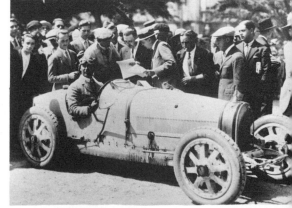

76. *The start of the 1926 European Grand Prix at San Sebastian. Costantini on the left, Wagner, Delage and Goux—the eventual winner. A fine picture with all the atmosphere of the great Grand Prix.*

77. *De Vizcaya on the 1,100 cc single seat car which ran in the 1926 Alsace Grand Prix. Note the straight front axles. Front springs were quarter-elliptic. One of the two cars entered came to England and was driven at Brooklands by Malcolm Campbell (see plate 83). The cars started life as the unsuccessful Type 36 with no rear springs, appearing briefly in practice for the Grand Prix d'Ouverture at Montlhéry, 1925.*

78. *Benoist in a T.35C in the Spanish Grand Prix at San Sebastian, 1928.*

79. *1928. L. Chiron with the 2·3 litre blown Type 35B, on the road between Molsheim and Saverne. The car now has larger tyres and brakes.*

80. *The up-and-coming young René Dreyfus at Antibes in 1928.*

81. *The famous Czech driver Madame Junek after winning the Coupe des Dames, Montl-héry, 1928.*

82. *Williams, an Englishman living in France, won many races in a Bugatti. Here he is at Monaco in 1929 in a blown 2·3 litre, 60 × 100 mm with enlarged radiator, set more forward, and larger brakes.*

83. *(right.) Malcolm Campbell and son Donald at Brooklands in 1928 with single seater Alsace G.P. car now converted to 2,300 cc.* (photo: Autocar)

84. THE 'TECLA'. *The success of the G.P. T.35 caused Bugatti to market a detuned version known as the T.35A which used the standard chassis and body, usually with wire wheels, and an engine similar to the T.38, with three main bearings and plain big ends. The car illustrated shows Mr J. C. Byrom in 1928; the alloy wheels were an extra.*

TYPE 35B 85 and 86. *An engine now in Portugal and perfectly restored.*

(*photos: J. Lacerda*)

87. *An original dash layout; note the typical clock and small tachometer. The Scintilla magneto does not use the plug lead holes which a Bosch magneto would call for.*

(*photo: J. Lacerda*)

88. *The unblown T.35 engine with two Zenith carburettors.*

89. *The G.P. gearbox, although similar to the Brescia box in internal details, is mounted quite differently on cross tubes. The forward universal on the propeller shaft has a square hole and block.*

was thus often known as the Targa model; engine numbers generally have the suffix T, the car originally being known as the 35TC. Brake drum diameter was also increased, and the tyre size, but the general layout was unchanged; these improvements may have followed later as only the enlarged engine and blower are referred to in the October 1926 catalogue.

Type 35C   A 2 litre version of Type 35B, with bore and stroke 60 mm × 88 mm, was produced in parallel with the longer stroke model from 1926, with the same blower and generally indistinguishable from it except by the absence of a compression plate about 6 mm in thickness as used on the larger model. Its first win was at the Milan G.P., September 1926.

Type 39   This was the catalogued (in the 1926 catalogue) 1·5 litre model, with a short stroke crank, resulting in a bore and stroke of 60 mm × 66 mm, more reasonable than the earlier modified 2 litre cars. Only a few were produced.

Type 39A   This is the usual designation of a supercharged version of the Type 39 (cf. 37 and 37A), the blower being a narrower version of the Type 35B unit and may have preceded the unblown version. Probably less than ten of this model were produced, but it has the distinction of establishing beyond doubt the success of the blown engine by winning the 1926 French Grand Prix (Goux). One of the 1926 works cars came to England and was driven in the 1926 British Grand Prix by Campbell.

Type 35A   An interesting version of the basic 2 litre model was produced under the catalogue description of 'Course Imitation' or unofficially the 'boy racer'; it was also known at Molsheim as the ' Tecla ' model after the make of cultured pearls. This had an identical body and chassis to the G.P. car, but used the Type 38 touring engine. This differed from the racing car in having a 3 ball bearing crank, and plain big ends (indeed as on the Type 30) and although capable of speeds of 90 mph or so (at 4,500 rpm), it could not achieve the performance of the G.P. cars. However, sold at a substantially lower price it was very popular in sporting as opposed to Grand

107

Prix circles ; lucky was the young man whose father bought him a real Bugatti!

Description of car

The chassis of the T.35 followed the 16 valve car layout, but with a number of notable improvements; the rear springs were swept in at the rear to lie within the streamlined tail of the body, and the rear axle was given additional location by a pair of tubular side rods. The gearbox was similar to the Brescia box, but carried on cross tubes, and the gear shift lever was on the right. The clutch was normal Bugatti. Brakes were much improved; a simple mechanical cable layout, with chain compensation longitudinally and bevel gears laterally, was used. The front cables were so arranged as to give a servo action with axle twist by passing over the top of the horizontal wheel axis. Brake shoes were initially lined with cast iron segments and brake cams had inset rollers. A new type of steering box, robust but simplified as compared with that on the T.30, was fitted and indeed was used in various sizes on all subsequent models. The front axle was produced with a novel form, the centre being hollow and the ends solid. This was achieved by forging the axle straight, boring a central hole right across, slotting out two square holes for the springs to pass through, and then forging down the ends to the solid again and finally bending to shape for machining and polishing all over.

Cast light alloy wheels with detachable rims were fitted, the brake drums being integral with the wheel. This construction was very light and effective although the spokes were not very strong against side shock loads: the later Type 51 well-base wheel had not only an integral rim but stiffening ribs inside the spokes.

The engine was similar to the Type 30; the blocks, cambox and camshaft drive were almost identical, but the crankcase differed by being split on the centre line, the lower crankcase carrying the engine-to-chassis attachment arms. The crankshaft had five main roller or ball bearings, and was built up and had roller bearing rods lubricated by oil jets. On blown models, a gear

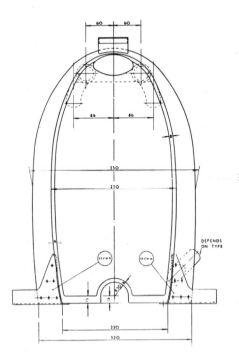

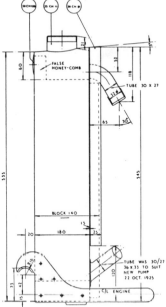

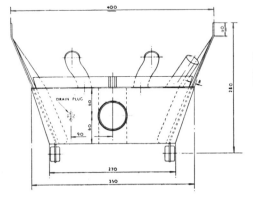

Fig. 16. *From an original Molsheim drawing of the classic T.35 horseshoe radiator, dated 19 April 1924.*

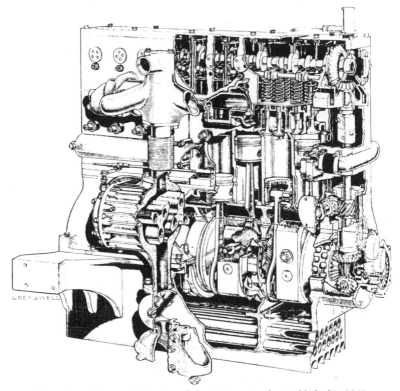

Fig. 17. *A Cresswell drawing of the T.35 engine first published in 1942.*

(*The Motor*)

train on the front of the engine drove the blower, a three bladed Roots-type drawing from a low mounted Zenith K type barrel throttle carburettor. To allow the blower drive to be fitted, the radiator of blown models was moved forward and usually (if not always) enlarged. Unblown models had twin carburettors, the manifolding being rather tortuous. Ignition was by magneto mounted on the dash and driven from the end of the camshaft.

A cross-shaft drove a water pump on the left, the early cars having a small Brescia type pump, later cars a larger unit. The oil pump was driven from a pair of helical gears off the crank-

The G.P. crankshaft is carried on 3 ge double row self-aligning ball races, split roller races and has a sixth ady ball race at the rear. The rods are piece with a single row of 8×11 mm lers in bronze cages. Alignment is by ans of cross tapered cotter pins. The nk illustrated is from a T.43 but is ntical with T.35B and T.51 assembly.

91. Subtle identifying features: the extra pipe to the front bearing is not present on the T.35A (or 38) 3 main bearing engines. The compression plate is normally present only on 2·3 litre (i.e. 100 mm stroke) engines.

92. The rear end of the G.P. chassis.
(photo: J. Thompson)

93. *Today a T.35 is a collector's piece. This is the Vizcaya car from Lyon 1924 (chassis 4325) beautifully restored.*

94. *The cockpit of car 4325. The magneto advance lever is a push-pull control, unlike the later production cars. The magneto is at camshaft height, not driven by a 2:1 step-up gear on the end of the cambox. An epicyclic train in the magneto achieved the same speed-up to engine speed to improve the spark at starting.*

95. *The most successful postwar Bugatti driver, Peter Stubberfield, several times record breaker at Prescott, in a single seat T.35B. This car was owned by Eyston in 1927. It has done the kilometre at Brighton in 28 seconds, crossing the line at 6,000 rpm. in top (130 mph).*

(*photo: P. Eggleston*)

shaft, and was mounted low in the front of the engine, instead of being driven off the water pump shaft as on the T.30. Early cars had hand starting only, but later ones had a starter motor carried on top of the gearbox.

(For fuller details of the engine and chassis see *The Grand Prix Car*, Vol. 1, 1954, by L. Pomeroy, Motor Racing Publications.)

Contemporary road impressions

The *Autocar* of 11 June 1926 had this to say on the car in an article headed 'The Enthusiast's Ideal':

If a year or two ago any firm had announced that it was prepared to offer to the public exact replicas of a car specially designed and built for the Grand Prix, it would probably have been deemed demented. Yet this is exactly what M. Bugatti has done with outstanding success. It is true that M. Bugatti is somewhat of a law unto himself, and that frequently he does things which no one would believe possible, and it is true, also, that the Brescia Bugatti was in some sort a racing car, though it now ranks as a sports model, but the 1924 Grand Prix Bugatti was something very different from every point of view.

When it first appeared for the race at Lyons, the little horizon-blue car captured the imagination instantly. It was so well finished, with its nickelled axles and controls, its almost show-polished engine, and its shapely radiator, that it was the kind of toy which an enthusiast had only to see to desire. Yet, however much of the toy there was externally, it soon appeared that there was no lack of speed or power. The brakes also were really powerful. That there was a fly in the ointment was certain – with a racing car this is always the case – and this time it was the cast aluminium wheels, but this has now been reduced to the status of merely a minor defect, and the car is just as desirable from the sportsman's point of view.

The real Grand Prix car, which actually has been sold in considerable numbers, has, among other things, a roller bearing crankshaft, but along with it M. Bugatti introduced two other models, both with the same sleek, shapely body – one an eight-cylinder two-litre, the other a four-cylinder one-and-a-half-litre, with ordinary bearings, and incidentally, ordinary wire wheels. It is, however, with the genuine Grand Prix racing car that we now deal.

The average every-day motorist would probably recoil from such a mount not only because he would deem it fierce and intractable, but also because it has neither hood nor mudguards. But, fortunately for the romantic and sporting side of motoring, there is another section of the community to whom this car is its heart's desire, precisely because all these fitments are absent, and because it is fierce; but certainly it is not intractable.

Quite what it is that alters the feel and character of a car when the mudguards and hood are not in place, and the windscreen merely a minute segment, is difficult to define, but it is so insistent that it might be said that the stripped car has a soul that is lacking in the sober touring mount. The whole car seems different, and to an enthusiast a hundred times better. True, on muddy roads the state of driver and mechanic beggars description, yet somehow, even this seems good. Goggles and a sound waterproof are essential, yet there is something thrilling in the feel of rain against the face, and the freshness of the cold air.

Concerning tractability, this car, which can lap Brooklands at well over the 100 mph gait, and probably at 114 mph or more after a little attention, can be driven at 10 mph quite comfortably through say, Kingston, handled without trouble in London traffic, and is perfectly suitable for reasonable speeds on the road.

Once the engine is hot, starting is an easy matter, nor is it difficult from cold, save that the engine must be allowed to warm before the carburettors respond correctly. As a normal touring speed can be maintained with practically no throttle opening, the feel of the car is better than that of an ordinary touring machine, because the engine is extraordinarily smooth and gives that rare sensation of great reserve power. Care must be used to avoid making too much exhaust noise, yet once the trick is mastered this is quite easy. The steering, cornering and brakes would prove revelations, not unnaturally, to the average driver.

At full speed the car is indeed something worth having. It has its tricks, of course, and is rather bumpy though a slight modification of tyre pressure or some readjustment of the shockabsorbers might make much difference.

On the road in racing conditions it must be almost ideal. For anyone who has to combine a racing machine with a touring car, the Grand Prix Bugatti cannot be beaten, and it has a most subtle way of gaining what can only be called one's affection, even after a short run, while it feels as though it would keep its tune.

During our test the car was taken on the track and lapped at over 100 mph without any preparation after its run on the road other than to change the plugs for a set of No. 268 K.L.Gs, which suit the engine exactly for high speed. Deliberately, the tyres and shockabsorbers, number plates and spare wheel were left in position as ordinarily used.

114

TYPE 37
4 cylinder racing model

IN 1926 THE 1·5 LITRE BRESCIA RACING MODEL WAS REPLACED with a new car which used the Type 35 chassis and body and was fitted with a 4 cylinder, 69 mm × 100 mm, 1,496 cc engine; this engine had a block and valve gear (three valves per cylinder) similar in detail to the 8 cylinder car, but the crankshaft was carried on five plain main bearings. Early models had jet lubrication but later a full pressure-fed crank was used. Wire wheels were fitted as standard in place of the light alloy G.P. wheels and ignition was by coil. A small blower (casing length 135 mm, compared with the T.35B unit which was 185 mm long) was also added on the Type 37A; this model, usually referred to with the suffix G.P. by Molsheim, had a successful racing history, the late Chris Staniland lapping Brooklands at over 122 mph in one of them. These racing models had dash mounted magneto ignition and usually the detachable rim alloy wheels.

The unblown model was first catalogued in the October 1926 catalogue, under the designation Grand Sport. The engine was also fitted to the Type 40 touring model described on pages 136–143. A full description of the engine by Max Millar follows at the end of this chapter.

Contemporary road impressions

In *Motor Sport*, September 1926, Richard Twelvetrees described a road test of an unblown Type 37:

One has only to glance at the 1,500 cc Grand Prix Bugatti, however, to observe that it is a distinct advance on any of its forerunners, and the manufacturers have introduced a new era for the sporting motorist by placing a real production racing car in the hands of the public. That is to say one can purchase one of these machines, drive it away, and as delivered it will be fit to win races and competitions without any need of 'hotting up'. The actual car [tested] is that belonging to Captain J. C. Douglas and is used daily as a runabout by Mrs Douglas for shopping expeditions in the West End, which supports the maker's claim as to docility.

The stability of the Grand Prix Bugatti and its wonderful steadiness in cornering at speed is largely due to the very low centre of gravity, the chassis being very low without detracting too much from ground clearance. The suspension comprises semi-elliptic front springs, located outside the frame members and provided with rebound clips on the forward halves. The well-known and tried reversed quarter-elliptic springs carry the rear axle, shockabsorbers of the Bugatti design being employed for both sets of springs.

Though the seats are arranged very low the riding is quite comfortable and plenty of leg room is provided on either side of the clutch and gearbox, this part of the mechanism being covered by a readily removable leather flap.

When the bonnet was removed for examination of the engine, I was surprised at the amount of accessibility, for from the external appearance of the car one is apt to imagine that the mechanism must be somewhat cramped. There is, however, plenty of room to get at everything, and any of the normal running adjustments can be made with extraordinary facility. The four-cylinder engine . . . revs up to well over 5,000 rpm almost as soon as the accelerator pedal is depressed. The overhead camshaft gear is enclosed in a neat square aluminium cover, which, conforming with the outline of the cylinder block, gives the engine a particularly neat appearance. Both the revolution counter and the Delco distributor take their drives from the rear end of the camshaft. . . .

I was fortunate in being able to see the best of this attractive little sports model in really expert hands, for Captain J. C. Douglas is certainly amongst the top notchers of demonstrators. I had expected to be whirled along the main roads at lightning speed, having to keep my eyes well skinned in case a man in blue hove in sight. Instead of which the car was driven gently along at a comfortable touring pace, running with remarkable smoothness though some very pretty work with the gears produced something quite out of the way as regards acceleration. The body work gives a good position, but, as might be expected, fails to provide the luxurious comfort to be found in some of the more elaborate sports tourers, and one has to remember that the rear wheel is very close when tempted to put the elbow too far over the side.

Leaving the traffic, I was treated to a turn of speed along a good

116

96. *The 4 cylinder T.37 two seater as equipped for road work. Introduced in 1926, this model replaced the famous Brescia in the 1·5 litre class; although not able to hold its own against the works 8 cylinder supercharged car, it nevertheless had a successful career in Voiturette races.*

TYPE 37

97. *The original model was often used in France without mudguards or road equipment other than lamps.*

(photo: Autocar)

98. *Count Czaykowski served an apprenticeship on a T.37.*

99. *Eileen Ellison and Cholmondley-Tapper, well known at Brooklands pre-war in their 37A.*

100. *A nicely-restored 37A at Prescott in 1972.*

101. *A 1927 T.37 (No. 37337), imported new into Australia by Cyril Poole who is at the wheel; this car was destroyed in an accident.*

102. *A T.37 in original, fully restored condition.*

103. *Right side; the magnet drive is non standard.*

TYPE 37 ENGINE

104. *Left side. The high mounted oil pump is non-standard but common, as a means of overcoming the usual wear of its worm drive from the crankshaft in the usual lower mounting.*

TYPE 37A

105. *A blower was added to the T.37 to make it more suitable for racing and making it very potent indeed.*

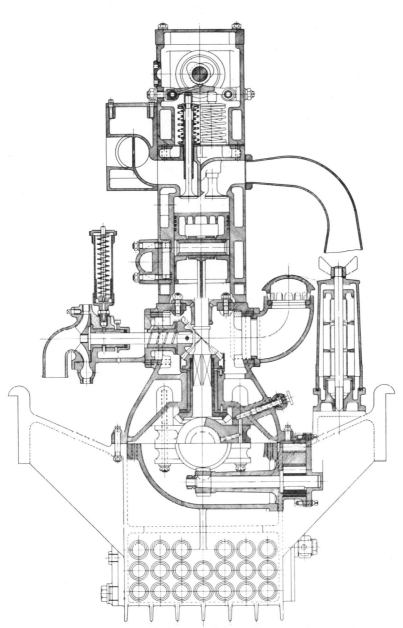

Fig. 18. *A Molsheim sectional elevation of the T.37 engine, the original drawing being dated 31 July 1925. The piston is shown in a 90 deg. section.*

121

wide open road, and again by using the gears with fine judgment Captain Douglas made the little bus hum along merrily at over 85 mph, with plenty more movement left on the accelerator pedal. When going at over 70 mph, he shouted to me to hold tight and by applying the brakes brought the car to rest in an incredibly short distance, though I was expecting a skid, and said so . . . I must say the Bugatti created a most favourable impression.

In 1933 a Type 37 road-equipped Grand Prix Bugatti was the subject of an article in *Autocar*, following Brian Twist's run in the car then owned by Mr R. J. W. Appleton. 'There is no car quite like a Bugatti to the enthusiast . . .' observed the former. This particular car, a 1926 model, had been converted from the splash to pressure-fed big ends, as fitted from 1928 onwards; it also had two Solex carburettors instead of the normal one, a Scintilla magneto and special connecting rods. It had lapped Brooklands outer circuit at 96·8 mph, did 17–23 mpg on petrol-benzole, and 7–10 mpg on alcohol. Acceleration tests produced the following: 10–30 on the 9 to 1 bottom gear in 4·4 second, and 6 seconds on the 7 to 1 second gear; 0–60 mph in 14·6 sec, and 0–80 in 30·2 sec, the former being accomplished in bottom gear, which is quite something and, incidentally, 6,000 rpm. It was pointed out that alcohol fuel was used and the carburation was unhappy on account of the cold weather during these tests. The brakes stopped the car in 30 feet from 30 mph, and approximately 85 yards from 70 mph which, as the author of the article comments, 'is pretty good'. He concludes: 'Finally, I drove the car back to the workshop and was fascinated by the ease of the steering, the smooth power of the brakes, the quite reasonable tractability in such towns as we passed through, and last, but not least, the wonderful Bugatti exhaust note'.

THE MODERN STORY OF A TYPE 37A

by P.M.A.H. from *Bugantics*, 21, 1, 1958

A little blue Bugatti – the 1927 Type 37A Grand Prix car belonging to A. F. Eminson of the Vintage Sports Car Club – showed itself during last season to be the fastest vintage racing car being raced at present in this country. It won the two main events in the V.S.C.C.

calendar – the Itala Trophy at Silverstone and the Seaman Vintage Trophy at Oulton Park. In this last race it was driven by D. H. C. Hull, who has been responsible for tuning the car for the last two seasons.

This model Bugatti has a supercharged 1½-litre four-cylinder engine, with a plain bearing crankshaft and three valves per cylinder. In the great days of Bugatti supremacy in racing the Type 37A was always rather overshadowed by the Type 35 series Grand Prix cars. In present-day vintage races, however, Eminson's car has at times beaten surviving examples of the eight-cylinder car, and with its less complicated engine, has the added advantage of being less expensive to maintain.

For the driver of average height and girth the cockpit is on the cramped side, and there is no question of 'slipping behind the wheel'; it would be truer to say that the driver has to insinuate himself there. Once in the seat, however, he finds the big wooden rimmed steering wheel nicely in his lap, although the throttle, brake and clutch pedals are so close together that plimsolls are almost essential footwear. Eminson has even had to buff away some of the rubber sole of one of his shoes so that it will not foul the pedals!

Both the handbrake and gear lever are on the right-hand side, outside the body, and although the gear lever is well placed it is awkward in that the gears are 'the wrong way round', and one moves the lever forward to change into top. On the left, beside the driver, is an extra oil tank holding about three pints, and a pump which enables the driver to replenish the sump with oil during races. There is another hand-pump on the left-hand side of the dashboard with which the driver can build up air pressure in the rear fuel tank in order to force the fuel forward to the engine, but once the engine is running this pressure is maintained by a mechanical air pump.

Among the instruments on the dashboard is the classic Bugatti car clock which was fitted to all Bugatti racing cars, and which, after nearly thirty years, still keeps perfect time.

To the enthusiast the view from the cockpit is inspiring. He looks over a single aero-screen down a tapering louvred bonnet, secured by two straps, and terminating in the traditional little Bugatti horseshoe-shaped radiator. On either side of the radiator he can see the front wheels, shod with Dunlop racing tyres. The whole car gives the impression of being splendidly small and handy.

When in motion this 37A makes all the well-known Bugatti noises. The getaway needs to be practised if the car is not to be stalled ignominiously on the line, and gears can be 'missed' on the crash box if the driver is lacking in skill.

123

On corners the handling of the car cannot be faulted as it has no tendency whatsoever to chase its tail. The hardness of the suspension, however, would appal the drivers of modern racing cars. At Oulton Park, which for the Bugatti is a very bumpy circuit, both Eminson and Hull have to wear racing body belts, a familiar sight at the old Brooklands meetings, but equipment not often worn nowadays. In addition the steering is fairly heavy, so that after an hour's race at Oulton the driver of the Bugatti is probably more tired than the driver of a modern all-independently sprung racing car would be after a three-hour British Grand Prix at Silverstone or Aintree.

The top speed is 110 mph at 5,500 rpm, and fuel consumption while racing about 8 mpg. Race averages at Oulton Park are around 8 mph down on those of the faster modern sports racing cars, but it is fair to say that the Bugatti would have little trouble in out-stripping the majority of standard production sports cars seen on our roads today. Its best time up Prestcott Hill is 49·7 sec, which contrasts with Peter Stubberfield's best time in his sprint Type 35B single-seater, which is down to 45 sec odd. [This refers to the old course.]

TYPE 37 ENGINE

by Max Millar

(Under the heading 'Another Famous Engine', this illustrated article first appeared in the *Autocar* on 19 September 1952

In the history of the car world during the years from 1911 to 1939, there were few names that could compete with that of Ettore Bugatti for his remarkable career and general attainments, and for his great success in the racing sphere; his name, moreover, is still regarded with as much respect and admiration among Bugatti enthusiasts as in the old days.

A biography of Bugatti by W. F. Bradley tells us that this great man (1881–1947) was a born artist as well as an engineer, and that for many years he not only designed his own cars but also made the drawings and supervised production in his shops at Molsheim. His cars were so outstandingly different from others that a mere superficial look at them at any time would be enough to excite great attention, but a closer examination reveals characteristics which indicate that Bugatti was an individualist in the field of design respecting almost every component, stud and nut in each of his creations.

124

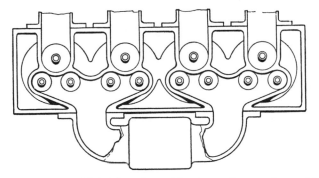

Fig. 19a. *How Bugatti fed 8 inlet valves with mixture from an internal induction manifold and single carburettor. The exhaust valves are ducted separately to a 'bunch of bananas' exhaust pipe.*

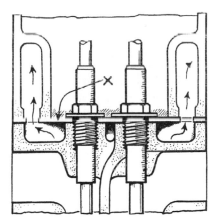

Fig. 19b. *Section of cylinder head showing how valve guides are employed to assist holding down the cover plate on the top face of the head.*

125

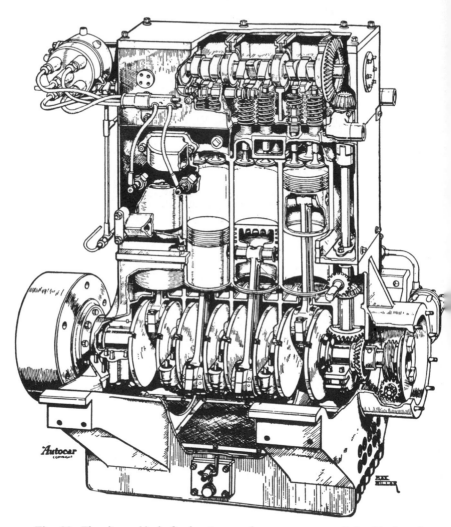

Fig. 20. *The disc-webbed, five-bearing crankcase, compact cylinder block and overhead valve gear are special characteristics of the Type 37 engine. The worm drive to the oil pump is a source of trouble. It is inadequately lubricated and the high rubbing velocity of the worm causes the pinion on the gear pump to wear out fairly rapidly.*

By his personal ability to design, experiment and carry through the work to the production stage, Bugatti was able to do what he liked, and the long list of road and racing successes was ample proof of his capacity as a practical engineer; but the aforementioned abilities enabled him to design with such a superb sense of proportion and finesse that the contemporary efforts of other makers often seemed crude and wasteful by comparison, and, of course, he gained immeasurably in regard to weight reduction in his chassis.

In discussing Bugatti's achievements in engine design, it would be difficult to select any one power unit as being more interesting than others; they all exhibited remarkable features in one form or another. He produced many types of engine ranging from 4 to 16 cylinder units and from 1,327 cc up to the enormous Royale of 12,760 cc (although curiously a 6 cylinder engine was never listed), and a number were supercharged; but a 1925 Type 37 4 cylinder 1,496 cc engine may be taken as representative of Bugatti design some twenty-five years ago, and it exhibits many of those novel features that reveal the Bugatti mind as a designer and engineer.

In general, the Type 37 engine is remarkably simple as a unit, the cast iron cylinder block being a rectangular component, with the heads and valve ports cast in as one-piece job. Three valves per cylinder (one exhaust and two inlet) are fitted, and they are operated by an overhead camshaft bevel driven through a vertical shaft from the crankshaft, in the time-honoured system so frequently seen on sports or racing engines. The cylinder block is bolted to an aluminium alloy crankcase split across the crankshaft centre line, the lower half forming the capacious alloy oil sump of 10 pints capacity, conventional in most respects except for one important point in that the four substantial bearer arms of the engine are attached to the lower and not to the upper half of the crankcase; the lower half, or sump, therefore, carries most of the dead weight of the engine.

The cylinder block of 69 mm × 100 mm bore and stroke has the four barrels cast together without interspace cooling, and they project into the crankcase for some distance. The block is machined all over externally and is flat sided, with the vertically disposed valves (inlets 26·5 mm, exhaust 36 mm) set to the maximum diameter available in the combustion chamber, with slight rebating of the cylinder walls to give clearance. The inlet valve ports are double siamesed; each group of four is connected with an intake from the induction manifold, and each exhaust valve is separately ducted in the cylinder head to individual exhaust pipes. The block, as a whole, is interesting in that Bugatti considerably simplified the coring and casting by not including the upper face of the head in the casting process, thereby leaving the ports and passages open to inspection

127

before machining. After machining, a flat aluminium roof about $\frac{3}{32}$ in. thick, drilled where necessary, was fitted on the top face of the head. This roof is held in place by the 12 threaded bronze valve guides, and by the six screw sockets that retain the overhead camshaft case in position. The firing order is 1, 2, 4, 3.

A study of the cross-section of the Bugatti engine reveals the extraordinary proportions and character of this power unit. Tall and narrow, the engine has a crankcase so tightly built around the circular webbed crankshaft that the minimum safe clearance has been given to the connecting rod big-ends; but the crankcase is more rigid in consequence, and there is a considerable saving in weight. The cylinder block is held to the crankcase by 10 small studs and nuts on each side; the nuts lie in a machined slot, which is covered by an aluminium strip held in the slot by spring-loaded balls; thus the flat sided effect of the cylinder block is preserved.

In view of the fact that the close spacing of the cylinder bores involved an equivalent restriction on the lateral proportions of the crankshaft and its webs, it is not surprising that Bugatti made the webs circular in shape and very narrow in width (11 mm) to leave enough room for the three inter-crank bearings of the five bearing shaft. The webs are not balanced, and the crankshaft (weight 37 lb) is machined all over. In the early engines of the Type 37 the big-ends were lubricated by horizontal jets in the crankshaft main bearings – jets that fed oil into shallow circular grooves in the outer faces of the webs and thence by drilled passages to the crankpins. But at a later date the crankshaft was drilled for direct pressure lubrication as between each journal and crankpin. Splash lubrication of the cylinder bores is regulated by horizontal webs cast in the crankcase below the mouths of the bores; the webs further increase the rigidity of the crankcase in that area.

Four of the main bearings have four slender studs and nuts for retention of the bearing caps, in place of pairs of larger size, and the rear main bearing is held by six studs and nuts instead of a possible two or four as is usual practice. The flywheel, if it can be termed such, is only 8½ in. in diameter, but it is of considerable length (weight, 22 lb) to accommodate the multi-plate, semi-wet Bugatti clutch.

The connecting rods (weight 2 lb 1 oz) are of normal design, but have slender shanks for a fast engine, and are notable for the amount of extra metal in the big-end shells, and for the bronze white-metal-lined bearings, riveted to the shells to prevent rotation. Alloy pistons (weight, with gudgeon pins and rings, 14 oz), with three compression rings and one scraper, are of conventional design; the gudgeon pins are held in the piston by an interference fit and endwise locating

128

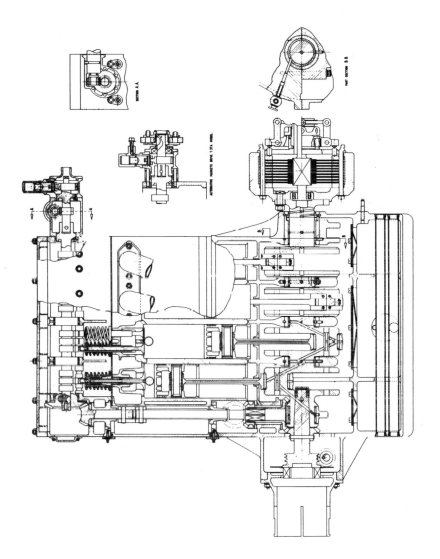

Fig. 21. *Longitudinal section of T.37 engine.*

rings. The 18 mm sparking plugs are fitted in the side of the combustion chambers, the electrodes shielded by shrouded recesses in the cylinder walls.

In this engine, Bugatti operated the inlet and exhaust valves from the single overhead camshaft through horizontal levers, two for each pair of inlet valves and a single one for each exhaust valve. The rockers butt against the hardened steel caps fitted on the valve stems and are each located laterally by an adjustable screwed peg in the side of the camshaft casing. The rocker spindles are drilled; oil fed through them from the oil pressure system lubricates the rockers, cams, and the camshaft bevel driving wheels and bearings; the four plain bush bearings supporting the camshaft are lubricated by splash oil caught in troughs above the bearings. The complete box-like camshaft casing, with flat-topped lid, is in shape just an upward extension of the cylinder block, and it heightens the general appearance of the tall, narrow engine.

Bugatti's penchant for tucking things in neatly, and for reducing weight and mass of metal in various places, is exemplified by his vertical drive to the camshaft and by the close association of the lower driving bevels with the front main bearing of the crankshaft. The vertical shaft is in two sections, linked together by a squared sliding joint, and at a midway level a further pair of bevels drive the horizontal spindle of the water pump. No ball or roller bearings are used in the drives; indeed, none is found in the engine anywhere. The upper portion of the vertical drive is enclosed at the side by an aluminium casting shaped to complete the box-like structure of the cylinder block and camshaft casing.

The oil pump, externally located on the nose of the crankcase, is driven transversely through a skew gear on a front extension of the crankshaft, which also carries the dog drive for the dynamo bolted to the front of the crankcase. The pump, drawing oil from the finned oil sump, feeds the main bearings through a high pressure filter and an external gallery pipe supplying the bearings through drilled passages in the crankcase webs. Two secondary pipes feed the hollow spindles of the overhead valve rockers, and the oil returns to the sump through passages in the cylinder block or downwards past the camshaft vertical drive. Cooling of oil in the sump is effected not only by external finning but also by horizontal air tubes, which greatly increase the total cooling area of the sump.

The simple, clean appearance of this Bugatti engine is enhanced by the layout of the water-circulation system, whereby the customary external piping is largely eliminated. Water from the pump is taken to the lower end of the cylinder jacket through an aluminium

130

manifold which feeds coolant through a series of spaced holes in the jacket to provide a directional flow upwards past the cylinder barrels. From the cylinder jackets the upward flow is further directed past the valve ports on each side and through another series of holes to the water manifolds cast in the sides of the camshaft casing; the return of water to the radiator is through two forward mounted elbows and hose pipes. Hot water for the induction pipe jackets is bled off at a central point from the cylinder block and is returned to the radiator via one of the elbows just mentioned.

Another feature indicative of the clean planning of the engine is the mounting of the coil ignition distributor (skew gear driven) at the rear end of the camshaft casing, and the neat rigging of the high tension leads. The water pump has an unusual feature in that it is equipped with a permanently-fitted grease gun for gland lubrication, and is fitted with a light external tell-tale spindle to indicate the quantity of grease remaining in the barrel. Throughout the engine are to be seen small square and hexagon-headed nuts of Bugatti design – many with special flanges, as in aircraft engine practice – and all external surfaces of the power unit are either machined or hand treated and polished.

With a weight of 15½ cwt, the Type 37 Bugatti Grand Prix two-seater model was capable of 95 mph at 5,000 engine rpm, with a rear axle ratio of approximately 4 to 1. Unquestionably, the fine road performance of this model, with an engine of only medium compression, was owed to the light weight of the chassis and ensemble, and to the fact that it could be handled and driven superbly by a competent driver. At the same time the conservative stressing of the engine gave a considerable degree of reliability, in terms of a sports car, and an unusual fuel economy of approximately 30 mpg, the engine having normally only a single Solex carburettor.

A later development from this engine was the Type 37A, which was fitted with a Roots-type supercharger; but not many – in comparison – of these units were produced, and the supercharged version never achieved the lasting fame of the Type 37. The Type 40 engine, also unsupercharged, was similar to the Type 37, but was a detuned version for a touring car, with a lower compression ratio.

The death of Ettore Bugatti in 1947 brought an end to an astonishing career, the details of which must be treasured by the many who knew him – a career that could not easily be emulated in the present world. The recent re-establishment of the Bugatti at Molsheim, nevertheless, offers good hope that some of the influence that Ettore so powerfully created will not be lost in future productions from the famous factory.

TYPE 38
8 cylinder

IN 1926 AND 1927 AN 8 CYLINDER 2 LITRE TOURING MODEL WAS produced, using an engine based on the Type 35A; this model, Type 38, replaced Type 30 but was similar in most respects. The model was listed in the British 1928 catalogue, but probably few were produced after 1927. In fact, Type 44 replaced it as the 8 cylinder touring model and Type 38 more or less grew into Type 43 by the time the G.P. supercharged engine was fitted. The chassis (which is described in detail in the *Automotor Journal* of 21 July 1927) was rather longer than in Type 30, having the same wheelbase as the later T.44, and the track was widened two inches from the earlier model. The front axle was of circular (but solid) section with the springs passing through the centre of the axle as on the G.P. cars. The rear suspension and axle were normal Bugatti; wire wheels on Rudge hubs had large brake drums and cable brakes run on almost identical lines to the G.P. cars. Hartford type (Repusseau) friction shock-absorbers were used in place of the Bugatti model seen on earlier cars.

The engine was virtually a 35A unit, with a 3 ball bearing crank and plain connecting rod bearings, the crankshaft itself being the same unit as on Type 30. There were two Solex carburettors and coil ignition. The clutch was normal Bugatti, but used a Y-shaped vertical yoke for withdrawal in place of the transverse diamond shaped lever used on Type 30 and other earlier cars. A new gearbox was used, carried in a casting straddling the frame as on the earlier cars, but the gear change was central, and the direction of change normal. Virtually all

(photo: R. Jarraud)

106. *This replaced the Type 30 in 1926; it used the 2 litre T.35A 3-bearing crankshaft engine in a chassis which was very similar to the later Types 43 and 44. It was the first Bugatti to have a flat based radiator, and a central change on a new gearbox, and used afterwards on Types 40, 43, 44 and 49. A few supercharged T.38As were produced but the crankshaft was scarcely up to it.*

TYPE 38

107. *A pretty Lavocat and Marsaud roadster body—virtually indistinguishable from a T.43.*

108. *A contemporary photograph of a Type 40. Introduced in 1926 and replacing the Brescia Modifié, it provided a characteristic Bugatti sports car costing originally only £365 complete, with economy of upkeep, typical roadholding and acceleration and a speed of 75–80 mph. The standard 3-4 seat Grand Sport body shown here was introduced in 1927–8.*

TYPE 40

109. *Jean Bugatti built this interesting 'fiacre' body on a Type 40 chassis and added a supercharger to it; it was owned until 1972 by Lidia Bugatti.*

chassis details other than the engine were used on the later Type 40, 43, 44, 49 series cars.

A few supercharged Type 38A cars were produced, using the small Type 37A blower, but the Type 30 crankshaft was not up to the extra loading and the engines did not last long.

As the editor of *The Bugatti Book* stated: 'There have been more successful models'.

TYPE 40
4 cylinder

TYPE 40 REPLACED THE BRESCIA AS THE 1·5 LITRE, 4 CYLINDER touring car, a type of car indeed on which Bugatti had made his name. The type is sometimes rudely referred to as 'Ettore's Morris Cowley', but if its performance was a little pedestrian it still had all the good road manners of the earlier models coupled with sensible bodywork and a degree of simplicity which the 8 cylinder models could not offer, and finally was sold at a reasonable price.

The chassis, although of shorter wheelbase, was similar to Type 38, and the axles, gearbox and general layout were the same. The engine was that of the Type 37, already described, namely an unblown 4 cylinder 69 mm × 100 mm, 5 plain bearing crank, plain rods and three valves per cylinder in a cylinder block and cambox which were similar to half of the 8 cylinder G.P. engine. As in the case of the Type 37 the jet lubricated connecting rod bearings on early engines were eventually replaced by a full pressure crank version. The crankcase casting itself had different attachment arms. The standard Molsheim bodywork on Type 40 was a close-coupled 4-seat torpedo touring car with a single left-hand door and a hatch on the long tail to provide access to a luggage compartment, a style also used on the T.43. But many proprietary coach builders fitted closed or convertible bodies to the model.

In 1930 a batch of about fifty Type 40A cars were produced, these having cylinder blocks from Type 49, with a 72 mm bore, but otherwise similar to the standard model. They mostly had two seat roadster bodies with a folding rear seat, along classic American lines.

136

Contemporary road impressions

A road test of this model was published in *The Motor*, 10 December 1929, the car being a Molsheim bodied tourer with a single left-hand door. The front seat was 36 in. wide with a reasonable 9½ in. of rear leg room. The turning circle was commendably low at 36 ft to the right and 34 ft to the left.

Bugatti cars have always been famous for their successes in racing, but they have generally been considered just a little too expensive for the young man with sporting tastes but a limited bank balance. The Type 40 Bugatti, however, possesses many of the excellent features of the 1,500 cc Grand Prix model, but sells at the comparatively modest price of £365.

The maker's claims as regards maximum speed are by no means extravagant: 70 to 75 mph is the speed with which they credit the car, and we found that it would lap Brooklands at 70·64 mph, in thoroughly unsuitable weather, whilst its maximum speed attained on test with the wind behind was 76·8 mph. Moreover, the car is fast on its gears and will reach 62·5 mph on third, while the acceleration is distinctly good.

The Type 40 Bugatti is one of those cars which one appreciates to the full only after having driven it some considerable distance. At first one is apt to find the gear change a little difficult. Indeed, the mechanically-minded Britisher rather shrinks from seizing the gear lever in a grip of iron and thrusting it without ceremony into whichever slot of the gate corresponds to the gear ratio required. Attempts to change gear as one does on the average British car – gently with two fingers – are seldom successful. As a matter of fact, the gear change is distinctly positive, and moreover very rapid. The higher the speeds at which the gears are changed the easier the manipulation of the gear lever becomes. On the intermediate gears the car is not quiet, but mechanical silence is never considered of great importance by the sports car enthusiast. On the other hand, the engine is quieter than most power units of its type, while the exhaust is by no means offensive.

The car is, above all, thoroughly roadworthy, and this surely is the greatest recommendation of all. One can swing round a bend or stamp on the brake pedal on a greasy stretch of road without experiencing the slightest qualm. Comfortable at low speeds, the springing becomes positively luxurious at a mile a minute or over; indeed, it is one of the best-sprung cars of its type which we have yet driven, and there is no need, for instance, to vary the shock-absorber adjustment even for widely different conditions, such as low speeds in town and an all-out lap on Brooklands track.

The steering for the first few minutes seems a little stiff, but this impression soon fades, and once on the open road no car could be more easily controlled; one can steer to an inch at any speed.

The clutch, of the multi-plate type, is smooth and light to operate, while the back axle is fairly quiet.

Another good feature of the car is that it seems to delight in being driven hard. The accelerator pedal can be kept fully depressed for lap after lap of the track, and the car will, if anything, gain in speed. This partly due to very careful consideration having been given to keep the oil cool. The sump, besides being deeply ribbed, is fitted with longitudinal tubes of large diameter, through which the air passes, thus cooling the oil very rapidly. The body-work is built on distinctly sporting lines and closely resembles that fitted to the famous 2,300 cc model which has done so well in races during the past year.

Mr Edgar N. Duffield also tested this Molsheim 'Morris-Cowley' for the *Automotor Journal* and reported in the June 1929 issue:

In 1913, using only eight valves with four cylinders, Ettore Bugatti astonished Europe. Later he added to his valve numbers. I have had four Bugattis – one 8-valve and three 16-valve; but to pretend that the £575 11·9 hp Bugatti chassis of 1923 was in the same class as this 1929 complete car at £365 is utterly impracticable. . . . Braking is now on all four wheels when one uses the pedal. The brakes are abundantly powerful, but also very quiet and smooth. Aforetime Bugatti brakes were at their best when used very inconsiderately, criminally so. Nobody wants, or is likely to get, better brakes than these. Repusseau shockabsorbers are standard equipment and lighting equipment by Marchal-Vaucanson. Wheelbase is 8 ft 11 in. The car was sent down to me by Colonel W. Sorel, the British representative of the Bugatti factory, in charge of a M. Mischall, a Molsheim-trained tester-demonstrator-service man. . . . I have never been to Brighton so quickly on any other car.

Mischall [see page 355] learned to drive on Bugattis, around the Bugatti works; learned to climb hills in the Vosges; learned the niceties of cornering and car-handling generally under the auspices of Bugatti stars. Never did he take any chances. He drove nicely, considerately, with beautiful judgment and every regard for his car; but quickly, you know, quickly! Bugatti gears are not sensationally

10. *T.40 with drop-head coupé body.*

11. *Jean Bugatti with a 'fiacre' bodied car, about 1930. Similar bodies were offered with T.44 and T.46 chassis. Today the style is called razor-edged.*

112. *The late Geo Ham, the famous French automobile artist with his Type 40 in 1927.*

TYPE 40A

113. *Jean Bugatti and 'Totosche', the Sicilian donkey given to Ettore by Count Florio, to commemorate his wins in the Targa Florio.*

114. *The engine of the T.40 is virtually identical with the T.37 except for the width of the engine bearers.*

(*photo: C. W. Davies*)

115. *4 cylinders, plain bearings and coil ignition—an original illustration.*

TYPE 40A ENGINE

116 and 117. Apart from the cylinder bore, and use of twin plugs, the T.40A engine is indistinguishable from that of the T.40. This beautifully restored engine is in the U.S.A.

(photos: H. T. N. Graves)

quieter than they were; but the whole car runs with a solidity and one-pieceness greater than ever; its suspension and steering are perfect. In those bad old days, dreadful stories . . . were told about slow running in top gear. Today one really can drive through Crawley at 10 mph on fourth speed regularly, steadily, without any unevenness. One can also take surprising gradients on fourth, with the rev. counter showing only moderate engine-speeds. Our rev. counter showed 3,600, 3,700 rpm mile after mile; but its speed is only one of its very real unquestionable merits because it is, all the while, in any circumstances, running on the level, up-hill or down-hill as joyously as one wishes, so thoroughly dependable, safe, trustworthy, a little Blue Devil!

A private owner's experience with a 1929 11·9 hp Type 40 shows a performance much above the average for a car of this size at that period. It reads:

At present I have a 1929 Type 40, and my previous car was a 1926 2 litre straight eight. I have driven these cars hard, but not carelessly, and have found that they are never 'sick or sorry'. There is no trouble whatever in starting. Maintenance cost is very small. Petrol consumption is 31 mpg, and speeds are as follows: Third, 65 mph, top, 82 mph. I have, however, made the following alterations which have definitely improved the performance: U type Zenith carburettor, Terry's valve springs, and slotted scraper rings. I have obtained a maximum of 4,300 rpm in top and can drive all day at 3,500 rpm without any strain. This is equivalent to about 60 mph. The old bogey of oiling up, which was evident in the very early models, is entirely absent in the later ones. The engine is noisy at low speeds, and the indirect gears are noisy.

TYPE 41 ROYALE
the Golden Bug

IN 1913, THREE YEARS AFTER STARTING AT MOLSHEIM, ETTORE Bugatti began to think of a large, luxury production. He wrote to his friend Espanet on 11 April 1913:

As for the 8 cylinder, it is being designed, but not yet being made. The 8 cylinder car that I spoke to you about will have an engine with a bore of 100 mm, but the stroke is not yet settled.

The car will be larger than the Hispano Suiza [this altered by Bugatti's own hand to 'Rolls-Royce'], *but at the same time lighter; the speed of the closed car will reach 150 km/h, I hope to achieve perfect silence, when I have the first car on test I will make a long trip and I will not forget to come to see you to know your opinion on my new machine.*

There is no need to tell you that the production of these cars will be very limited and made with irreproachable care. All these cars will be delivered after tests of at least 1,000 km, and will have a guarantee of five years; the car will be extremely expensive, but will not be compared with any vehicle of this type.

If I succeed in achieving what I am looking for it will certainly be a vehicle and a piece of machinery beyond any criticism.

The war came shortly after, and Ettore's talents were turned to aeroengines, which undoubtedly derived from this design. When the war was over he experimented with a smaller 3 litre, 8 cylinder car (Type 28), but this did not go into production. In 1926, however, the project for a super-car was revived and the Golden Bug (so known because the prototype was much gilded) was born. This fantastic car, indeed probably the most fantastic car ever to be produced, turned out to be a straight eight of about 15 litre capacity (77·8 hp R.A.C. rating) and naturally enough has been the subject of much Bugatti-lore, most of it untrue! It is said that Ettore designed the car after being piqued by an English lady's reference to Rolls-Royce at a dinner party, but his letter of 1913 seems to put his dream of a super-car in a proper historical perspective. It has been said too, that the

Golden Bug, or Royale as it was called in France, was a car of kings. But if a few kings may have seen the specification (no catalogue was ever produced), no king ever got as far as placing an order!

Contemporary description

In the *Autocar* of 11 June 1926, Mr W. F. Bradley wrote, in an article headed 'The Golden Bug – Remarkable straight eight of nearly fifteen litres engine capacity which is being built in limited numbers of M. Bugatti at Molsheim':

While there is obviously but a limited market for a very costly high-grade car – a car which lays claim to be the best in the world – every motorist, rich or impecunious, is likely to have at least an academic interest in such a machine. Recently, during a visit to the Alsatian village of Molsheim, M. Ettore Bugatti gave us an opportunity of examining such a motor car, on which he has been at work for several years, and which will make its appearance at an early date.

It would be difficult to compare this new car with anything existing, for in the first place it has an engine of exceptional size, with eight cylinders of 125×150 mm, bore and stroke, giving a cubical capacity of 14,726 cc, and in building it no expense has been spared to attain perfection, so far as that is humanly possible. The size of the car is very much greater than that of any other private passenger vehicle, for it has a wheelbase of slightly more than 15 ft and a track of about 5 ft 6 in. It will carry a comfortable seven-passenger body, and as a model M. Bugatti has taken a body off an eight-cylinder Packard chassis and has placed it on the first of his own chassis with less rear overhang than usual.

There is no intention of producing this car in big series, but at the same time each one will not be a toolmaker's job with no interchangeable parts. Instead, most elaborate machinery is being laid down, and jigs and dies are being made so that the parts will be rigorously interchangeable, while the instructions accompanying the drawings permit no tolerance anywhere. The selling price of the car is not known, but it will be not less than that of a Rolls-Royce imported into France in the regular way. The 'Golden Bugatti', as it has been termed by those who have seen it, will be produced concurrently with the present models.

In full running order this Bugatti will weigh slightly less than 50 cwt, but to propel this weight it has an engine developing 300 hp at 1,700 revolutions, thus giving a ratio of less than 20 lb per horse-

145

(see page 157 for details)

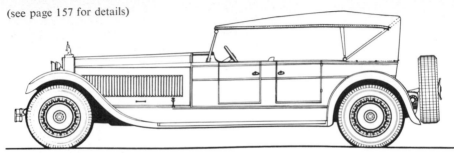

No. 1   *41100 The prototype chassis fitted with an American built body from a Packard.*

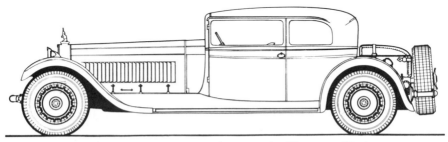

No. 1a   *The fourth body on the prototype chassis was by Weymann of Paris.*

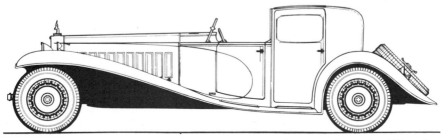

No. 1b   *The so-called Coupé Napoleon designed and built at Molsheim, the fifth in fact to be fitted to the prototype chassis retained by the family.*

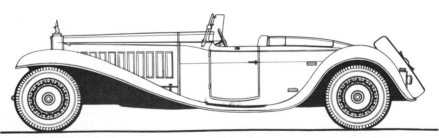

No. 2   *41111 The Roadster body designed and made at Molsheim for Mr. Esders.*

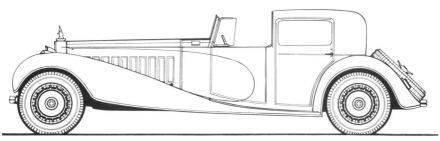

No. 2a *The second body fitted this chassis, 41111 was a Coupé de Ville by Henry Binder of Paris.*

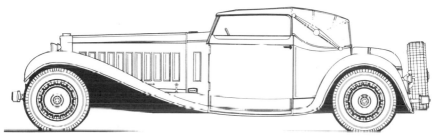

No. 3 *41121 Drophead Coupé by Weinberger of Munich.*

No. 4 *41131 Four door Limousine body by Park Ward of London.*

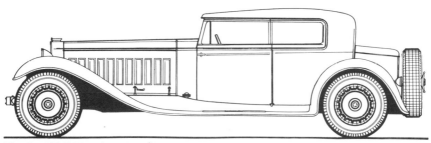

No. 5 *41141 Two door Coupé body by Kellner of Paris.*

power. There are three gears, one being an emergency or starting gear, the second being the direct drive, and the third a geared-up ratio for very fast travel.

The engine weighs 770 lb, of which 238 lb are accounted for by the cast-iron cylinder block, and 220 lb represent the crankshaft, without the flywheel. Examined externally, it is difficult to understand how the engine is built, for it appears to be a huge block of aluminium, with carburettors added on one side and exhaust pipes on the opposite side.

The peculiarity lies in the casting, which is an extraordinary piece of work, for the eight cylinders, measuring 55 in, from end to end, form a single block with an integral head, having water spaces completely around each cylinder barrel, and the water-jacket extending right down to the nine crankshaft bearings. The main-shaft is carried, not in a separate crankcase, but in the cylinder itself. In other words, this casting, with its water-cooled main bearings, constitutes practically the complete engine; the light aluminium casings built around it act as dust excluders and oil and water retainers, and in no way add to the rigidity or solidity of the whole.

The crankshaft has circular webs; as already explained, it is carried in nine plain bearings, the pistons are a special aluminium alloy, the connecting rods are I-section, and the big-ends have white-metal bearings. By reason of the machinery installed and the processes employed, there is no hand scraping at all, and it is claimed that the rods and their bearings come off the machine rigorously exact to a thousandth of an inch, and any rod and piston can be changed for any other. The valve arrangement is similar to that of other Bugatti engines, there being two inlets and one exhaust, with overhead operating gear.

Three bronze hangers on each side attach the engine to the frame, but instead of the bolts being secured to the outer aluminium casing, as might be thought at first sight, they go right through the cast-iron cylinder block. Dry-sump lubrication is fitted, there being two scavenging pumps and one feed pump from a tank on the forward face of the dashboard. Double ignition is used, by magneto, and battery and coil of a special type.

Quite separate from the engine, immediately under the driver's seat, are a light flywheel and clutch contained in an aluminium housing. The gears are in the rear axle, which has a central housing of aluminium and two tubes containing the drive shafts. Straight bevels are used for the direct drive. The indirect gears consist of a reduction one for emergency work, such as starting on hills, and a high ratio for very fast travelling.

148

118. *The first Royale (No 41100) with a Packard body. The photograph is reproduced from a Bugatti booklet, and unfortunately the caption proved incorrect. No royal personage ever owned a Royale.*

119. *Bugatti experimented with coach bodies on the prototype chassis, first a 2-door one and then this heavy 4-door version.*

120. *The first car was rebodied with this magnificent Weymann coach and won first prize at the Concours d'Elegance in Paris in 1929.*

121. *After a crash the car (plates 118, 119) was again rebuilt with a 'Coupé Napoleon' or Sedanca de Ville body. This car is now in the Schlumpf collection.*

122. *Dr Fuch's cabriolet by Weinberger of Munich (No. 41121) and now in the Ford Museum at Dearbon.*

123. *A fine view of one of the most beautiful bodies ever built and designed by Jean Bugatti who stands beside it. Mr Esders ordered the car but did not drive at night and needed no lamps.*

NO. 41111

124 *and* 125. *Other views of the car in 123. From any angle a most beautiful car.*

126. *Kellner 2-door saloon (No. 41141); now in U.S.A.*

127. *Berline de Voyage, 4 doors. folding rear hood, believed to be Bugatti coachwork (No. 41150); now in U.S.A.* (*photo : Dr Skitarelic*)

The frame members are special by reason of their dimensions, for they have a depth at the centre of 10 in. The front springs are semi-elliptics, having their rear extremities received between semi-circular bronze blocks. At the rear there are two sets of quarter-elliptic springs, one pair being behind the axle, outside the frame members, and the other set, which only come into play when a heavy load is carried, being ahead of the axle and beneath the frame members.

A front axle of the same general type as that used on the racing cars is employed. The construction of this is very unusual. It is a straight forging bored out from end to end, and having a greater thickness of metal outside the spring seats than is really necessary. After being bored out, the two extremities are hammered up until they are almost solid, the axle is heated and shaped, and the finished article is a one-piece axle, hollow in the centre and solid at the extremities.

The tyres for this car have had to be specially made Rapsons. They are straight-side balloons of 1,000 × 180 mm, mounted on special aluminium wheels forming a single casting with the brake drums.

There are innumerable details of construction which attract attention. All the brake rods are on roller bearings. The wearing parts of the universal joint can be changed in five minutes. The radiator filler cap is a bevel-faced valve with a hinge and a quick release catch. At the same time the entire filler cap can be lifted off and replaced by another if repair is required. Instead of an automatic oiling system for the chassis parts the design is such that attention has to be given only once every month or six weeks.

There is no intention of exhibiting this car at either the Paris or the London shows, for it is recognized that it will not appeal to the ordinary purchaser, and those who are likely to be interested in it will have other opportunities of examining it.

The following year Bradley returned to Molsheim and tested the car, as reported in the *Autocar* 18 March 1927. He added a few technical details of the construction:

Double ignition is fitted, by magneto and by coil and accumulator, with two plugs per cylinder. There are two carburettors on the right-hand side, while the exhaust occupies the whole of the left-hand side, the pipes being dropped down at the centre of the engine and covered with an asbestos lined polished aluminium cover to deflect the heat from the bonnet.

The engine has no flywheel, and the clutch is mounted separately in a casing under the forward seats. The change-speed mechanism is

153

in the rear axle and consists of a geared-down indirect gear for starting and a geared-up indirect gear for fast running. On direct drive, through the spiral-bevel gears, the car has a speed of 95 mph at 2,000 rpm, while the geared-up indirect gives 125 mph, at the same engine speed.

There is a brake on the drive shaft to the rear of the clutch housing, and a foot-operated set on the four cast aluminium wheels. The wheels and the brake drums, it is interesting to note, are one casting, the spokes of the wheels being set so as to form a slight helice and thus direct a draught of air on the drums. The tyres, as already stated, have had to be built specially. They are four-ply Rapsons of 980×170 mm.

He went on to recount his experiences of a road test with Ettore at the wheel.

One might be excused for imagining that a car of this size and power would have to be employed entirely on main highways. Probably M. Bugatti divined that this suspicion was lurking on our mind, for, on taking the car out, he quickly turned off the national highway and entered narrow, twisty, hilly lanes with a particularly greasy surface. Further for a considerable portion of the time he handled the car in that dashing manner which so much appeals to young bloods.

This was done to prove the stability of the car on bends at high speeds, and it must be admitted, the demonstration was most convincing. Merely out of habit, the side of the car was gripped, but it was soon realized that even when cornering violently there was no tendency to be thrown sideways. To use a hackneyed expression, the car ran as on rails, with the difference that it was much more steady than anything on rails we have ever ridden in.

A considerable amount of traffic was met with, mostly consisting of farmers' wagons hauled by two horses, but no difficulty was experienced in passing them on the narrow roads. The same route had been covered earlier in the day on a sporting type Bugatti of normal dimensions, and the only disadvantage of the 300 hp model was that it needed reverse to get round a hairpin bend that the smaller car had taken on a single lock.

In view of the price of the car, we expected a high degree of flexibility and good, steady pulling at low engine speeds, and were not disappointed. The low emergency gear was used for starting, although it was quite possible to get away on direct drive, and the rest of the running was done on high. This included short, steep gradients with sharp bends on which the car was throttled down to 3 mph and then accelerated rapidly. Among the tests was the climbing of a short, steep hill on direct gear at the lowest possible speed and in a most silky manner. The same hill was taken on the indirect gear in order to show the terrific acceleration. On a straight road outside Strasbourg an opportunity was afforded of making use of the geared-up indirect gear, which was found to be just as silent as the direct drive.

A car of this price can obviously have but a small market, and probably some of the objections one would normally bring against it fall to the ground because of its special construction. The absence of a detachable head and the cylinder design make it impossible to change a valve, or even to grind in a valve, except by dismounting the engine, but the reply to this is that by reason of the construction, the high-class material, and the perfect workmanship, repairs are not necessary except at very long intervals, and the accessibility desirable on a normal car becomes unnecessary with this engine.

Royale sales technique

Bugatti seems to have adopted a sales technique as arrogant as the design of the car! In *Bugantics*, 13, 4, July 1950, Mr H. Dale tells the story of meeting Mr Ladopoulo in Cairo, and how Mr Ladopoulo had negotiated the sale of a car to Prince Mohamed Abdel Said: no sale took place on account of the price. Mr Paul wrote from Molsheim on 22 December 1933:

I thank you for advising me of your intention to acquaint His Highness Prince Mohamed Abdel Said with the 'Royale' Bugatti chassis.

I am, however, afraid it may not be possible to transact such a business without His Highness having been able to see and, the case arising, test the car.

The best way would be to take advantage of the forthcoming visit of His Highness to Paris in order to show him M. Bugatti's personal car, which is a small town coupé on the same chassis, and arrange an interview with him.

For such a special chassis I have never considered it necessary to publish a catalogue. There is, in fact, no need whatever of advertising such a model, the prospective buyers of which, who are essentially aristocratic, are inaccessible by the means adopted for standard cars.

To enable you to appreciate the main characteristic features of the chassis I am sending you herewith typewritten details thereof.

I am also sending you for handing to His Highness, photographs o, the recent 'Royale' models delivered: Bugatti Roadster – to Mr Armand Esders, Paris; Park-Ward saloon car to Captain Foster (London).

Finally, a Grand Luxe Kellner Saloon which was made by those

155

Coachbuilders for the Olympia Exhibition, London, and the preparation of which we are on the point of completing.

To give you an idea of the proportions of the Town Coupé designed by M. Bugatti, I enclose herewith a diagram, from which you will be able to appreciate the extremely elegant lines of this car.

The cost of the complete chassis supplied with five wheels fitted with tyres, accessories, tools etc., and covered by an unlimited guarantee, is fixed at 500,000 French francs.

I shall be pleased to furnish you with any additional information you may desire to have, and meanwhile remain,

Yours faithfully,
A. Paul,
for E. Bugatti

Attached to the letter was a data sheet as follows:

CHARACTERISTIC FEATURES OF THE TYPE 41 'ROYALE' CHASSIS

The engine is an 8 cylinder monobloc type of up to 13 litres capacity.

The camshaft, as in all my designs in the last twenty years, is located above the cylinders.

Three valves are provided for each cylinder, two admission and one exhaust. The exhaust valve incorporates a special cooling device.

The Bugatti-make carburettor has been specially designed to ensure perfect delivery, both at extreme slow speed and at the highest speeds, that is to say in order to ensure homogenous combustion, unvarying whatever the speed. It is also possible with this carburettor to correct the proportions of air and fuel in such a manner as to obtain the highest efficiency both in hot and cold countries.

The fuel supply is looked after by electric pumps.

The gearbox is integral with the rear axle. It comprises only three combinations: a first speed for starting – a second direct mesh, which is utilized on all roads, and a third super-multiplied speed which can be utilized on long, straight runs.

The brakes act directly on the four wheels and incorporate a self-regulating device which permits automatically taking up wear on the linings. The braking stresses are extremely low.

The car can attain any speed desired by the designer.

It is characterized by remarkable road-holding qualities and unequalled ease and smoothness of drive. In a word, it possesses perfect docility and can easily be driven by a lady in spite of its size.

Moreover, it is strictly silent running at all speeds.

The dimensions of the chassis permit of providing extremely spacious coachwork affording 7 to 9 seats.

The production programme

Although a batch of 25 was hinted at (and probably hoped for) only six or seven cars were built at Molsheim. The engine itself was later produced in some numbers for the Bugatti railcar. Production cars had a stroke of 130 mm, unlike the prototype tested by Bradley, giving a capacity of 12,763 cc.

The six cars which were completed still exist and their history can be traced as follows:

No. 1 (No. 41100)   This car, the prototype, was built in 1926–7, and was originally fitted with a Packard touring car body. It was next fitted with a curious 2-door coupé and then an ugly stagecoach body; then it was re-bodied once more with a magnificent Weymann body which won many prizes. This car crashed on a trip from Molsheim and was burnt out, but was rebuilt. It was until recently in the possession of the Bugatti family at Ermenonville, fitted with a remarkable fixed head coupé body, often called a coupé Napoleon; Jean Bugatti was concerned with the body design.

No. 2 (No. 41111)   This started life as a 2-seater roadster, produced to the order of Mr Armand Esders. It was subsequently re-bodied with a coupé de Ville by the coachbuilder Binder. It is now in the U.S.A.

No. 3 (No. 41121)   This car was built to the order of Dr J. Fuchs of Germany in 1931 and fitted with a cabriolet body by Weinberger. Its story is told by Mr C. A. Chayne on page 156 and it is now in the Henry Ford Museum at Dearborn.

No. 4 (No. 41131)   Delivered in 1933 (orders were slow in coming) to Captain C. W. Foster in England; this car was fitted with an English Park-Ward 4-door limousine body and, after a sojourn in the U.S.A., is back in France.

No. 5   This car was fitted with a 2-door sedan body by
(No. 41141)   Kellner and remained in the possession of the
Bugatti family for some time, being used by L'Ebé Bugatti.
It was exhibited at the Olympia Motor Show in 1932, and
listed at £6,500 – more than double the finest Rolls-Royce at
the Show! It is now in the U.S.A.

No. 6   This car also remained in the Bugatti family for
(No. 41150)   some time, fitted with a Bugatti designed (and
possibly built) coupé body, known as a Berline de Voyage. It
is now in the U.S.A.

Mr C. A. Chayne formerly of the General Motors Corporation tells the story of his Royale, which now rests in the Henry
Ford Auto Museum at Dearborn:

THE STORY OF CAR 41121

This car was ordered by Dr A. Joseph Fuchs in 1930 and was
delivered in 1931. The chassis was built in Molsheim, of course, and
the body by Ludwig Weinberger in Munich. The original cost was
equivalent to $43,000. The writer first saw the car during the practice
days for the Vanderbilt Cup Race at Roosevelt Speedway, Long
Island, in 1937. After this we lost track of the car, and it finally
developed that the block had been frozen and cracked, apparently
during the winter 1937–38, and, as Dr Fuchs was unable to have the
car repaired in this country, it was left in his backyard on Long Island,
covered with a sail, for a number of years.

I understand that the car was at one time taken to a shop in New
York City for inspection, but they did no actual work on the car.
Finally, in early June 1943, I received a telephone call from a friend
in New York to the effect that the car had been sent to a junkyard in
New York City and, if I wanted it, I had better move fast. I immediately telephoned Charles Stitch, who operates a foreign car shop
in New York, had him buy the car and store it until I could make
arrangements to have it brought to Flint. Because of the war and
early post-war business obligations, I was unable to start serious
restoration until the latter part of 1946. This work was completed
in time to take the car east for the 1947 Glidden Tour of the Veteran
Motor Car Club of America.

When we disassembled the engine, we found that the outer walls of the cylinder block had been badly cracked and bulged, both above and below the crankcase cover plates. Since the casting is very large and very complicated, it was decided not to attempt to weld the cracks, but instead to resort to the old reliable patching procedure. We knocked out the loose panels, milled the bulged panels flush with the sides of the case, and attached a plate of $\frac{5}{32}$ in. cold rolled steel on each side of the block. These plates, of course, had to be notched to clear the crank cheeks and the connecting rods, since the water jackets on this engine extend around the upper halves of each of the nine main bearings. After screwing on the plates we filled the casting with salammoniac solution, flushed it thoroughly, allowed it to dry and then made sure of the seal by filling it with a resin type casting sealer under pressure which was then set permanently by baking the case for several days at a moderate temperature. While this procedure may have been more elaborate than was absolutely necessary, we accomplished the purpose of sealing the jackets and they have not leaked to this day.

We found that the freezing had squeezed the cylinders badly out of shape and it was necessary to rebore to about 0·30 in. oversize. I was fortunate enough to find aluminium piston castings that could be machined to fit. No work was necessary on the crankshaft or bearings. The crankshaft, by the way, is in two pieces, joined at the centre main bearing, and has circular cheeks to which the counterweights are bolted. Connecting rods were magnafluxed and shotpeened. The engine has a full pressure lubricating system, except that the wrist pins are oiled by splash.

The water pump was badly corroded, consequently in the rebuild we modified it rather extensively, and fitted it with a modern 'permanent' type of seal. New valves and valve springs were made and installed, and it was necessary to make a new camshaft as the original one was very badly rusted, there being no ventilation provisions in the cam boxes. Fortunately, there were a few narrow areas on the original cams in good condition which permitted us to check the cam shapes and new master cams were made. The camshaft is also in two pieces joined at the centre bearing.

The camshaft drive is very unusual. At the top of the vertical shaft are two bevel pinions having opposite spiral angles. These mesh with two bevel gears, one of which is fixed to the camshaft. The second gear is concentric with the first, but drives through a friction clutch. As the second pair of gears is one tooth off from an even two to one ratio, the friction clutch merely loads these gears so that the thrust on the vertical shaft is balanced by the opposing

159

spiral angles. Just one more example of M. Bugatti's rugged individualism.

The major modification to the engine was made in the intake system. The original design consisted of a very large barrel-throttle air-valve carburettor, fitted to a single manifold with the four branches coming out of the bottom of the manifold. With the branches arranged in this manner it was obvious that all of the liquid in the manifold would drain into the centre four cylinders, and I could not develop any enthusiasm for spending time and money restoring the engine only to risk scoring one or more of the centre four cylinders on a cold morning start. I, therefore, designed short elbow connections and installed four single Stromberg carburettors with a ½ in. balance tube connecting the four elbows. Carburettors were balanced on a flow bench (including the idle settings) and no changes have been found necessary. The new intake system is completely satisfactory under all operating conditions. Since the water outlet manifold was originally cast as a jacket on the top of the intake manifold, the installation of the four single carburettors made it necessary to design and build a new water outlet manifold which was equipped with a large thermostat and by-pass leading to the intake side of the water pump.

The radiator was a honeycomb type, having square tubes which were badly corroded, and it was necessary to re-tube the core.

No work was done to the clutch, which is located under the driver's seat. The clutch is a typical Bugatti wet-plate design. The connection between the engine and the clutch is through two heavy fabric universal joints, there being no flywheel on the engine. Starter and generator are mounted on the clutch case.

The transmission is part of the rear axle, and is driven by a short shaft from the clutch. The transmission has two forward speeds and overdrive, and of course a reverse. Low speed is used solely for the purpose of starting the car and the shift to second which is direct drive, should be made at a fairly low car speed. All driving is normally done in direct. For high speed driving, the overdrive may be engaged at any speed above 75 mph. We did not find it necessary to open up the transmission or rear axle, and checked the ratios by measuring the number of turns of the drive shaft necessary to rotate the rear wheels one turn.

Another major modification was made to the braking system. This was, of course, of the well-known Bugatti cable design. The chain and bevel gear equalizers were badly rusted and would have had to be completely replaced. I found, however, that one of the American brake manufacturers made a 'slave' cylinder which could be bolted

160

128. *The magnificent Royale engine which Bugatti developed out of the Type 34 aeroengine.*

(photo: Lenton–Atlantic)

129. *The crankshaft and connecting rod assemblies are massive.*

130. *The Chayne car (No. 41121), see page 158, after restoration in the U.S.A.*

131. *The left-hand side of the engine.*

132. *A row of engines adapted for Railcar duty.*

133. *Steering box de-*
tails: ball bearings for
low friction. The centre
in is slightly eccentric
allowing the worm wheel
to be meshed with the
worm, a feature from
the T.30.

134. *The crankcase. It*
is good to see water
all round the cylinder
walls, although the pros-
pect of removing the
crankshaft in order to
grind in a valve is not so
pleasing.

135. *The driving compartment of the coupé Napoleon*

(*photos:*
L'Automobile)

136. *The
Royale wheel.*

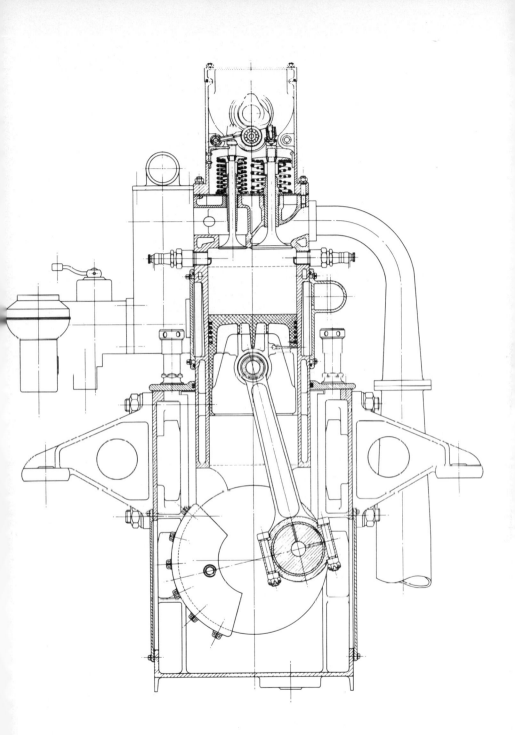

Fig. 22. *Transverse engine section of the Type 41 the Royale.*

to the outside of the backing plates, then by reversing the cams the operating levers could be made to apply the brakes with a push instead of a pull, and I ended up with about as nice a hydraulic brake system as anyone could desire. I heartily recommend the procedure to anyone trying to restore a car having old style mechanical brake.

The tyres, of course, were a problem, but I succeeded in locating a 7·50–24 tractor tyre mould, having a ribbed tread and had tyres made in this mould with full rayon carcasses. The ribbed treads were 'siped' to give the necessary anti-skid characteristics. Hub-caps, with the well-known Bugatti monogram, and trim discs were added to the wheels to improve their appearance.

Paint and trim, of course, had deteriorated very badly during the 'weathering' years in a Long Island backyard. The car was originally fitted with beautiful pigskin upholstery, but this was so brittle that it was hopeless to attempt to restore it, and have it in keeping with the rest of the car. The original front seats had cushions that were luxuriously thick, but did not leave enough room between the cushion and the top of my 6 ft 3 in. I therefore installed front seats (new bucket type), and a new cushion and back in the rear seat, these being trimmed in dark green glove leather. The car is painted oyster white and dark green, matching the leather, and with a dark green top. The original leather covering on the trunk was also not usable, and while I had the body of the trunk restored, it is now fitted with a zipper cover, made of the same material as the top.

The electric wiring has been completely replaced and the car is fitted with legal sealed beam driving headlights. I kept the original Scintilla headlamps, but the beam they produce is highly illegal; and consequently they are never used for driving. The front fender lamps were converted to take two filament bulbs and new tail lamps fitted so that the car now has a direction signal system and back-up lights, in addition to the usual licence and stop lights. In order to have horns that are in keeping with the majesty of the car, I fitted a pair of Strombos air horns. The radiator cap ornament which shows in some of the pictures, is a design I developed for use on all of the cars in my collection.

The wood rim of the steering wheel had to be replaced and I used Tenite II in a colour to match the green upholstery. I might note in passing that the steering wheel is equipped with four horn buttons on the underside of the spokes, near the rim.

Originally the car had a very beautiful stop watch mounted in the centre of the steering wheel but, as this was missing, I replaced it with a cap having a Tenite insert with the Bugatti ornament in silver letters.

TYPE 43
100 mph Grand Sport model

TYPE 43 PROBABLY SHARES THE DISTINCTION WITH THE BRESCIA, the Type 35 G.P. and Type 57 in being one of the four really great Bugatti models. Fast, exciting and fitted with a reasonable four-seat open body, this 100 mph model must have been a remarkable car in 1927 when it first appeared. Even today a Type 43 has a performance equivalent to a good TR 3 or M.G.A.: 0 to 90 mph in a shade over 30 seconds, a standing kilometre in under 35 seconds, and 105 to 106 mph without a great deal of difficulty. At a list price in 1927 of £1,200, however, the model was expensive.

Basically the car stems from Type 38, using a similar chassis but of slightly shorter wheelbase, with Type 38 axles, brakes, steering, radiator and gearbox, but with the T.35B 2·3 litre supercharged G.P. engine, and detachable rim alloy wheels from the G.P. cars. The standard model had a Molsheim body of narrow, torpedo shape, with a single left-hand door, and a removable hatch in the tail giving access to a luggage compartment. This model was very suitable for sporting events such as the Alpine Trial, as well as long distance touring (across the national routes of France) and yet was also very suitable for hill-climbs and track racing. Many models were seen on the Brooklands mountain circuit, and teams were entered (with drivers such as Sir Malcolm Campbell, Earl Howe, Divo and Conelli) in the Ulster T.T. and long distance races in the late 'twenties and early 'thirties. In the early days of the Bugatti Owners' Club the car was often seen in rallies and sprint events.

167

In 1930 the model became more respectable, sometimes being fitted with coupé bodywork; a special model known as the 43A was produced with an American-style roadster body with a rumble (or dickey) seat and even a small door for golf clubs. This was the period of North Atlantic influence rather unsuited to the type and it was soon out of production. The engine was too rough and noisy to be suitable for college-educated coachwork! (Fig. 23, page 177).

In December 1928, Bugatti prepared and may or may not have issued a data sheet labelled 'Super Grand Sport 1929, Type 43A', which was fitted with the 16 cylinder engine (60 mm × 84 mm, 3,850 cc) used on the Type 45 (see page 192). This car appears in the illustration to be identical with the normal Type 43 Torpedo bodied model except that the bonnet line is slightly raised; the axle ratio was 15:52, and the weight 100 kg up at 1,200 kg. The list price was a rather astronomical 400,000 francs or about £5,000! Fortunately, there is another Molsheim data sheet of about 1931 in date giving authority to the roadster model being Type 43A so the embarrassing intrusion of a 16 cylinder Type 43A will be ignored.

The construction of the standard car has been fairly well documented in recent years in issues of *Bugantics*, 1958–60.

Description of model

The *Autocar* of 18 March 1927 has this to say in announcing the new model:

There are indications, in France at any rate, that the supercharger, after being confined practically to racing cars, is to come into more general use. One of the most important steps in this direction is the introduction, by M. Bugatti, of an entirely new model fitted with a compressor.

The name of Bugatti is so closely associated with racing and sporting type cars that one would almost naturally imagine a super-charged model from this factory to be the fastest and the raciest of the firm's products. It is surprising, therefore, to find that the new model, a straight-eight of 2,300 cc, has been designed for all-round work and is the most flexible car in the Bugatti series. As a proof of this, M. Ettore Bugatti, during a trial run we made with him in

Alsace, stopped the engine, engaged top gear, and then started away by pressing on the starter button and rapidly accelerating without gear changes to a speed of 90 miles an hour.

The new model is a development of the cars which won the Targa Florio race, in Sicily last year. It appears to be the intention to deliver this car with a four-seater sporting-type open body. No attempt has been made to bring the body out beyond the frame members; there are no running boards; there are two doors [eventually one] on the left side only, and wells are provided for the passengers' feet. Protection is given by a fixed wind-screen, a very light folding hood is provided, and there is provision for baggage in the pointed tail. Briefly, the body is a sporting type, but one providing quite a reasonable amount of comfort for four persons.

Considered technically, the chassis has a close resemblance to other Bugatti types. The eight cylinders, cast in two blocks of four, but so close coupled that at first sight they appear to be one set, have a bore of 60 and a stroke of 100 mm. There are two inlet valves and one exhaust per cylinder, mounted vertically in the fixed cylinder head and operated by an overhead camshaft.

The built-up crankshaft is carried in five bearings – two spherical ball bearings at the extremities and three intermediate roller bearings [in fact the centre bearing is also ball]. The connecting rods are I-section forgings in one piece, with roller bearings assembled on the shaft.

The distinctive feature of the engine resides in the compressor, which is a Roots type, mounted horizontally on the right side of the engine and driven from the timing gear at engine speed by means of a horizontal shaft with fabric couplings. The carburettor is a Solex placed under the compressor, and not visible on raising the bonnet; indeed, it can only be reached by opening a trap in the sheet metal underpan.

The induction piping consists of a vertical branch flanged to the compressor and two horizontal arms, each one feeding four cylinders. There is a relief valve in the vertical arm to prevent damage to the blades in case of a blow back.

Separate lubrication is provided for the compressor from a small tank on the forward face of the dashboard, and a lead to each of the two ball bearings. As the quantity of oil required is very slight, the flow is connected up with the throttle, and is only opened at a given engine speed. While the carburettor is lacking accessibility, the rest of the engine is quite get-at-able, the water and oil pumps, plugs, oil filler, overhead camshaft etc., being easily reached.

The engine is separate from the gearbox, and has independent

169

electric generator and starting motor. The clutch is of the multiple disc type; there are four speeds forward and a reverse, and the change-speed lever is in the centre, with right-hand steering. The rear axle has a final gear ratio of 4·15 to 1. Springing is by means of semi-elliptics in front, these passing through the hollow, forged and nickel-plated axle, and by quarter-elliptics, with their thin ends forward, at the rear of the car. Spoke-type, cast-aluminium detachable wheels are used, the spokes being designed to direct a current of air on to the brake drums which form an integral part of the wheel.

During a test run made in the neighbourhood of Molsheim, it was fully realized that the car possessed a very high turn of speed. With a special gear ratio it is claimed that it can attain 125 mph on the level, while with the standard gear ratio it will run up to 112 mph. More impressive than the maximum speed, however, was the high average speed, due to the extremely rapid acceleration, the wonderful stability of the car on the road, and the high power-to-weight ratio.

Empty, the weight of the car does not exceed 20 cwt and, although figures regarding power output are withheld, it is known that the engine runs up to 6,000 revolutions, and it is not a difficult matter to estimate the power obtained. Most of the run was made on greasy winding lanes at the foot of the Vosges, with a certain portion consisting of an unmetalled track across country, and even under such conditions the suspension was good. Running at 80 mph, the stability of the car was really amazing, there being no tendency to slide on the greasy turns, and the brakes proved exceedingly powerful.

During the Targa Florio race the cars showed themselves perfect, and the new commercial model does not appear to be in any way inferior to the racing type. The compressor is silent at all speeds, and, judged from a sporting standpoint, the car is quiet.

The petrol tank has a capacity of nearly 16 gallons, and the fuel consumption is stated to be at the rate of between 17 and 18 miles to the gallon.

Contemporary road tests

The foregoing description of the car was probably sent in by Mr W. F. Bradley who was the *Autocar* European Correspondent at that time. He owned one of these cars himself and an account of his experiences was given in the *Autocar* of 26 July 1929:

On being introduced to the supercharged straight eight 2,300 cc

Bugatti most motorists give expression to a feeling of fear. This model has all the characteristics of a racing car, and is indeed a racing car with a touring body; it looks fast, and it really is fast, but six months' experience with one on French highways has proved that it is one of the safest cars a motorist could handle.

Its maximum speed is about 112 mph: its gear ratio and the size of tyre used give 20½ mph per 1,000 rpm; thus at 5,500 rpm the road speed, ignoring slip, is 112 mph. I must confess that I have never driven the car at this speed, although there is no doubt that the Bugatti is capable of attaining it. I have, however, touched 5,000 rpm, or 102½ mph, and on good roads have held 4,500 rpm (92½ mph) for comparatively long periods. A very good cruising speed on Continental highways is 3,500 rpm, or about 70 mph. This engine speed is so much below the maximum that nothing is stressed: plugs stand up well to their work, oil consumption is low, and there is a very big margin for momentary acceleration when required.

One soon becomes satisfied with the knowledge that the car is one of the fastest on the road, and the greatest pleasure is obtained not in attempting to obtain the maximum from it (indeed, that is all but impossible except on a track), but in its wonderful acceleration, its high degree of flexibility, and its remarkable steadiness at all speeds, and particularly when one is negotiating winding hills.

The 2,300 cc Bugatti possesses a wonderful degree of flexibility; it is possible to engage top gear, move away by using the electric starter, and gain speed rapidly. To do this the engine should, of course, be warm and the road level. Starting in this abnormal manner a speed of 82 mph can be attained in 54 sec. There is no necessity to keep the engine reving fast to secure even running. It will glide along perfectly at 30 mph, and from this speed will jump into action, at the slightest touch of the accelerator, in a most impressive manner.

Using the four-speed gearbox the acceleration is really amazing. From a standing start the kilometre can be covered in 35 sec, and a speed of 70 mph is reached in 30 sec [probably a misprint for 90 mph]. To go from 1,000 rpm (equivalent to 20½ mph) to 3,000 rpm, or 61 mph, the period required is 34 sec, while 4,000 rpm, or 82 mph, are attained in 54 sec. These acceleration tests from 20 mph upwards were, of course, made without using the gears. It is evident that the power curve rises rapidly after about 1,400 rpm, for tests made from a standing start, with the use of the gears, showed that 82 mph could be attained in 54 sec, or in exactly the same time as required for running from 20 to 82 mph without the gears. [There is something wrong with these figures as the car would do 0 to 80 mph in about 25 seconds, not 54.]

171

This wonderful acceleration, combined with efficient brakes, makes it possible to put up amazingly high averages without excessive maximum speeds. A run from the gates of Paris to Le Touquet was accomplished in 2 h 25 min, or an average of 54·7 mph. The start being made at 5.00 p.m., much traffic was encountered for the first half hour, and during that period the speed was not much higher than that of the average car. On some of the more deserted and well-surfaced French highways, distances of 60 miles have been covered in the hour, and averages of more than 50 mph for long distances have been maintained without at any time touching 80 mph. This Bugatti has been driven right across France without use of the gears, and it is very rarely indeed that a hill is encountered which calls for a third.

Racing experience is doubtless responsible for the extraordinary performance of this car. It sits on the road in such a manner and it steers so wonderfully that never at any time during the 6,000 miles I drove it did I feel that it was being taken into a bend just a little too fast for safety. In other words, the margin of safety is so high that even on curves which previous experience with other cars had told me were ticklish there was a feeling of perfect security.

This does not contribute to recklessness. It has to be realized that the car is fast, and that consequently the driver has a much briefer period in which to act in case of danger. Keeping this fact in mind, the Bugatti is much safer than some cars having a decidedly lower speed. Of the many passengers carried in the car, some of them experienced motorists and some entire novices, all were impressed and apprehensive at first, but invariably they expressed unlimited confidence at the end of an hour.

The car was used for all kinds of work, varying from short runs in Paris to 400-mile non-stop trips. Some country police objected to its racy appearance and signalled me to stop when following more silent and less speedy looking cars. The Paris police, however, were much better judges and never alloweu themselves to be misled by the fast appearance of the car.

Petrol consumption depends largely on the manner in which the car is driven. If handled much as in a race, the consumption will be as high as 12 mpg, but if the driver is satisfied with less meteoric acceleration the figure can be improved to 16 or 17 mph. A petrol-benzole mixture was recommended, but the car was run entirely on pure petrol without any inconvenience. Oil consumption is low, but a good quality oil should be employed, Castrol R being recommended.

Compared with a normal car, the Bugatti calls for minor attentions, as distinct from repairs. As a matter of fact, the engine, being a racing type and never being run at anything like its maximum by

172

137. *Supercharged 2,300 cc T.43. One of the classic Bugatti models. As fitted with this standard 3/4 seater Grand Sport body, these cars were capable of 110 mph, which was a very high speed for a fully equipped road car in 1927, the year they were first produced.*

138. *Friderich at the wheel of a T.43 at a Nice speed event.*

TYPE 43

139. *Williams the Bugatti driver, and his wife competed in the 1928 Monte-Carlo Rally in a T.43.*

140. *A fine action shot of G. Bachelier in a T.43 in the B.O.C. hill-climb at Chalfont St Peter, May 1932. There were few of these events which did not see a couple or more 2,300s.*

141. *The well-known Evans brothers at Brooklands about 1932, Denis in a 43, and Kenneth in a C-type Montlhéry M.G.*

142. *A T.43 in the Craigantlet Hill-Climb. 1959.* (photo: B. E. Swain)

143. *G. T. Shapley (seated) and Dr J. Harrison in a T.43, much used at pre-war Brooklands*

144. *The Shapley car, restored, in the sixties.*

145. *A works-entered T.43 in the 1928 Ulster T.T., driven by Dutilleux. Malcolm Campbell is in the pits behind the driver.*

146. *The engine of Type 43.*

the average owner, is very long lived; but it pays to keep it spotlessly clean so that loose nuts and connections, possible oil or water leaks, and other minor defects can be detected instantly. While the clearance is sufficient for the open road, it is not at all liberal, and precautions have to be taken if lanes and tracks are traversed. In such cases the exhaust system is likely to suffer.

Fully equipped, with tanks filled and tools aboard, the weight of the car is 2,433 lb.

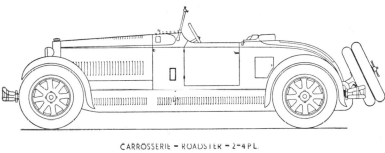

CARROSSERIE - ROADSTER - 2-4 PL.
sur chassis 1 p. 43

Fig. 23. The Type 43A roadster produced about 1930, and complete with trap door for golf clubs.

The Editor of *Motor Sport* also described his test of the car in May 1930 and confirmed Bradley's account of its attractions. In the issue of December 1932, the same journal tested a second-hand car (GU 17) belonging to Colonel Giles of the Bugatti Club and for sale at that time at £525.

A few strokes on the hand pressure pump, a touch on the starter-button and the engine fired. In a few moments we were threading our way through the West End traffic, the engine proving docile and flexible with the ignition half-retarded, third and top gears being used except where the traffic was very dense. The exhaust was inaudible, but the gears gave an occasional joyful shout as we trod on the accelerator.

Out in the country, driving the car was sheer joy. Light steering with adequate caster, almost unconscious cornering and terrific acceleration in the gears made it impossible not to put up a high average speed. Top gear acceleration was also surprisingly good, and from 50 mph the speed passed easily to 80. This top gear performance is very useful in populous areas, where the stirring howl of gears and supercharger gears is apt to be misunderstood.

177

10 to 30 mph took $3\frac{1}{2}$ seconds, 10 to 40 mph, 8, and 10 to 80, 23 sec: this is a terrific performance and compares well with that of the double-camshaft model – 10 to 80 in 19 seconds. The engine revs happily up to 5,000 giving a limit in second and third gears of 60 and 80 mph. On two occasions on short sections of straight road we reached 99 mph and there was obviously 10 or more mph in hand if road conditions had allowed further accelerations. Colonel Giles, the owner of the car, has reached 110 on Salisbury Plain.

As is usual on Bugattis, the brakes require considerable effort in order to attain full stopping power, but from 40 mph, applied really hard, they brought the car to a standstill in well under 50 feet. This figure is the best we have ever encountered and was only possible on a road of abnormally good surface, the co-efficient of friction being well over 1, but even on a normal tarmac road not more than 54 feet should be needed.

A wartime reminiscence

Wartime nostalgia for racing and sports cars was partly satisfied by a series of articles entitled 'Talking of Sports Cars' in the *Autocar*. No. 164 of 6 August 1943 was the story of Mr A. C. Whincop and his Bugattis:

There is something about the combined surge of power, the complete feeling of mastery, the beautiful balance of the chassis and steering, the blend of supercharger whine, exhaust, gear and axle notes, and the smooth slice of the gear changes on the Grand Prix boxes which cannot be expressed on paper. It is just there and has to be experienced to be believed. . . .

My car, like others of its type, had an engine almost identical with that of the Type 35B G.P. 2·3 litre, from which its power unit was copied. The maximum revs are between 5,000 and 5,500 rpm, at which bhp should be 140 in the Type 35B and 115 in the Type 43. These can be improved. . . .

The engines are well balanced, and the optimum revolutions can be felt quite clearly by the sensitive hand; on my car it was quite clear – 5,100–5,200 rpm on the gears, and 5,300 rpm or what you could get on top gear, never exceeding 5,500 rpm in any circumstances, as it is quite pointless to do so from the power point of view, and has, of course, other possibilities. The extreme smoothness right up to maximum revolutions makes it almost impossible to state any cruising speed, 2·3s just ask to be driven at full throttle where conditions permit, and usually are. If you want to cruise on English roads, well, try it, but you will usually find your speed mounting rapidly until you are holding your own strictly private Grand Prix. I have never met a car to equal the demand of the 2·3 Bugatti to be driven faster, and it is only really content when accelerating at full throttle in a rising crescendo of sound or is flat out on top gear at about 5,300 rpm, with the deep howl of the supercharger drowning everything in a perfectly tuned wavering top note of sound, as you blissfully watch the supercharger pressure – which is normally about + 7 lb per in^2 – gradually build up to about + 9.

My Type 43 (TR.4551) was amongst the first produced, being built in October 1927. Its life I know nothing of until 1935. . . .

I collected 'Two-three 1' early in 1938, and used it as a general-purpose car throughout the year, covering ten thousand miles with no overhaul, and the sole replacement of one fabric universal joint. Only two speed trials were indulged in, so that my bank manager might have an opportunity of forgetting a blown-up 1½ litre, but those two hill-climbs showed some promise, returning a first and second for the sole trouble of changing the plugs and jets. I mention this as rumour has spread it that Bugattis are not quite so reliable as they might be, and are apt to be difficult. Personally, I have found them extraordinarily reliable, with the exception of the four-cylinder models, provided they are carefully assembled by someone who is both interested and competent, and are thoroughly maintained, when little trouble should be encountered.

Plugs should not be a problem; my Type 43 would start, warm up, run in traffic and compete on Champion R.1s, never oiling in traffic, and only very occasionally when warming up, and only then when Castrol R has been used, as the engine was completely happy on Castrol XXL. For maximum performance sparking plugs should be scrupulously clean and gapped at 0·015 in.; also, if R.1s are used for much competition work their life is naturally short; in races of over three laps I used Champion R.11s, but then considerable care was needed before the start. For normal touring R.7s should be ideal, though never having had difficulty with R.1s oiling I have not had the need to come down to a relatively soft plug. If trouble is experienced with the oiling of plugs in any of the single-camshaft Bugattis it will almost invariably be found to be the result of excessive wear in the inlet valve guides, where the clearance should be 0·003 in.; if it is as much as 0·008 in. the plugs will not unnaturally oil up, this condition being rectified by the straightforward task of unscrewing the old guides, carefully reaming and fitting new ones, and recutting new valve faces and seats if necessary before reassembly.

I mention this point as many Bugattis have run for ten years and

179

more without the owners thinking of the valve guides needing to be replaced, this probably being the root of the story that Bugattis oil their plugs. One must admit that the design of the heads of the single-camshaft cylinder blocks does involve operating at high sparking-plug temperatures, but this need cause no trouble. . . .

. . . I carried out my original idea and had fitted a Brescia gearbox casing, which gave the chassis the same bracing as with the standard gearbox, and Grand Prix cogs, also the normal outside G.P. right-hand gear change. This modification, together with an aircraft fuel line of truly imposing dimensions, completely rejuvenated my twelve-year-old 2·3, which then handled and felt like a brand-new thoroughbred racing car. . . .

My Type 43 in her present condition has a genuine maximum of 108 mph when stripped, this being represented by 5,300 rpm on a 13:54 axle ratio, using 5·25 by 19 in. tyres and making allowance for wheelspin. With road equipment the speed seems to be cut down to about 106 mph, with more, of course, under favourable conditions.

Modern Road Impressions

There is no doubt that the Type 43 is one of the most drive-able models for today's owner who wants to use the car on the road. It has an excellent performance as already indicated and is surprisingly comfortable even on poor road surfaces. For long distance touring across France a regular pace of 65 mph (around 3000 rpm) seems an optimum, and on one occasion a trip of no less than 475 miles was accomplished returning from Molsheim to London in one day (in 1970). The main weakness from the practical point of view is a tendency to overheat in modern traffic conditions in towns and then to soot plugs – oiling up is not a problem if the bores and pistons are in good shape. With road use the crankshaft needs re-rolling every 6,000–8,000 miles. Fuel consumption is rarely better than 18 m per Imperial gallon, and oil consumption is mainly due to leakage and thus about 500 mpg! Fortunately Dunlop racing tyres, 5.00 × 19, which suit the car admirably are still being made.

147 *a and b. The 17·8 hp straight eight T.43 engine showing the Bugatti Roots-type supercharger. This model has a bore and stroke of 60 × 100 mm, 3 valves per cylinder, single overhead camshaft and full roller-bearing crankshaft.*

148. *T.43 chassis frame, typical of Bugatti construction and braced mainly by engine and gearbox.*

149. *3 litre T.44, originally produced as the T.28 in 1920 and then shelved until 1928. It was the first 8 cylinder, plain bearing, touring car to offer refinement as well as Bugatti-like performance.*

TYPE

150. *With French coachwork, shining new at Molsheim about 1928.*

151. *The Bugatti daughters in a T.44 coupé, Lidia on the left, L'Ebé in the car.*

152. *A very elegant and attractive coach body on a Type 44.*

53. *A T.44 in the Netherlands, with Mr G. Prick of the Dutch Bugatti Club.*
(*photo: E. J. de Flines*)

54. *The T.44 engine at the Olympia Motor Show, London, 1928. Note the high-mounted oil pump.*
(*photo:* The Motor)

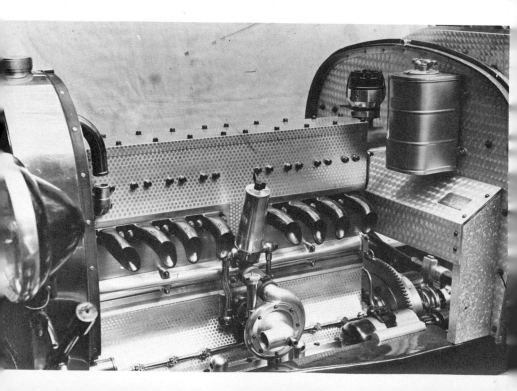

TYPE 44
8 cylinder refinement

AT THE END OF 1927 BUGATTI ANNOUNCED A NEW 8 CYLINDER production car of 3 litre capacity, derived from the prototype Type 28 exhibited in 1921, and replacing the 2 litre Type 38. In effect this new car was the combination of a new engine, with the single overhead camshaft driven from the centre of the crankshaft, and nine plain main bearings, and a chassis very similar to Type 38 or Type 43. The engine of the new car had the smooth torque of earlier models and a new degree of silence, which resulted from the elimination of the roller bearing crankshaft.

The general appearance of the engine is similar to that of Type 38, or other unblown 2 litre engines of the Type 35 family. The crankshaft is in two halves, with the camshaft drive bevel keyed to the centre. The shaft is carried completely in the upper crankcase which bolts to the lower case which itself is bolted to the chassis. A vertical shaft in the centre of the crankcase drives the camshaft through bevels and the usual dog coupling. A further pair of bevels drives a cross-shaft on the centre left-hand side of the crankcase; this drives the water pump, on the left between the exhaust manifolds, and through a further pair of skew gears and an extension shaft, a low mounted oil pump. Early models had the pump high mounted without the ex tension drive shaft. Early models too had 'Bugatti' lubrication by jets, but later engines were converted to full pressure feed. A relief valve was used on this oil system – a surprising in novation for Ettore!

The clutch, gearbox and back axle were virtually Type 40 or 43 units. The front axle was of the circular type with the springs passing through it, again as on Types 40 and 43. Brakes were of large diameter and similar to those on Type 43. In fact, the hubs and wire wheels of a Type 44 are often used as replacements of the alloy wheels on the 43.

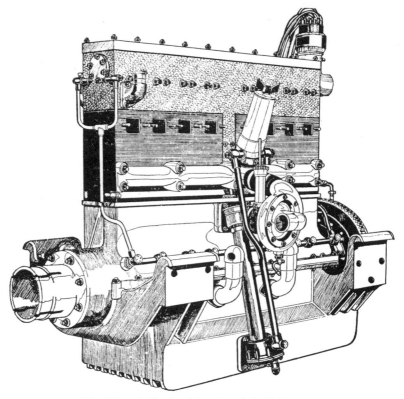

Fig. 24.   *A Shepherd drawing of the T.44 engine.*

Contemporary comment

Edgar Duffield described the car in the *Automotor Journal* in 1928:

Up to 1923 the Bugatti was still finding itself as a touring car. Maitre Bugatti would not agree, I know, but that was so, according to British ideas. But this new three-litre is really a very wonderful machine, and really a touring car, although it will bowl along the Cobham fair-mile at 75 to 80 mph with a lot of throttle opening to

186

spare. And the notable thing is the refinement of this car's performance and its very marked engine flexibility.

The motor is an overhead and mushroom-valved straight eight with bore and stroke of 69 mm × 100 mm, giving a Treasury rating of 23·6 and a capacity of 2,992 cc. The camshaft is overhead and the crankshaft has nine bearings. Cooling by pump; ignition is by battery and coil; a Schebler Automatic carburettor Autovac fed from a 13-gallon tank. Each cylinder has two inlet and one exhaust valves. The clutch employed is the Bugatti patented multiplate, running in oil, the discs being alternately of steel and cast iron. The complete car, with a genuine Weymann four-doored saloon, very elaborately finished and equipped, is priced at £850. In very many, if not all, details his design of today is almost as much ahead of its confrères as it was in 1914. Bugatti first showed the world what could be done with 1½ litres of gas before even he had begun to employ 16 valves on a four-cylindered motor.

This Bugatti is decidedly sporting; yet it is just as emphatically smooth and sweet, and the flexibility on fourth speed is remarkable. When I ran Bugattis, for 2½ years, I thought myself quite lucky if I got more than 400 or 500 yards of fourth speed in London. From my home, then alongside Hurlingham Club, to my office in Kingsway I travelled mainly on second. Occasionally I would get a few minutes of third. But to get more than a couple of furlongs on fourth was to have something about which to telephone home. This 3 litre straight eight could be driven from 'The Bear' at Esher to Aldgate Pump on fourth speed, using third only for restarting after traffic lights. It is just as refined as it is fast; just as amusing a car in the hands as ever the little beggars were. But it is a gentlewoman's car, whereas up to even five years ago I regarded Bugattis as cars only for the strong, silent men. For what my judgment is worth, the 23·6 hp Bugatti is one of the five best, most interesting, most friendly, companionable and altogether delightful motorcars that can be bought in London today.

Contemporary road impression

In July 1928, *Motor Sport* carried a short road test report on the car – a 4-door saloon model:

At the last Olympia Motor Show, Ettore Bugatti departed from his previous practice of building only racing or sporting models, and surprised his many followers by introducing the first serious attempt at a Bugatti touring car.

This was the new 3 litre, 8 cylinder model, which differs in size and in certain features of design from any other type of Bugatti. To begin with, excepting only the formidable 'Gold Bug' of some 15 litre capacity, this new car is the largest Bugatti (by some 700 cc) that has yet been produced.

Secondly, in view of the larger size of the engine, and in order to ensure the minimum of vibration, the designer has wisely used the maximum number of bearings to the crankshaft, namely, nine, an interesting point when it is remembered that five bearings are considered sufficient for the 2,300 cc supercharged model.

In the past there have been many enthusiasts who were prepared to sacrifice docility and flexibility for the undisputed 'pep' common to all Bugatti models, but even the most enthusiastic could not claim that their cars were comfortable touring vehicles. The 3 litre model was introduced to remedy this state of affairs and, with a view to testing its success or failure in this direction, I was very pleased to accept the loan of Colonel Sorel's private car for a day's trial.

The car in question is fitted with a low built fabric saloon body of a type which is becoming increasingly popular among sportsmen who realize that the extra comfort more than outweighs the almost imperceptible sacrifice of performance.

Settling ourselves aboard in the heart of London, we, driver and crew, at once realized that a comfortable day was before us, for seating accommodation, suspension and ventilation seemed to be extremely adequate.

I was immediately impressed by the ridiculous lightness of the major controls and in particular of the clutch pedal. The latter was almost incredible and suggested those Olympia models in which a special (and quite useless) clutch spring is fitted to gull the unsuspecting buyer.

That the spring pressure was perfectly adequate we soon discovered on moving off.

In traffic, the car proved a delight to handle as either the top gear crawl or the second gear 'buzz and jump' method could be indulged in at will. It was soon realized that all the drawbacks of the more 'racing' Bugattis were absent, giving place to real docility, smoothness and silence at low speeds and at the same time not excluding such desirable traits as splendid acceleration and deceleration. Although it is hardly likely that a top gear fiend will ever drive one of these cars, yet if such should be the case, he would find that the engine would readily respond to his crude and lazy methods, in a manner surpassed only by the large and woolly American. On the other hand, once the rapid changes of engine speed have been mastered, the

155. *The later T.44/49 engine with low-mounted oil pump. The fan is usual only on the T.49.*

156. *The type 44 was occasionally raced. Here is Phillipe de Rothschild in the 1929 'Fuel Consumption' Grand Prix at Le Mans.*

157. *Chiron and Bouriat in the 16 cylinder car at the Klausen Hill-Climb in 1930.*

16 CYLINDER RACING CAR

158. *Chiron: standing kilometre sprint, Geneva. 1930.*

gearbox artist will find the lever a joy to handle, as no effort is required and even if an error of judgment is made, the fact is only betrayed by a slight crunch from the machinery.

Tests showed that the corrected speeds on the various gears were approximately as follows: 1st gear, 30 mph; 2nd, 40 mph; 3rd, 60 mph. All these speeds were obtained with great rapidity and without fuss or vibration; when accelerating or decelerating a period lasting for about 1½ mph on the speedometer, is passed through at speeds corresponding to about 55 mph on top gear. This period was so short and withal so slight that it could not possibly be described as a fault, and seems to be an unavoidable feature of many high efficiency engines.

When we arrived at the track, we attempted a few speedy laps. All went well until half way round the Byfleet banking when the rear of the car swung from side to side in an alarming manner, indicating that the tyre pressures were more suited to road work than to high track speeds. After borrowing some of Mr Dunlop's potted air for our Michelin Balloons, we motored a fast lap to test the behaviour of the car with the harder tyres. This time the steadiness was remarkable and the speedometer registered 95 mph for a considerable portion of the lap; unfortunately, the stopwatch *did* stop on this run so the speed was not checked. On attempting a second lap the rather touring plugs showed acute signs of distress and we were compelled to stop to allow them a respite. We then restarted and the stopwatch records recorded a lap speed of 77 mph, although the car was still suffering somewhat from tired plugs and failed to persuade its hopeful speedometer beyond the 90 mph mark.

There is little doubt that on the first lap over 80 mph was averaged, as the car was running infinitely better before the plugs 'cooked'; we were very sorry not to be able to attempt some all-out laps on a new set of 'Bougies'.

We then forsook the speedway for the public roads once more and I was again impressed with the delightful running of the car. The lightness of all controls, the liveliness of the engine and the really powerful brakes made traffic driving and cross-country spurts equally joyous and enabled high averages to be maintained with a complete absence of effort or danger.

Here we have a car with most of the virtues of a racing car, including an honest maximum speed of 85 mph, combined with economy (25 mpg) and tractability to satisfy the most fastidious owner.

TYPES 45 & 47
16 cylinder racing models

IN 1928 BUGATTI DESIGNED A PAIR OF EXTRAORDINARY 16 cylinder engines similar in conception to his aeroengines, and intended to be fitted in a G.P. racing car (Type 45) or a Le Mans regulation-bodied Grand Sport car (Type 47). The engines were identical, except that the G.P. engine was 60 mm × 84 mm, 3·8 litre, while the sports version was reduced in stroke to 66 mm, to bring it within the 3 litre class. The design consisted of two 8 cylinder engines somewhat similar to the Type 35 ones, geared together, each bank fitted with a rear mounted blower. The crank, however, differed notably from the T.35 having nine roller main bearings, but plain big ends.

These cars, according to *Motor Sport*, March 1928, were originally intended for the 1928 French Grand Prix which was abandoned and, according to this journal, work on the cars was also abandoned. Three cars were, however, built, two being at the time of writing in France and the third, having 'escaped', is now in the U.S.A. The cars had three outings in 1930 in hill-climbs making F.T.D. on each occasion, but the crank gearing was defective. There was at least a proposal to fit the engine in a T.43 chassis but, as far as is known, nothing came of it. The T.47 chassis itself seems to have formed the basis of the later T.54 G.P. car.

The type was, however, described in detail in the *Autocar* of 12 April 1929:

Sixteen cylinders, forty-eight valves, two crankshafts, two camshafts, a power output of 250 and a weight of roughly 500 lb, or 2 lb per horse-power, are the outstanding features of a most unusual engine produced by M. Bugatti. The mere mention of sixteen cylinders

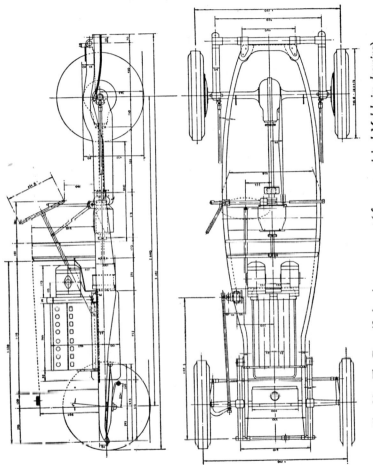

Fig. 2⁵. *The Type 45 chassis arrangement (from an original Molsheim drawing).*

193

suggests a bonnet of almost interminable length, but this Bugatti is shorter than the firm's eight-cylinder model of the same bore and stroke, for its cylinders are not in line, but in two banks of eight, each engine being complete in itself and the two being united by gearing.

It was during the war that Bugatti conceived the double eight engine for use on aeroplanes. A few were built, but for some reason or other the idea was not pushed, and now the dual power plant has been brought forth as a four-litre model, each engine having a capacity of two litres. It could be best described as a super-sports car, for it has been catalogued and plans have been laid for its production, but it is doubtful if many will get into the hands of the public before 1930. The intention is that it shall participate in races – the 24-hour event at Le Mans, records and hill-climbs – this year, and be openly offered for sale after it has proved its merits.

While, naturally, the number of motorists likely to be interested in the purchase of such a car is limited, for it is a costly model, it is such a distinct departure from anything that has yet been built that no motorist can fail to be attracted by it. The cylinders have a bore and stroke of 60 by 84 mm (3,800 cc). One of the features which immediately attracts attention is that the cylinder blocks are not designed to be bolted down to a crankcase, nor do they carry crankshaft bearings. They are rectangular cast-iron blocks, machined all over, having eight cylindrical borings, and, in accordance with the usual Bugatti design, three vertical valves in the head.

The overall length of an engine is determined first by the cylinder bores, secondly by the number and length of the main bearings. The Bugatti blocks measure 22 in. from end to end, while the totalized diameters of the cylinders is just a fraction under 19 in., and yet in the remaining space of a little more than three inches it has been possible to lodge nine crankshaft bearings. This result has been obtained by having forged steel bearing supports fitted on to the bottom of the cylinder blocks and held to them by studs. Eight of these supports carry roller bearings; the central bearing is plain. The feature of the connecting rods is that the bronze caps are riveted and brazed to the rods and have an exceedingly thin white metal lining. If the white metal should melt, the resultant play in the big end would not be sufficient to prevent the running of the engine.

The two blocks of cylinders are united at the front by a steel plate, the outer ends of which are received in trunnions on the frame. At the rear there is a steel housing, which unites the two blocks of cylinders, contains the timing gear, and also serves to carry the engine in the frame.

194

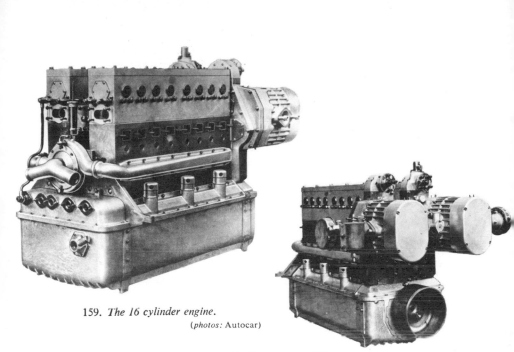

159. *The 16 cylinder engine.*

(*photos:* Autocar)

160. *Rear mounted blowers.*

161. *After lying derelict at Molsheim for many years the 16 cylinder prototypes have been restored and are now in the Schlumpf collection.*

162. *A handsome town carriage on the long wheelbase T.46 chassis. A far cry from the G.P. models in production alongside it, though road-holding and performance were typically Bugatti, with the added attraction of a really comfortable suspension. Introduced in 1928, a 3-speed gearbox on the back axle followed Royale design. Bugatti alloy wheels were an optional alternative to normal wire wheels.*

TYPE 46 (see page 201)

163. *A remarkable photograph of Ettore on the occasion of the completion of the 500th [sic!] Type 46 chassis, surrounded by his family, agents and drivers. Well-known personalities which can be identified include L'Ebé, Lidia, Czaykowski, Chiron, Loiseau, Dreyfus, Friderich, Sabipa, Paris agent Lamberjack, Docime and no doubt many others. This was probably chassis 46500 rather than the 500th.*

164. *A new 46S saloon discovered in Marseille in 1960.* (photo: F. Sipp)

165. *The 16" brakes.*
(photo: Autocar)

166. *The original factory finish.*

TYPE 46 ENGINE

167. *At the London Motor Show, 1929.*
(*photo:* Autocar)

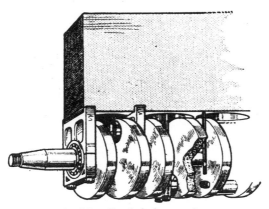

Fig. 26. *Crankshaft mounting.*

(drawing: Autocar)

The crankcase is nothing more than an oil collector and a dust excluder. It is a light cast aluminium casing, with side pieces which can be lifted off so as completely to expose the crankshaft and the main and connecting rod bearings. Examined superficially, the engine is a complicated piece of mechanism, but in reality the design assures a high degree of accessibility. In addition to the rods and bearings, which can be seen and felt after lifting away a quickly detachable cover, the oil pumps are equally accessible, and, as the crankcase is only a shell, any main bearing or any piston and rod can be reached after five minutes' preliminary work.

All the timing gear is at the rear. The mechanism consists of a spur pinion on each crankshaft, each one meshing with an intermediate pinion on the clutch shaft, from which the drive is taken in the usual way through the gearbox to the rear axle. There is a train of spur pinions up to the two overhead camshafts – one for each block of cylinders. These pinions are made use of to drive the two magnetos carried on the dashboard, with their distributors immediately in front of the driver, and also the two Roots-type compressors. The induction pipes are between the two banks of cylinders; the plugs are mounted horizontally on the outside, and the valves are placed vertically in the head and do not differ essentially from those of other Bugatti engines.

Three pumps are relied on to assure the lubrication of the engine, and they are driven off the front end of the crankshafts by worm gearing. One of the pumps scavenges the base chamber, another delivers oil at a pressure of more than 100 lb per square inch to the connecting rod bearings, while the third sends oil under low pressure

199

to the overhead valve mechanism and other parts. It is because of the forced pressure feed to the connecting rod bearings that the central crankshaft bearing is plain. Oil is delivered direct to this bearing, then passes through oil ducts in the crankshaft to the connecting rod bearings. The oil supply is maintained in a tank within the chassis.

The water pump is on the front of the engine, but, like the other accessories, it is driven from the rear, use being made of a long shaft which passes between the two blocks of cylinders. There are two inlets from the radiator and two outlets, one going to the outside of each line of cylinders. A Zenith carburettor is bolted up direct to each Roots blower.

The engine develops its power at between 5,000 and 6,000 rpm, although it is claimed that it has been run under load up to 7,000 rpm. It weighs little more than the normal two-litre straight eight; it is shorter because of the special cylinder and crankshaft construction, and, as the width is only $14\frac{1}{2}$ in., there is no difficulty in lodging it under an ordinary bonnet behind a narrow radiator.

There is nothing particularly distinctive in the chassis. As to the speed of the car the makers prefer to give no information, but with the power available and the low weight of the chassis it ought to be wonderfully fast and have extraordinary powers of acceleration.

TYPE 46
5 litre luxury model

IN THE AUTUMN OF 1929 A NEW, LARGE CHASSIS WAS ANNOUNCED, with an 8 cylinder, 5·3 litre engine and a wheelbase of nearly 12 feet. This offered to those who could afford a luxury car, if not a Royale, a chassis on which the finest coachwork could be carried, and with the traditional flexibility and good road manners of a Bugatti. Two years later a blower was added to the 46S (Sport) model, giving it an even better performance than the standard coach. Type 46 was one of the best of the large Bugatti models. It was the forerunner of Type 50 which differed only in the engine, and was in many ways a small Royale. It was Ettore's favourite model; nearly 500 were produced well into the 1930s, although there was some difficulty in selling the last few, which accounts for the recent appearance of three or four brand new chassis.

Description of car

In the *Autocar* of 20 September 1929, we read:

The newcomer differs from its predecessors, however, in being far removed from the racing type and having all the qualities of silence, flexibility and comfort so much sought after by present-day motorists. M. Ettore Bugatti is generally looked upon as one of the chief exponents of the ultra-sports model, although such types really constitute but 5 per cent of his production. In his new straight eight he has sought to meet the requirements of a larger class of owners.

The engine has a bore and stroke of 81 mm × 130 mm (5,227 cc) and its overall length is 3 ft 1 in. In general design it is similar to the 'Golden Bug' – the 14 litre straight eight being built at Molsheim in limited numbers for the favoured few who can purchase the most expensive car in the world.

Rigidity is a most desirable feature in any engine, and it is secured by mounting all the auxiliaries direct on the cylinder casting. The

201

crankcase serves only to collect oil and to exclude dust, and does not carry any moving component. It might be remarked that any engine with cylinders and crankcase in one casting falls into this category, but the feature of the Bugatti is that the cylinders are extended downwards, with suitable ribbing for rigidity, to allow the nine bearing crankshaft to be mounted directly upon it. These crankshaft supports are machined and ground to very fine limits; very thick bronze bearing caps with a minimum of white metal are fitted, and the lower cap is held in the usual way by studs. The crankshaft is a one-piece forging, with circular webs, and of very big diameter.

As in the case of other models of this marque there are three vertical valves per cylinder, operated by an overhead camshaft driven by bevel gearing from the front. The entire engine is assembled with its two oil pumps – one scavenger and one feed pump – its water pump at the front, its dynamo and the distributor, the last mentioned being driven from the rear end of the camshaft; it is only after completion that the single-piece aluminium crankcase is added.

The engine is carried in the chassis by means of four forged hangers bolted to the cylinder casting and having at their outer extremities a cup containing a rubber block to give an elastic attachment to the frame member. The entire crankcase can be dropped in a few minutes to give complete access to the main and connecting rod bearings, the oil pumps, and the front end drive for the camshaft and auxiliaries. In addition, there are big inspection plates on each side of the crankcase through which connecting rods, can be examined and withdrawn.

One of the patented features of the engine is the rubber-mounted flywheel. Instead of the flywheel being keyed directly on the crankshaft, a hub is fitted, and between this and the flywheel a thick rubber ring is interposed. This acts as a very efficient vibration damper and gives a slightly flexible drive. The clutch, a multiple-disc type with Ferodo facings, running dry, is in the flywheel. A multiple-jet Smith carburettor is fed with petrol from a rear tank by means of a couple of Autopulses. The whole of the lubricating oil is contained in a dashboard tank, connection between this and the oil-collecting base chamber being by means of flexible metal pipes. The oil filter projects from the tank, on the engine side, and can be dismounted immediately for cleaning without the use of tools.

The three-speed gearbox is a unit with the rear axle. A tubular cross-member carries the pedals and also receives an aluminium housing which encircles the clutch and acts as a support for the starting motor. This aluminium housing is rigidly secured to the tubular cross-member, but merely fits over the rear of the engine

168. *Type 46S supercharged engine.*

169. *The T.46, along with the T.50 and the original T.28, has the 3 speed gearbox in the rear axle.*

(*photo:* Autocar)

170. *The T.46 has a ball change and a steering wheel with the wood rim extended down the wheel spokes.*

(*photo:* F. Sipp)

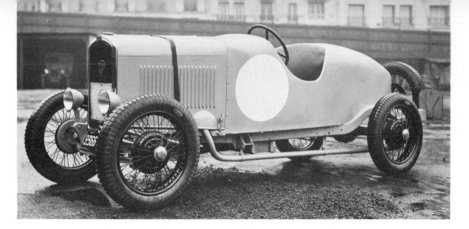

171. *The 1931 Peugeot 201X car fitted with the 4 cylinder supercharged 1,000 cc T.48 engine.*

TYPE 48 _(see page 208)

172. *The engine, virtually half a T.35 unit.*

crankcase, so as to allow relative movement to take place at times between the two units.

A vertically divided two-piece aluminium casing is used for the gearbox and the differential housing. The axle tubes are of chrome nickel heat-treated steel, the whole weighing only a couple of pounds more than the standard axle on the other models. The propellor-shaft is of the open type, with a fabric-type joint in front and a metal joint at the rear. The aluminium brake drums have an internal diameter of $15\frac{3}{4}$ in., and as the tyre size is 32 in. $\times$ 6 in., the brake drums are only a little less in diameter than the wheels. The position of the dynamo is somewhat unusual, it being under the floor-boards and secured by clips to the right-hand frame member. It is driven by means of a one-piece rubber belt from a pulley on the front end of the propellor-shaft.

Contemporary road impressions

There was a report of a road test of a Type 46 (No. 46219, still in existence) in *The Motor* of 1 April 1930:

A really solidly built, beautifully sprung, comfortable saloon car with exceptionally rapid acceleration throughout its speed range; that is the 32·5 hp or 'five-litre' Bugatti. It combines the luxury of a large limousine, the flexibility and top-gear performance of a thorough-bred town carriage with the perfect road-holding, the speed and acceleration of the best type of sports model.

Although in the appearance of the square-cut eight-cylinder engine, the shape of the radiator, the design of the rear springing and a certain lowness of build the new five-litre has a good deal in common with the famous racing cars from the Molsheim factory, the whole 'feel' of the car – its control and the manner in which it is driven – is different. Whereas with the sports models a lightning change-up is made after accelerating to the full on each of the intermediate gears, the driver of the five-litre is encouraged to get into top gear as soon as possible and to stay in top. The car then handles in a manner reminiscent of a large American car. It will creep through traffic at three or four miles an hour on top gear, will climb practically any main-road hill without there being any need to change down, and will accelerate, whenever the opportunity occurs, with surprising rapidity. Instead of the acceleration 'tailing-off' however, at high speeds, it continues almost the same until the maximum is reached.

Of course, if one does change down to second speed – and the change is singularly easy – one can leave most other cars far behind. So the driver of one of these new, big Bugattis always has this second gear, as it were, 'up his sleeve', although to all intents and purposes his is a 'top-gear' car.

Possibly because of its low build and its admirable driving position, the Bugatti does not strike one as being a large car. Yet it is as wide and as long as most full-sized automobiles and, inside, it is as roomy, or roomier, than most. In traffic, however, it is handled with exceptional ease.

There seems always to be such an enormous amount of power in reserve that one drives the car instinctively in a very gentlemanly manner. What does it matter if anyone 'cuts in' ahead, or if exigencies of traffic compel one to slow to a crawl at the beginning of a steep ascent? The moment the accelerator is depressed the Bugatti leaps forward. The other cars fade into the background and the gradient seems to flatten as we devour it.

The suspension, by reversed quarter-elliptic springs at the rear and by half-elliptics in front, is all that can possibly be desired. Although all road shocks are completely damped out and one can take a culvert or hump-backed bridge at speed and scarcely feel it, there is a firm, secure feeling about the whole car that is most reassuring. There is no rolling on corners; one can swerve to the side of a steeply cambered road and yet feel completely at ease. Moreover, the springing is just as good at walking pace as it is at 90 mph.

The steering is absolutely accurate and pleasantly direct; it has a marked degree of self-centring action and, after rounding a bend, the steering-wheel spins back automatically to the 'straight-ahead' position. It is only at very low speeds that this caster action has the effect of making the steering just a shade heavy on sharp corners. At anything above 10 or 15 mph the steering is feather-light.

The clutch is very smooth in action and light to operate. The engine is most efficiently balanced and is delightfully smooth-running in consequence. It is quite inaudible at low speeds.

We put the Bugatti through our usual brake and acceleration tests at Brooklands and were particularly impressed with the liveliness of the car. As it was new we did not wish to overstress the engine. For this reason we made no attempt to exceed 50 mph on second gear although at that speed the power-unit was so quiet and there was so much throttle in hand that we could quite easily have exceeded by a large margin the figure mentioned. In the same way we were contented with a flying half-mile at 82 mph on top gear and a lap at slightly over 79 mph and did not keep the car fully extended long enough to reach the ultimate maximum. We were assured by the concessionaires, however, that by using an alternative back-axle ratio, a speed of 96 mph should be obtainable.

Even when driving off the home banking at nearly 90 mph the car was beautifully quiet mechanically, while the body was completely silent.

The brakes were singularly smooth in action and absolutely safe. Judging by the size of the drums, they should last for an indefinite period.

We found that the Brooklands test hill could be climbed on top gear if approached at 25 mph and the accelerator depressed only when the car was actually on the gradient. From a standing start on first gear the test-hill was climbed in $12\frac{2}{3}$ second, equal to an average speed of 19·37 mph. This is quite exceptionally good, especially when the weight of the car – 35 cwt 3 qr 2 lb – is taken into account.

The car we tried had a very smart Weymann body of the sportsman's coupé type, but far more roomy than is usual. There was plenty of room for those in the rear compartment and ample headroom.

The five-litre Bugatti is undoubtedly a very fine car and one which, in our opinion, will meet with an excellent reception in this country.

TYPE 48
the Peugeot 201X

ETTORE BUGATTI HAD DESIGNED A BABY CAR IN 1912, WHICH HE licenced to the Peugeot Company. Contacts were evidently maintained with that Company since years later (in 1931) he designed a supercharged 1,000 cc engine for use in a special series of Peugeot 201 cars, known as the 201X; about twenty of these cars were made, mostly with cabriolet bodywork. Peugeot were anxious to produce a high performance sports car and the choice of a Bugatti engine was no doubt appropriate.

The engine, known as Type 48, was virtually half of a Type 35 engine, 60 × 88 mm, capacity 996 cc, and used half of the normal roller bearing, G.P. crankshaft and a single cylinder block, although the cambox had a rounded top. Another Molsheim feature of the car was the reversed, Bugatti-style, quarter-elliptic springs at the rear, but the transverse front spring was Peugeot. The wheelbase was 2·47 m and the track 1·15 m.

The Peugeot 201X had an unhappy history: the famous race driver André Boillot was killed in one of these cars on 5 June 1932, while practising for the Côte d'Ars race. He had had a long period of success as a driver for Peugeot and had just completed a few days previously a 24 hour run in a Peugeot 301C averaging 68 mph without a relief driver.

One example of the T.48 engine is known to exist today.

173. *The last single-cam car produced and replacing T.44.*

TYPE 49 (see page 213)

174. *A T.49 coach owned until recently by the celebrated racing driver Jules Goux.*

175. *A 1934 coupé by James Young of Bromley. Many Bugatti experts consider the Type 49 to be the finest of the closed-bodied cars. Weight had not increased to the point where road handling suffered.*

176. *Lord Cholmondely, an enthusiastic Bugatti owner, had this splendid 'canné' coach fitted to his Type 49.*

TYPE 49
ENGINE

177 *Introduced in 1930, this model was an improved T.44, having an increased bore of 72 mm, stroke of 100 mm, and a capacity of 3,257 cc. Single overhead camshaft and 3 valves per cylinder were still employed, also a single Schebler carburettor with Autoflux petrol pump. New features were a fan and twin coil ignition with 2 sparking plugs per cylinder (long since abandoned, incidentally, by all present-day users of this model and the similarly equipped 5 litre and T.40A, in favour of single ignition) which were reported to give greatly improved acceleration and general performance similar to the T.57; also dry clutch and ball type gear change.*

178. *The left side of the T.49 engine is very similar to that of the T.44. The fan on this engine has been removed.*

179. *18 inch bolt-on alloy wheels were standard on the T.49.*

180. *The T.50 chassis introduced in 1930 with the first twin overhead camshaft engine; it was super-charged and had a remarkable performance.*

TYPE 50 (see page 221)

181. *A magnificent stagecoach-style body with ponyskin covered trunk.*

TYPE 49
the last single-cam car

MANY EXPERIENCED BUGATTISTES BELIEVE THAT THE FINEST OF ALL touring Bugatti cars was Type 49, which replaced Type 44 in July 1930 and continued in production for three years or so. It was the last single-cam engine produced and was virtually an enlarged Type 44, the bore being increased from 69 to 72 mm, a fan being added, the clutch being dry (except on a few early cars) and the gearbox having a ball change lever. The cylinder blocks had two plugs per cylinder supplied from a dual Scintilla distributor. Bugatti alloy wheels were usually fitted and an enlarged radiator, but otherwise the car was very similar in all respects to the later series Type 44. A long chassis version was also available.

The front axle was of normal Bugatti design with the springs passing through the axle; the rear axle was also the same as on the 43–44 models but now had helical bevel gears, ratio 12×50, for silence. The brakes were operated by the normal compensated cables and on this model at any rate were excellent. Inside the car one could notice a speedometer in place of a tachometer and a neat cluster of instruments and switches in a solid walnut dash. The steering wheel had the simple steel centre with walnut rim as on earlier models and the racing cars – the larger touring cars (T.46, T.50 and later T.57) had more complicated constructions.

The model was eventually replaced by Type 57, but had in comparison with it a 4 in. narrower track and 8 in. less wheelbase in standard form. These reduced dimensions and consequent weight saving gave it better handling than the later model. It did not have the performance of a Type 43, nor of the T.57, but was an admirable touring Bugatti which compared very favourably indeed with any other car of the 1930 period.

Contemporary road impressions

The Motor, 1 November 1932, reported a road test of the car:

A FINE FRENCH CAR CAPABLE OF OVER 80 MPH, YET REMARKABLY
FLEXIBLE AT LOW SPEEDS

The Type 49, or 3·3 litre tourer, combines all those qualities for which the Bugatti is famous, with an unexpected flexibility and silence at low speeds on top gear. It is, indeed, a car with a dual personality – a comfortable carriage and a lively sports model.

It will lap Brooklands track at over 80 mph, and it will crawl through traffic and round street corners on top gear with never a sign of snatch. By means of dash-controlled, friction-type shock-absorbers the suspension can be instantly adjusted to give safe, bounce-free riding at any speeds from 10 to 80 miles an hour on any kind of surface.

So quickly and easily does the Type 49 reach a speed of a mile a minute that, on the average main road, it is possible to cover long distances in an astonishingly short space of time. So safe does the car feel that one has no hesitation about driving at the maximum whenever road conditions permit.

The car is, of course, beautifully finished. The engine is polished in a manner calculated to turn most enthusiasts green with envy. It is smooth running, too, except for a slight 'period', which could possibly be cured by adjusting the damper on the end of the crank-shaft. The exhaust is quiet, as is the rear axle. Indeed, the only unit that lacks refinement is the gearbox. This is a four-speed box of ordinary type, with no 'silent' gears. It is not easy to change gear with, and it is noisy on the lower ratios.

The gearbox has particularly well-chosen ratios, allowing, as it does, of a speed on top gear of over 80 mph with third and second gear maxima of 60 mph and 40 mph without over-revving the engine. The gear-change is exceptionally rapid, which probably accounts for the difficulty in gear-changing except at high road speeds, with the result that it is possible to make a remarkable get-away from a standstill. It only takes 20⅕ sec to accelerate from a standstill to 60 mph using the gears, and changing up approximately at 25 mph, 40 mph and 60 mph. On second gear the car will accelerate from 10 mph to 30 mph in 4⅔ sec, the top-gear acceleration between the same speeds being 8⅔ sec.

In the course of our Brooklands tests, which were, of course, additional to our trial on the road, we lapped the track in 2 min 2⅘ sec, which is equivalent to 81·11 mph. The half-mile was covered in 22⅘ sec, which is equal to 78·95 mph. It may be considered by those unfamiliar with Brooklands track that this result is somewhat strange. All Brooklands *habitués* know, however, that with a certain direction of the wind it is possible to lap the track at a higher average speed than can be maintained over half a mile.

The brakes, needless to say, proved to be exceptionally good, the pulling-up distances being better than is usually considered possible; at any rate, from low speeds. Several repetitions of the brake tests gave an average of 7 ft 6 in. from 20 mph, 23 ft from 30 mph, 50 ft from 40 mph and 78 ft 6 in. from 50 mph. It is to be assumed that the brake linings were well bedded down in the process, for the stopping distances, although very good, were not so remarkable at 60 mph and 70 mph, when they measured 131 ft 6 in. and 211 ft respectively. It was not considered worth while readjusting the brakes to get super-lative results at these high speeds. The car pulled up dead straight on every occasion except one, when a rear wheel locked as the result of passing through a pool of water.

On the road the car handles delightfully. The steering is remarkably free from any reaction, is very light and fairly direct. Moreover, the amount of caster action given to the front wheels is not so great that it makes steering in reverse difficult.

Although carrying a really roomy four-seater body the Type 49 Bugatti is of handy dimensions, the wheelbase and track being 10 ft 7 in. and 4 ft 2 in. respectively. There are not many cars with engines this size which have such a narrow track, but the car is so steady on corners and the road-holding generally so good that one does not realize that the track is not the standard width of 4 ft 8 in.

Last winter we were able to make a long run on a similar model to that now described, covering some 320 miles in the day on a give-and-take road, including long straight stretches and a good deal of winding, hilly going, at a higher average speed than we have ever yet succeeded in maintaining for such a long distance.

We found that many main-road bends, which on the average car we would treat with the utmost respect, could be rounded on the Bugatti at such high speeds that it would be wiser not to quote them in this article. This run was accomplished without the slightest fatigue, which speaks well for the comfort which the suspension and bodywork afford and the freedom from worry engendered by the perfect road-holding and controllability.

As an instance of the remarkable hill-climbing properties of the

215

Type 49, we may mention that the steep, winding roads leading out of Lyme Regis, in Dorset, in the direction of Exeter and Dorchester, were both climbed so fast on top gear that we were obliged to cut out for every bend. There are very, very few cars capable of equalling this performance.

For whatever purpose the car is used it invariably demonstrates itself to be a thoroughbred.

182. *The T.50 was fitted with a variety of remarkable examples of the French coachbuilders' art, in this case 'carrosserie profilée'.*

183. *A handsome drophead body.*

184. *The late Mr. Ken Purdy's T.50 on the Thompson Circuit, Connecticut.*

185. *Louis Chiron racing at Le Mans in 1931.*

186. *One of the fabric-covered cars made for Le Mans came to Britain.*

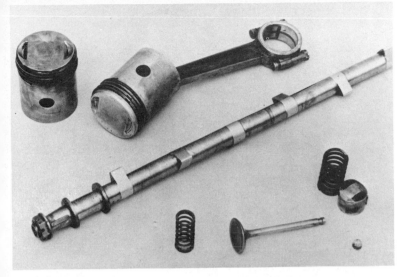

187. *Valve, camshaft and connecting rod detail on T.50 engine.*

(*photo: John Caperton*)

188. *36·6 hp 8 cylinder. This impressive looking engine was the first twin overhead camshaft Bugatti model. With a bore and stroke of 86 × 107 mm, a capacity of 4·9 litres and large Bugatti Roots-type supercharger with 2 carburettors mounted below it, the performance was pretty vivid, 5–112 mph on top. The very large supercharger runs at twice engine speed and is reasonably silent at cruising speeds, the maximum supercharge pressure being 6·8 lb/in². This photograph evidently shows the prototype engine; the blower was later more heavily ribbed.*

216

189. *The left side of the engine in plate 188 with original factory finish.*

190. *The normal T.50 engine with heavily ribbed blower and 3 blower relief valves, although the centre one seems later to have been eliminated.*

TYPE 50
twin-cam, 5 litre luxury car

IN 1930 BUGATTI PRODUCED A NEW LARGE LUXURY MODEL
replacing the 5·3 litre Type 46. It would perhaps be more
accurate to say that it replaced the Type 46S, since it was supercharged and sold as a Grand Sport car. The chassis and transmission were identical with the earlier 5·3 litre car, but the
engine was completely new. Later a longer wheelbase Type 50T
(T = Tourisme) was introduced. The bore and stroke were
86 and 107 mm, giving 4,972 cc (not 4,840 cc as given, un-
accountably, by Brixton Road publicity, but not Molsheim, and
repeated frequently in *The Bugatti Book* and elsewhere). The
crankshaft was carried on nine plain bearings. The new and
significant change in cylinder head layout was the abandonment
by Ettore of vertical valves and the use of 90 degree inclined
valves, two only per cylinder and operated directly by twin
overhead camshafts.

The story has been told elsewhere that Bugatti saw and
eventually acquired in exchange for three Type 43s, a pair of
Miller racing cars that had been raced at Monza in 1929 by
Leon Duray; this is certainly true, the cars having only recently
returned home. What is probably also true is that he copied
their cylinder head layout and the use of cups between cams
and valves. He had never shown that he had any understanding
of cylinder head-combustion chamber thermodynamics and
it is more than probable that he realized that the time had come
to follow the clearly established practices of others, also
successful in the racing car business. After all Duesenberg had
copied his 8 cylinder engine ten years previously!

221

The engine is a fine piece of engineering, with a massive cylinder block with fixed head. A vertical shaft at the front of the engine driven off the crankshaft by bevels, drives a pair of oil pumps through spur gears, the sump being of the dry type. An intermediate pair of bevels drives a short shaft lying across the front of the engine, then a further pair of bevels drives the longitudinal blower at twice engine speed. The top end of the vertical shaft drives the camshaft through five spur gears and idlers and a final pair of bevels. Twin Schebler carburettors were mounted below the blower. Ignition was by coil. The engine was reputed to develop 44 hp at 1,000 rpm, 113 hp at 2,000 rpm, 175 hp at 3,000 rpm and 200 hp or more at 4,000 rpm. At peak revolutions the speeds on gears were 47 mph on 1st, 85 mph on 2nd and 110 on top, although so high a maximum speed was probably unobtainable. The acceleration of the car was remarkable and the handling, steering and brakes excellent. Dash controlled shockabsorbers were used.

The clutch, gearbox, chassis, axles and brakes on the Type 50 were identical with those of Type 46. Wheels were of the cast alloy type, with Royale hubs. Many magnificent bodies were mounted on the Type 50, a model which was at the peak of Bugatti's luxury cars, overlooked perhaps by the fantastic Royale. It was used occasionally for racing, a team of regulation-bodied touring cars being entered in the 1931 Le Mans 24 hour race. The car driven by Rost crashed, due to a burst tyre, and unfortunately killed a spectator; the team was then withdrawn, the other drivers being Conelli, Varzi/Chiron and Divo/Bouriat. The normal Type 50 engine, no doubt with increased power, was used in the Type 53 F.W.D. car and the Type 54 G.P. car, although its weight was a fault.

A special racing engine, with a light alloy crankcase and known as the 50B was later developed from the standard engine; details are given on page 300. The famous Wimille 4·7 litre single seater car appears to have been classified by the factory as a T.50 derivative judging by its chassis number (50180).

TYPE 51
twin-cam G.P. racing car

THE CLASSIC BUGATTI RACING CAR PROBABLY REACHED ITS ZENITH in the 1931, 2·3 litre version of Type 35B, fitted now with a twin-overhead camshaft cylinder block and known as Type 51. The engine consisted of a crankcase, roller-bearing crankshaft and blower with drive from the T.35B, with a new block carrying 95 degree inclined valves, two per cylinder, and intermediate cups between the cams and valves as on Type 50. A single central 18 mm plug was used; manifolds were also new. The camshaft lubrication was by pressure pipe from the main oil gallery on the left-hand side of the crankcase, feeding the blower gears, the timing gears (four connections) and the camshafts.

Improved wheels with non-detachable rims were introduced, rather neater in appearance than the earlier G.P. type and with strengthening ribs inside each spoke. Externally, however, the car was virtually indistinguishable from a T.35B, although the experienced eye can notice the lower location of the blower relief hole in the bonnet, due to the difference in inlet manifolds, and the location of the magneto on the left-hand side of the dash, since it is driven by the left-hand, exhaust camshaft. A number of 1,500 cc, 60 mm × 66 mm, cars were produced under the designation T.51A; a few 2 litre cars, 60 mm × 88 mm, were also produced, but there is some doubt that the designation T.51C (by analogy with the T.35C) is official. About forty cars in all were produced. On test the 2,300 cc engine gave 187 hp at 5,200 rpm, and the 1,500 cc a surprising 158 hp.

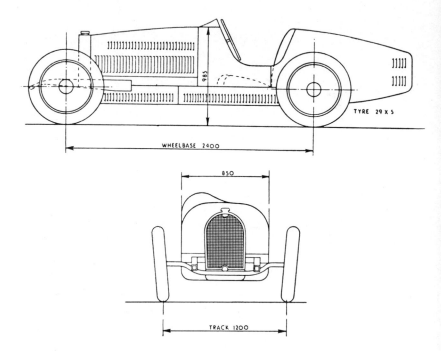

Fig. 27. *The fine lines of the classic T.51 racing car.*

Racing successes

The type made a good start to its racing career, Chiron winning the 1931 Monaco Grand Prix and Varzi the Tunis G.P. He and Chiron jointly won the 10 hour French Grand Prix of that year at Montlhéry, covering 782 miles. From then on many examples were to be seen in races all over the world, and the car was very popular at Brooklands. It has been said that the car was no faster than a good single-cam version, but given an equal degree of tune it probably was. The exhaust valve seats probably

224

191. *2·3 litre, twin overhead camshaft, 8 cylinder, G.P. car, perhaps the finest racing Bugatti of all time.*

TYPE 51

192 (below). *Chiron at Monaco, 1931.*

193. *A few cars were produced as 1½ litre versions, and Veyron and others took the Class 24 hr. Record in this one.*

194. *1931 Grand Prix of the A.C.F. Varzi entering the car with Chiron looking on anxiously. Refuelling and changing four wheels in 46 sec!*

195. *J. L. Burton at Brooklands 1938.*

(*photo: Louis Klemantaski*)

196. *F. E. Wall at Prescott, with the ex-Sarginson T.51.*

197. *The B.O.C. T.51 presented to the Club by Ettore Bugatti in 1939 (see page 229). The position of the blower relief hole identifies a T.51.*

198. *The engine of the Type 51.*

SOUTH AFRICA

199. *The late 'Tiny' Hindle (see page 292 and Fig. 28) with his T.51 and T.59.*

200. *The T.51 alloy wheel had a no detachable rim and the spokes were ribbed give them increased strength over the earli T.35 style. The wheel illustrated, on a T.43, fitted with a pre-war sports tyre.*

cracked less often! Mr A. C. Whincop wrote in the *Autocar* of 13 August 1943:

The Type 51 was first built in 1931, it being half Ettore's answer to the Monoposto Alfa Romeo which was breaking down Bugatti's amazing run of European successes since 1926, if the brief reign of the 1½ litre Delage in 1927 is excepted. The other half of Ettore's answer was the double-camshaft 4·9 litre G.P. car, which in spite of its very much greater capacity and new chassis design was no faster on many circuits than the 2·3; and was definitely slower on the corners, through the 'magic' having failed on that one chassis. As a result of Ettore's two answers, the years 1931 and 1932 provided probably the most colourful racing we have ever seen with Monoposto Alfa Romeos, 2·3 and 4·9 Bugattis, Maseratis of various capacities, and an occasional short-chassis Mercedes-Benz, all fairly evenly matched in spite of all giving their performance in such different ways. The Monoposto, however, had that little extra power which enabled Alfa Romeo to depose Bugatti from the supreme position in motor racing. The Type 51 can well be content with its successes during this period, which earned it the reputation of being the most reliable and the most pleasant racing car of its vintage to handle.

The engine is almost identical with that of the Type 55, which was, of course, by normal Bugatti practice, developed from it. With careful tuning the 51 engine in really good standard condition should give about 170 bhp at 5,500 rpm. The chassis, apart from small modifications and a new type of aluminium alloy wheel, integral with the brake drum as in the old wheel, is almost unaltered from the Type 35B.

My particular car is alleged to have been driven by Divo in the Bugatti team before it was brought into this country, in which case its history makes even more interesting reading. [This reference was to car 51140, still in existence.]

The B.O.C. car

At the Bugatti Owners' Club dinner in London in February 1939 Jean Bugatti made the astonishing announcement that his father and he were presenting the Club with a T.51 G.P. car for use by those club members who could not afford a car. The car arrived a few months later and was tried out at Prescott successfully – rather too successfully by one member who disappeared off the course onto the trees below the last bend on

229

the hill. The war came shortly afterwards; the subsequent story of the car has been communicated by Mr A. Rivers Fletcher:

Early in 1943 the B.O.C. decided to sell the Type 51 Bugatti which had been presented to the Club by Ettore Bugatti in 1939. Although the car was a wonderful gift it proved to be rather a white elephant in that it was so difficult to decide who should drive it. Obviously, the people with the requisite amount of experience already had suitable cars of their own, and there were clear difficulties in handing over such a potent and expensive piece of machinery to an inexperienced person. No doubt, the B.O.C. Council must have been very loath to part with the car but in retrospect it was a wise choice. The war was on and in any case there did not seem to be much prospect of any motor racing for a long time.

At that time I was working with my great friend, Peter Monkhouse, at the Monaco Motor and Engineering Company Limited at Watford. We were completely involved with war work of a fairly secret nature, but Peter was mad keen to get a suitable racing car organized for himself for post-war racing. He had always been very keen on Bugattis and was most enthusiastic at the prospect of buying the Club car. He did a deal with Eric Giles on behalf of the B.O.C. and on Easter Monday in April 1943 Peter and I travelled down to the Giles' home in Surrey by railway train. We brought with us a pair of trade registration plates and a roll of four inch width canvas. Eric Giles had promised to fasten a batten across the radiator stone guard extending to the front wheels and another batten across the tail of the car so that we could stretch the canvas across from wheel to wheel making some sort of impromptu wings to comply with British law. We also brought with us a bulb horn from a child's fairy cycle! Thus equipped we set off in a very Grand Prix Type 51 Bugatti on a sixty mile detour round London – it was very nearly legal! Anyway, we certainly had a method of giving audible warning of approach! There was a rear view mirror on the scuttle, there were mudguards – at least we said they were mudguards – we were using trade plates, and maybe the requisite insurance was valid. The Type 51 had been filled with racing fuel on the outbreak of war, and although it had tended to separate out, we drained it out, shook it up and re-filled the tank before setting off. It was a fantastic journey. Peter drove nearly all the way though I had a short spell. We were cheered by numerous military convoys who were, no doubt, surprised to see and hear a Grand Prix car being driven in such a manner and in such a place. We came across several policemen but they obviously did not believe their eyes or ears, so we were well past them before anyone could do anything about the situation. At one roundabout near

230

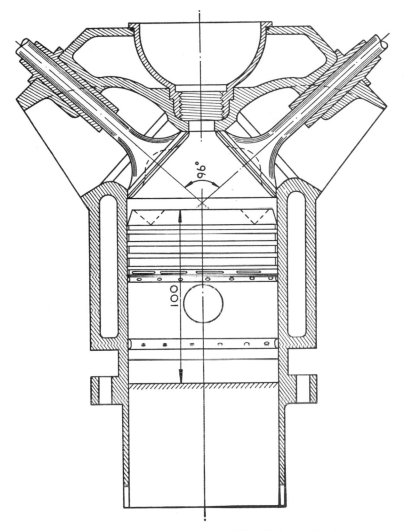

Fig. 28. 'Tiny' Hindle drawing of the T.51 cylinder head and piston.

Beaconsfield a military policeman gave us the thumbs up signal, and indicated to us to do just one more circuit of the roundabout for their delectation; Peter was driving and gave them the works – second gear with plenty of wheel spin and all the resultant tail wagging and pleasant odour!

The car was carefully stored at Monaco until racing cars could be got out again after the war. Peter drove the car at the Cockfosters Rally on the first occasion when racing cars were used in England in the new peacetime. He had offered to lend the car to our Patron, Lord Howe, to open the course, but Lord Howe declined the offer, wisely saying that something always happens if you borrow somebody else's car however carefully you drive it. Anyway he did use a Bugatti for the opening ceremony, as he used his own immaculate black and blue Type 57 SC coupé.

The first competition in which Monkhouse drove the Type 51 was in the V.S.C.C. sprint at Elstree in 1946 in which he made Fastest Time of the day, second place being taken by Roy Parnell driving Reg Parnell's Delage. This was on Easter Monday, just three years after the car had been collected from Eric Giles' home. Peter also got a second place in a short race at Gransden Lodge in June that same year, and of course he used the car at Prescott and in other sprints and hill-climbs during the next two years. Mrs Monkhouse won the prize for fastest lady driver driving the car in the Brighton Speed Trials, and in May 1947 Peter achieved 47·78 seconds at Prescott.

By that time the car had been modified by Peter's excellent mechanic Jack Jaguard, gearing up the supercharger to give more boost, and fitting a Wilson help-yourself gearbox instead of the original Bugatti clutch and gearbox.

Later in that year, in June, Peter in the Type 51 on the Holyhead Road near Dunstable was involved in a horrid shunt hitting a heavy lorry head on. The car was completely written off, but fortunately no one was seriously injured.

Peter Monkhouse was tragically killed in April 1950 in the Mille Miglia in a Silverstone Healey driven by Phillip Wood. Peter was a great personality, a brilliant engineer and an extremely good driver. He was unconventional in many ways, and almost desperately outspoken; he was one of those 'larger-than-life' characters that motor racing seems to throw up from time to time. Thinking back to the Peter Monkhouse days, it is sad to think that both the other characters who used to race Type 51 Bugattis at Prescott against Peter have also died tragic deaths, Kenneth Bear was killed driving his Type 59 in Jersey and 'Twink' Whincop died in tragic circumstances a few years ago. All those of us who remember them do so with great affection.

(The serial number of this car seems to have been 51155, originally delivered to King Leopold of Belgium.)

201. *At the opposite end of the dimensional scale to the Royale, and introduced about the same time, the versatile Ettore produced an electrically propelled scale model G.P. for the baby of the Bugatti family, Roland, shown here at the wheel. The catalogue of the period, in saying it is not a toy but a real little car, concludes naively: 'Commes toutes les Bugattis elle est inusable'! These little model racers were always available for hire in pre-war days, on the promenades at Nice and Cannes. Maximum speed 15 km/h.*

BABY BUGATTI

202. *The son of Dr S. Scher, the well-known American enthusiast, in an electric 'Baby'. The production version had a longer wheelbase which spoiled the scale effect.*

203. *While the fathers were tempted with the Royale, the sons could try out a T.52. A visiting prince from North Africa.*

204. *Le Patron's personal vehicle for factory inspection and local journeys. It was propelled electrically and exhibited in the 1931 Paris Salon.*

TYPES 52 & 56
electric vehicles and the Baby Bugatti

AT THE 1927 MILAN AUTOMOBILE SHOW, BUGATTI SHOWED AN attractive miniature children's Grand Prix Bugatti; this was originally built for young Roland, the second son of Ettore, born in 1922. This children's car was later put on the market, the correct factory reference being Type 52. It was listed as the Type 'Baby' for children of six to eight years of age; it had a speed of 10 to 12 mph, driven by a 12 volt accumulator. It was six feet in length and weighed 150 lb, and had pneumatic tyres on detachable wheels, with brakes on all four wheels, the brake shoes consisting of a one piece expanding annulus of wood. Transmission was by a single stage gear train from an electric motor mounted on the rear axle, the left-hand wheel being free on the axle. Reverse could be selected by a change-over switch in the motor field windings. A throttle-like lever operated a stepped resistance to vary speed. The prototype evidently had a wheelbase and track of 1·8 m × 0·9 m; no doubt to increase leg room, the production models had the wheelbase lengthened at the expense of aesthetics to 2 05 m.

These Baby Bugattis were much sought after in France and were often seen on the promenades at Deauville and other smart resorts. Today they are collectors' pieces.

Type 56 was a two seat electric runabout built by Bugatti more or less as a personal transport. At least some consideration was given to marketing it since a data sheet was produced. The chassis frame was a combination of wood and steel, with full-elliptic springs, and steering tiller; the tyres were 26 in. × 3·50 in. Six 100 amp/hour 6 volt batteries in series provided

235

the energy for a 36 volt 1 hp motor mounted on the axle and driving through gears by a mechanism very similar to that used in the Baby car. Speed control was by means of a right-hand lever. Foot and hand operated drum brakes were fitted. The total weight was under 800 lb, and a maximum speed of 16 to 18 mph was claimed.

A small batch of these electric vehicles was made and at least two survive, one in Switzerland and Bugatti's personal vehicle, returning to Alsace to the Schlumpf collection via Illinois.

TYPE 53
4-wheel drive car

IN 1932 BUGATTI ANNOUNCED A REMARKABLE 4-WHEEL DRIVE racing car, which apart from an experimental Christie car in the early 1900s, seems to have been the first time such a construction has been attempted in the racing field prior to the advent of the Ferguson car in 1961. If the chassis was completely new, the power plant was based on the Type 50, 4·9 litre engine, and was as used in the Type 54 G.P. car (see page 246). The original conception of the car was based on an Italian design which Jean Bugatti saw and persuaded his father to adopt, for development at Molsheim.

J. A. Grégoire, the well-known designer of the Tracta, Hotchkiss and other front-wheel drive cars has written (*L'Aventure Automobile*, Flammarion, Paris 1953):

About 1930, [Bugatti] met me one day, looking more red-faced and jovial than ever, and said, 'That won't work, that front drive car of yours'. I knew, of course, that he had designed and built a 4-wheel drive racing car which was causing him some trouble. And he added 'when you want to take a corner with this car, you can't hold the steering wheel and the car tries to leave the road'. Asking him how he managed the transmission to the front wheels, he explained to me that it was by normal universal joints. I tried hard to explain to him the causes of the trouble and the need for constant velocity joints, but he would not admit the clearly demonstrated facts. He condemned for always, as a result, front-wheel drive and regarded me with the benevolent sympathy accorded to a fanatic, until the decisive demonstration of Citroen.

One of the cars, only two being built, competed in a few hill-climbs in France, breaking the record at La Turbie, 1932, in the hands of Louis Chiron, and then being crashed by Jean Bugatti at Shelsley Walsh in that year. Dreyfus broke the La Turbie record again in 1934, exceeding 100 km/h for the 6·3 km course for the first time. It is still in France at the moment of writing, the other of the pair being missing.

237

Description of car

The *Autocar* of 25 March 1932 carried a comprehensive description of the car:

A four-wheel drive racing car with independently sprung front wheels has been produced by Bugatti and is expected to make its appearance in some of the leading Continental races this season. M. Ettore Bugatti does not claim to have invented four-wheel drive. But if many have thought of building a racing car having power delivered to each of its four wheels, it has remained for Bugatti to develop the idea and, after two years' labour, to produce an original and exceptionally efficient racing machine.

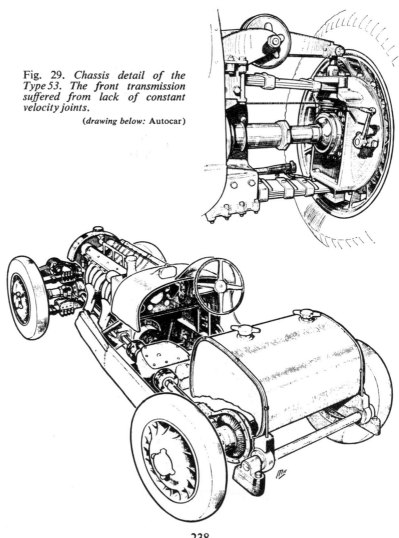

Fig. 29. *Chassis detail of the Type 53. The front transmission suffered from lack of constant velocity joints.*

(*drawing below:* Autocar)

205. *The unique four-wheel drive model produced in 1931. The bodywork is reminiscent of the 1920–22 T.13 cars.*

TYPE 53

206. *The only Bugatti to have independent suspension.*

207. *Chiron and Varzi at the Klausen Hill-Climb, 1932, with a pair of T.53s.*

208. *Jean Bugatti in the paddock at Shelsley Walsh in 1932, where he managed to crash the car, after which it was not repaired. The type had had some success at Klausen and at Chateau Thierry.*

(photo: A. D. Johns)

209. *The 4·9 litre T.53 twin-camshaft supercharged engine was virtually identical with the T.50 and T.54 G.P. engines.*

210. *A T.54, road converted and formerly owned by Dr S. Scher, with engine basically similar to the T.50 and a 9 ft wheelbase, this model was a formidable car in its day but, due to bad handling, it was invariably 'too fast for owner'. However, the late Achille Varzi won the 1933 Avus races, lapping at 136 mph, with Count Czaykowski a close 2nd, on another 'four-nine'.*

TYPE 54

211. *Around 1949 J. M. James owned this extremely potent 4·9 litre T.54 and is seen competing at Lulsgate. This car, a full G.P. model, once owned by Earl Howe, was converted for road use by the late L. G. Bachelier in 1936.* (photo: Louis Klemantaski)

212. *Kaye Don, in his large red 4·9 litre T.54, often in the air at Brooklands in the middle 'thirties. This car was later driven by Dudley Froy, the engine being finally installed in Dick Wilkins's specially built B.H.W. and raced in 1939 by Reg Parnell.*

213. *Chiron at Monza, in a Type 54, with his mechanic Wurmser.*

It is pointed out that, unlike other Bugatti models, this car is not intended for sale to the public. It is a special racing machine, designed for special conditions, under which it is almost unbelievably efficient. The advantage of four-wheel drive over rear-wheel drive is the absence of wheel slip and, consequently, vastly improved acceleration. The car, therefore, will show to greatest advantage on a hilly, winding course necessitating frequent braking and acceleration. On an easy, straight-away run there is no advantage in driving on four wheels – at any rate with engines of the size usually employed for road racing. There is, indeed, a disadvantage, for the more complicated transmission entails a power loss of about 4 per cent.

Any person who has handled a modern racing car, and particularly a machine such as the 4,900 cc supercharged Bugatti, is prepared for speedy acceleration. But the new Bugatti four-wheel drive is a revelation, even to the initiated. With an engine developing 300 hp wheel slip is inevitable if any attempt is made to transmit the whole of that power through two wheels to start away or to accelerate from low speed. But with only 75 hp going to each wheel the effect is amazing. Opportunities of appreciating this were given during a recent visit to the Bugatti works in Alsace, but as the car has not yet been seen in public it would be unfair to the maker to give any definite figures. It is sufficient to say that it is practically impossible to produce a skid; that for cornering on a rough or greasy surface the four-wheel driver is immensely better than the rear-wheel driver, and that its acceleration is so rapid as to be almost disconcerting to even experienced drivers.

The main interest lies in the method of transmitting the power to the four wheels. Behind the engine but connected to it by a universally jointed shaft, is a special gearbox, the housing of which extends right up to the chassis frame members, thus tending to stiffen the chassis. The gearbox contains three shafts (ignoring the reverse pinion shaft); the primary shaft, an intermediary shaft, and the driven shaft carrying a differential. Whatever the gear used, the power must go through the intermediary shaft, so that there is no direct drive. There are two sets of sliding pinions, one giving first and fourth speeds, and the other second and third. The reason for this is that for hill work second and third are the gears most frequently used, and quick changes from one to the other are essential. First is a starting-off gear, and fourth is only occasionally used.

As can be imagined, the gearbox is a very sturdy construction, with short stiff shafts and pinions well calculated for the immense stresses they have to withstand. From the extremities of the differential shaft in the gearbox the power is carried forward by means of an open shaft alongside the engine to a pair of bevel gears in a front axle

243

housing, and rearwards to what is practically a normal-type Bugatti rear axle housing, with the exception that the differential is considerably out of centre. The car thus has three differentials; one in the gearbox, one in the front axle, and one in the rear axle.

There is little to be said about the rear axle construction. It is a built-up type, with a vertically divided differential housing in aluminium and steel tubes which would appear fragile did they not have the proof of experience behind them. A truss-rod is used on the axle housing, and suspension is of the well-known Bugatti type, by quarter elliptics having their thick ends rearwards. A pressed-steel torque arm, with the usual elastic attachment at the front end, is made use of.

At the front everything is new. From the gearbox the drive shaft is carried forward through the steel bulkhead through the left-hand rear engine hangar, in which it has a steady bearing, under the forward left-hand engine hanger, and has a metal universal joint connection to the bevel-pinion shaft. The method of transmitting the drive to the front wheels, and at the same time of assuring independent suspension of the steering wheels, is somewhat similar to other makes known to motorists, with the special advantages of lightness and extreme rigidity.

The two chassis frame members are united at the front by a two-piece aluminium casting not altogether symmetrical, each one consisting of a deep channel section rail and the half of a differential housing. The two are united by means of the differential housing, which, as can be judged, is out of centre, for the propellor-shaft runs by the side of the engine. Two very broad transverse springs, each one having five leaves, are carried in the upper and lower channels of the aluminium cross-member. Under load the springs are perfectly flat; their vertical movement is comparatively small, and they are so well guided in the channels in which they are housed that there can be no horizontal movement and no torsion under braking and driving stresses such as occur in racing.

There are no stub axles, but the four extremities of the springs are attached, by means of ball and socket connections, to flanges on a cast-aluminium circular plate which fills the functions of the usual steering knuckle and has the main steering levers bolted to it. Double-arm friction-type shockabsorbers, which also act as radius arms, are attached to this disc by means of ball and socket connections. The differential-drive shafts, which of course are of unequal length, have a metal universal joint at each extremity, the outer joint being in the vertical axis of the wheel. As in the case of other Bugatti cars, the wheel is a single aluminium casting, together with its brake drum, and has helical spokes to assist in cooling. Steering is on the

244

right, most of the parts being the same as those used on the normal cars.

As can be readily appreciated, the front of the car is entirely changed from the usual Bugatti design. Because of the front-wheel drive the radiator has reduced height, and, in consequence, has been made much wider than that of other cars. The head resistance has been increased, but an attempt has been made to nullify this by means of a cowling in front of the radiator which encloses all the central portion of the springs, the frame cross-member, and the differential housing. This gives the car a blunt bullet-shaped appearance when seen head on, with a very pronounced impression of power and speed.

The weight is carried equally on the two axles with petrol tank filled and in full racing trim. As the tank empties there is a slight excess of weight on the front axle.

The engine used on this car is much more familiar than is the chassis. It is the straight eight of 86 by 107 mm, bore and stroke, with the two overhead camshafts driven from the front, and a Roots-type blower placed fore and aft on the right-hand side and driven by means of bevel gearing from a cross-shaft. The most pronounced feature of this engine is the cylinder construction, the block of eight being a single casting, milled all over, with the nine bearings for the crankshaft direct on the casting, and the hangers secured to it direct.

This gives an exceedingly rigid construction to which the crankcase is merely an attached light housing to retain oil and exclude dust without in any way adding to the rigidity of the unit. There are two Zenith carburettors under the blower. Ignition is by magneto, driven off the end of the right-hand camshaft, with plugs placed vertically in the cylinder head. Dry sump lubrication is used, with the oil supply contained in a big tank on the left-hand side of the inclined dashboard, under the bonnet.

With a view to obtaining desirable rigidity and also as a precaution against fire, there is a stout sheet-steel bulkhead immediately behind the engine, and fitting closely around the clutch housing and having a hole cut through it just big enough for the drive shaft to pass through. Unlike the smaller racing models this engine has a one-piece crankshaft with plain bearings and split-end connecting-rods. It was used last year in several races, notably at Monza, but detail improvements made during the past winter have resulted in increased power, the output, it is claimed, being now slightly in excess of 300 bhp.

As an engineering production this car stands out as one of the most notable achievements of the past few years. Having been on the road, secretly, for the last six months, it is fully tuned up, and its public appearance will be watched with exceptional interest.

245

TYPE 54
the 4·9 litre Grand Prix car

IN 1931 BUGATTI FITTED A NUMBER OF ELONGATED G.P. CHASSIS with the Type 50, 4·9 litre engine under the designation Type 54. The engine was that used on the 4-wheel drive Type 53 described on page 235, in turn a racing version of the T.50 power plant. The chassis layout seems to have been similar to that from the 16 cylinder Type 47, and the transmission was unusual for a racing car in having 3 speeds only, the gearbox otherwise being normal G.P. type. Mr W. F. Bradley wrote in the *Autocar* of 11 September 1931:

The new racing Bugattis possess the distinction of having been designed, built and put on the road in 13 days. In view of the Italian models [12 cylinder Alfa Romeo and 16 cylinder Maserati] prepared for the Monza race it was realized that something faster than the twin-cam 2,300 cc racing machine would have to be prepared. . . .

The [engine] is attached to a frame cross-member in front, the rear attachment being to a steel bulkhead completely separating the engine compartment from the driver's compartment. The two axles are of the normal Bugatti type, but are of a wider track than for any other of the racing cars. [The engine power was quoted as 300 hp at 4,000 rpm.]

The frame is that used later on the T.55, with rear springs not waisted in and the frame retaining full width at the rear. The engine and radiator were originally in the normal position, but were soon moved rearwards in an attempt to improve road holding, the front engine attachment no longer being direct to the front cross member, but direct to the frame side members.

The T.54 first appeared at the Monza Grand Prix in 1931, in the hands of Varzi and Chiron. Chiron retired after a tyre

246

TYPE 55

214. With the introduction of the T.55 2·3 litre supercharged sports car, Bugatti really had a winner. The engine, basically similar to the all conquering T.51 G.P. model, was mounted in the 4,900 T.54 G.P. chassis, and it had G.P. pattern aluminium wheels with brake drums integral, and the latest multiplate dry clutch and separately mounted 4 speed gearbox as fitted to the T.49. On top of this was mounted a really lovely low-built 2 seater body designed by Jean Bugatti, with deep cutaway sides and long, graceful mudguards in a continuous sweep from front to rear.

215. The business-like frontal aspect.

216. *Bugatti-designed coupé T.55. Rather noisy with a closed body, the model had, even bý.today's standards, a remarkable performance.*

217. *A T.55 coupé on a Kandersteg Hill-Climb.* (*photo: Charles Renaud*)

failure had cut a brake cable and left him with no brakes, although he tried to continue. Varzi finished 3rd also being delayed with tyre trouble. This was a race of giants, the other cars being 12 cylinder Alfas, or 16 cylinder Maseratis. For the next two years the T.54 was raced by the Works, alongside the 2·3 litre Type 51, but it did not have a particularly successful career, being heavy and rather uncontrollable. Kaye Don and Czaykowski both drove 4·9 litre cars in the 1933 Brooklands Empire Trophy. Varzi won the 1933 Avus race at 128·48 mph, and in the same year Czaykowski, who had just gained the World's Hour Record at Avus at over 130 mph, met his death in the car in the final of the Monza Grand Prix, skidding on an oil patch. 10 September 1933 was a tragic day as he, Campari and Bozzacchini all died.

Only a few of these cars were built.

TYPE 55
twin-cam, Super Sport model

IN 1932 BUGATTI INTRODUCED A NEW GRAND SPORT MODEL replacing the Type 43. This used the T.51 twin-cam supercharged 2·3 litre engine in a T.54 chassis and was fitted with a beautiful 2-seat roadster body, reputedly designed by Jean Bugatti himself. Certainly, with its long sweeping wings, G.P. wheels, rounded tail and rear mounted spare wheels, the car set a standard in appearance and purposefulness which has never been beaten and rarely equalled in the sports car world.

Its performance matched its appearance – 110 to 112 mph, and dazzling acceleration. Mr A. C. Whincop wrote of this car, as he had done of Types 43 and 51, in the *Autocar*, 13 August 1943, in the series 'Talking of Sports Cars':

The engine is almost identical with that of the Type 51 double camshaft supercharged 2·3 litre Grand Prix car, with all eight cylinders contained in the one block, and only two valves per cylinder operated by the twin overhead camshafts. The remainder of the engine is very similar to that of the Type 43, but the result of this improvement in design is to increase the bhp from the 115 of the earlier model to 135 bhp in the Type 55 at 5,500 rpm. There is also a very great increase in power low down in the engine speed range, which results in greatly increased acceleration. Maximum speed is not so noticeably improved, the same standard ratio of 13:54 being used, although, as with all 2·3 Bugattis, this can be altered at will, ratios of 12:54, 13:54, 14:54, 15:54 and 16:54, all being interchangeable on the Types 35B, 43, 51 and 55.

Chassis details are, rather surprisingly, very similar to those of the Type 43, although the two cars look so totally different, and the actual chassis of the 55 is the same as that of the Grand Prix 4·9 litre. There are, of course, a number of small improvements, such as Tele-controls fitted to the Hartford shockabsorbers. The body fitted has such perfection of line that although designed in 1932 it will still be completely modern when this war finishes [it still is]. I feel that the appearance of the body in combination with the increased acceleration of the Type 55 is responsible for the impression that there is so much difference between it and the Type 43 which it replaced. In reality they both give almost exactly the same impression when driving, and, if anything, I prefer the handling of the earlier model, which, in spite of its 2 in. longer wheelbase, seems just a fraction lighter and more positive in control. They are both so perfect in this respect, however, that the impression was possibly caused by petrol rationing preventing me from becoming anything like as familiar with the 55 as I was with 2·3 No. 1, which seemed literally part of oneself when driving.

Unquestionably, the most spectacular feature of the later model is its acceleration, which is really terrific; when the first car was imported into this country and was road tested by a contemporary journal in 1932, figures were recorded of 10 to 80 mph in 18 seconds and 10 to 100 mph in 40 seconds; these figures can have been surpassed by very, very few standard sports cars ever produced, irrespective of engine capacity and price. Whilst V8 and V12 engines in specially lightened chassis show the most amazing acceleration up to 60, 70 and occasionally 80 mph, the graph is usually conveniently cut off before that extremely telling figure of 100 mph is reached, this acceleration at the upper end of the speed scale being all important for road racing, if not for sprint events.

My particular car was built in 1934 and was first owned by Embiricos, who used it for Continental touring and for one or two races, although he owned a Type 51 at the same time. Delving through the files of the past shows that he once covered a half-mile at Brooklands at 124 mph with it stripped for racing and running on 'dope', although AUL 23 must have been fitted with a 14:54 axle ratio and at least 5·50 by 19 in. tyres to achieve that speed, as well as being at the absolute peak of tune. Her maximum when I sold her, on a 13:54 axle with 5·50 by 19 m tyres, seemed to be about 5,400 rpm on top gear when using a fifty-fifty mixture of 'Discol' and neat benzole which I still possessed in 1940 to test the car. Careful attention to the jets proved that the engine showed an uncanny desire to be allowed to run up to its maximum of 5–5 on the gears, but my fuel supply soon ran out and I can only give this estimate of about 112 mph as the maximum speed, allowing for wheelspin. Even on 'Pool' the engine ran smoothly with little trace of pinking and showed the same desire to rev, although this naturally had to be restrained for fear of doing damage.

251

I notice that when AUL 23 was road tested by the *Autocar* in 1937 as a second-hand version, a poor top speed of slightly over the 100 mph was recorded, the only suggestion I can make for the rather poor performance being that at about that time she had been fitted with a new block, the old one having been cracked by frost, so the engine may have been slightly tight. Alternatively, the car may have been put up for test without the little attention necessary to obtain maximum performance: that is, a new set of plugs, larger jets than the standard touring ones, suitable fuel such as 'Discol' or 'Discol' and benzole, and a careful check of ignition timing and contact breaker points. These small items need watching, for whilst the Type 55 is a standard sports car it also has to be remembered that the engine is only very slightly modified from the racing example.

The brakes on the Types 43 and 55 are identical, being of straight-forward design, cable operated in 13 in. drums cast integral with the aluminium wheels; they are fully compensated so that equal pressure is provided on all four brake toggles, though slightly greater leverage is provided for the front wheels, this giving the maximum of controllability if on occasion late braking into a corner has to be indulged in. This advantage is such that it seems well worth sacrificing the slightly greater efficiency, on straight braking, of brakes operating very much more powerfully on the front wheels, since the arrangement in question gives complete confidence at all times. The hand brake operates on the rear wheels only and has a completely separate layout.

My only criticisms of the Type 55 are:

1. The gearbox; again the touring version is very heavily built, resulting in great strength, and in this case a very quick gear change indeed, but the change is a rather heavy one with a tendency to drag when coming out of gear. To my mind, the very lightly built Grand Prix box is such a delight to handle, with its finger lightness that it is almost sacrilege not to fit it to a Bugatti, for it allows the most effortless tunes to be played on it up or down. This modification, as with the Type 43, can easily be made if it is so desired.

2. The fabric universals can be replaced with Hardy Spicers with advantage.

3. Personally, I prefer air pressure (hand and engine pumps) to petrol pumps for engines of considerable power. This is, of course, a purely personal preference, as are the others above, and I am quite sure all Type 55 owners will not agree with me as the basic design is completely sound.

252

Contemporary description

The model was fully described and illustrated in *The Motor* of 14 June 1932:

Here is a really comfortable, well-sprung car with superlative road-holding characteristics and a performance that is altogether exceptional.

Fig. 30. *Type 55 engine.*

(*drawing:* The Motor)

The power unit has eight cylinders in line, the bore and stroke being 60 mm and 100 mm respectively and the capacity 2,270 cc. There is one inlet and one exhaust valve to each cylinder, these being operated by two overhead camshafts, while the supercharger, of the Roots type, is fitted midway along the off-side of the crankcase with the carburettor underneath it and placed so low that it is reached by opening a trap-door in the undershield below the level of the chassis frame members. The supercharger is driven through a short flexibly jointed shaft from a train of gear wheels driven in turn from the forward end of the crankshaft.

Forced-feed lubrication is naturally employed, all oil pipes being external so that they can be readily dismantled and cleaned. Cooling is by pump, the centrifugal type waterpump being situated well forward on the near side of the crankcase. The ignition is by a single eight-cylinder magneto mounted in typical Bugatti fashion directly behind the facia board and accessible through an opening in the latter. It is driven through a short shaft with a flexible coupling at each end from the rearmost extremity of the nearside overhead

253

camshaft. The other camshaft at its rearmost extremity drives the A.C. mechanical petrol pump and the revolution counter.

The dynamo is driven from the forward end of the crankshaft, while the starter motor is situated beneath the engine and behind the deeply ribbed base-chamber. The supercharger is lubricated separately from a small reservoir on the engine side of the scuttle dash. This tank is provided with a tap which can be operated from the driving seat and two other small cocks are connected to the accelerator pedal so that the flow of lubricant to the blower bearings starts immediately the accelerator is depressed.

In order to ensure easy starting, an Athmos fuel injector similar in operation to the well-known Ki-Gass, is fitted on the dash and connected directly to the double-T type induction manifold. While talking of dashboard controls, it is interesting to note that the advance and retard lever operates directly on the magneto contact breaker, while the two small levers that on earlier Bugatti models used to govern the ignition setting and throttle opening, are now used to open or close small ventilators in the top and at each side of the scuttle. The adjusting knobs for the frictional-type shockabsorbers, to which they are connected by Bowden wire, are also situated on the dash.

A large petrol tank containing over 100 litres (22 gallons) of fuel is slung between the rear dumbirons, its contents being registered on a neat dial in the facia board. It is not necessary to use a strong 'dope' mixture for ordinary running, 25 per cent of benzole in the petrol being sufficient. Champion R.3 plugs are normally used and are placed centrally in the cylinder heads between the valves.

The exhaust manifolds are welded up from steel tubes, each group of four being welded into a collector manifold from which a large bore pipe conveys the exhaust to a flat oval-section silencer hidden beneath the near-side wings, which are extended to form graceful curved running boards. Between the exhaust manifolds are situated the oil filling orifice and a tap for draining the cooling system in frosty weather.

The transmission consists of a Bugatti patent multiple-disc clutch, a short shaft with a flexible coupling at each end connecting this to the separately mounted four-speed-and-reverse centrally controlled gearbox, whence a large-diameter open propellor shaft with a flexible joint at each end conveys the drive to the straight-bevel type rear axle, the direct drive ratio being 3·6 to 1 [generally lower].

The intermediate gear ratios, together with the compression ratio of the engine, the blower pressure and certain other facts about the car are not published by the makers, who consider it against their

254

policy to issue such details. On top gear, however, 5,000 rpm – an engine speed which is said to be readily obtainable – is equivalent to 112 mph. The speedometer, incidentally, is calibrated up to 130 mph.

The well-known Bugatti patent cast aluminium alloy wheels are used, the flat thin spokes being stiffened by ribs cast at right angles on their reverse faces and the rims being made to take well-base tyres instead of the bolted-on type popular in Continental racing circles. This model is sold with Dunlop racing tyres. In this way, the purchaser is safely guarded against any risk of the tyres not standing up to really high speeds in hot weather. Another 'safety first' feature is that the axles, tie-rods, steering arms and all similar connections are left in the bright polished state, so that they may readily be inspected for fine cracks which might develop in the course of racing over very rough circuits.

Needless to say, a car capable of such high road speeds requires superlative brakes. Those on the Bugatti are unique because the steel-lined aluminium brake drums are cast integrally with the wheels [in fact pressed in], and the shoes, complete with linings, can be instantaneously renewed simply by removing a wheel which only means undoing its central lock-nut operating on the well-known Rudge-Whitworth system. The brakes are normally adjusted by a threaded turnbuckle conveniently situated at a suitable point on the brake-operating cables [not strictly correct].

One of the most interesting features about this car is the driving position, which is exactly similar to that provided on the Grand Prix racers. Instead of reclining in a semi-prone position with his feet on the same level as the seat, as in most sports cars, the driver sits upright, with the pedals situated low down in exceedingly deep floor wells.

The body on this new model is an exceedingly attractive streamlined two-seater, having a very large and properly carpeted luggage locker in the stern. On the model we inspected, a new and graceful colour scheme of black and red was arranged, the effect being one of more or less oval red panels, which added to the naturally fleeting appearance of the complete car.

It will be gathered from the foregoing that the new Type 55 super-sports 2·3 litre supercharged Bugatti is an ideal car for travelling safely from point to point at really high speeds and in complete comfort. Considering its performance, it is really very reasonably priced at the figure of £1,350.

An article headed 'Stability Supreme' in the *Autocar* of 8 January 1937 described a test of a second-hand Type 55 which was first registered in October 1933, and had covered over 14,000 miles. This was the 1933 Olympia Show car, AUL 23, 10 to 30 mph acceleration in 7·9, 6·0 and 4·0 seconds in top, third and second gears respectively. From rest to 50 mph in 8·7 seconds and 60 mph in 13·0 seconds, using the gears. 98·9 mph timed quarter-mile, still accelerating. The road-tester writes:

An engine of this kind is not expected to be quiet; while the exhaust note was distinctly moderate, there was considerable mechanical noise, also gear and probably axle noise from the straight teeth used, these all being principally noticeable at low and moderate speeds, but blending into an efficient general 'scream' when travelling fast . . . so excellent were the stability and general handling that the car was 'wished' round corners, rock-steady and feeling completely safe, yet the suspension was really comfortable for a machine of this kind . . . it weighed 23½ cwt . . . the change needed knowing, but except that first and second gears would 'hang' if one revved up high on them it was a beautiful movement, quick and satisfying.

Modern Road Impressions

Apart from an appearance which to most Bugatti owners is unexcelled in sporting 2-seat cars, the T.55 has a performance which also puts it at the front of all Bugatti road cars. It can out-perform a Type 43 in acceleration and top speed, and is very comfortable except for the tall driver who finds the leg room inadequate, but cannot adjust it. The gear change is slow and the flexible gear lever cannot be manhandled as quickly as a Type 43, but on balance is better than on the earlier model. The main advantage in practice is in the engine since the combustion characteristics of the twin cam engine allow a better mixture from the carburettor and the engine is not prone to sooting as in the case of the T.43.

Accessibility is not so good on the T.55, the body and mudguards being more enveloping but once the car is in good condition this is not particularly important.

256

218. *Some Type 55s were fitted with special coachwork, in this case a Figoni drop-head.*

219. *A Molsheim photograph of the original T.55 engine layout; the finish is truly original. The modern restorer should note the lack of geometrical precision in the mottling of the dash!*

220. *The first of the famous T.57 series, introduced in 1934 and fitted with a factory built, 4 door pillarless Galibier saloon body; speed 95 m.p.h.*

TYPE 57

221. *The radiator. Note the flutes on the horseshoe.*

222. *Stelvio coupé.*

TYPE 57
twin-cam 3·3 litre splendour

IN 1934 MOLSHEIM INTRODUCED WHAT WAS TO BE THE MOST celebrated non-racing car that Bugatti ever produced. It remained in relatively large scale production (an estimated 750 cars) until the end of 1939 or early 1940, and a few were even produced after the war. It was on this model that Ettore's son Jean exerted his influence to a considerable extent, refining the car and generally making it fit to compete on equal terms with the sophisticated automobiles of the middle 'thirties – Delahayes, Delages, Bentleys and so on. The days of semi-racing road cars were over and there was no market for extravagant Royales or 5 litre Types 46 and 50; but a reliable, high performance Bugatti could still sell when fitted with fine bodywork drawing on the best in French creative ability as to line and colour. The Ventoux, the Stelvio and the Atalante bodywork catalogued and sold on these chassis was a credit to Jean Bugatti's imagination and the skill of French coach-workers. (*See page* 418).

The Type 57 was more or less new from stem to stern, except the bore and stroke which were the same as the Type 49, 72 mm by 100 mm. The engine had a 5-bearing (strictly 6-bearing) crank, and twin overhead cams with articulated rockers or fingers in place of cups, the cams being driven by a helical gear train from the rear of the crankshaft as opposed to the earlier front drive of the Type 50 and 51 constructions. The gearbox was mounted integrally with the engine and the classic Bugatti clutch was replaced by a single plate unit. The gears were of constant mesh, second, third and fourth engaged by dog-clutches. The rear axle started off with a taper-roller bearing mounting for the pinion, but this was replaced later with the normal earlier ball bearing construction. Suspension was standard at the rear and front, except that the original fifty or so

259

cars had a split, articulated front axle, although this was not continued into production on this model, most of the earlier cars having the axles soldered up. Brakes were mechanical along normal Molsheim lines. It is a matter of historical interest that Jean Bugatti produced an independently sprung front axle assembly in 1934 but either it was unsuccessful, or more likely, his father would not let him introduce so radical a departure from the Bugatti design tradition.

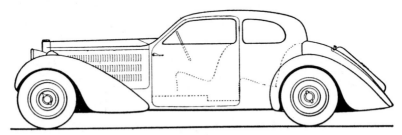

Fig. 31. *Ventoux; 4 light.*

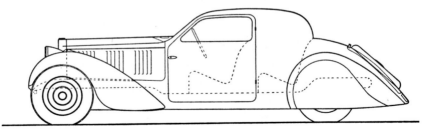

Fig. 32. *Ventoux; 2 light.*

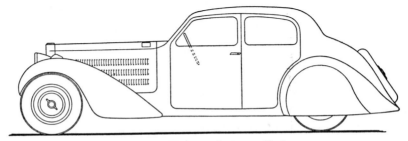

Fig. 33. *Galibier; early type, pillarless.*

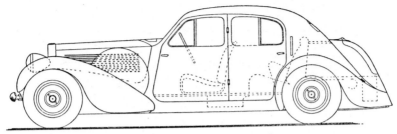

Fig. 34. *Galibier; later type, 4 door.*

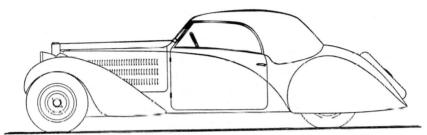

Fig. 35. *Stelvio; usually without hood irons.*

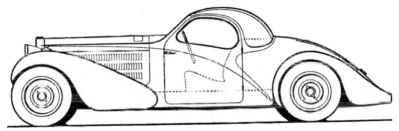

Fig. 36. *Atalante on a T.57 chassis; the 57S is lower.*

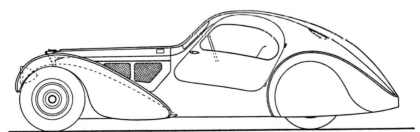

Fig. 37. *Atlantic.*

261

Development of the type

The original model was in production from 1934 to 1936. A few special cars were produced for sports car racing, for example the 1935 Ulster TT, the model sometimes being called 57T.

Type 57S   A short chassis, low slung sport version was introduced in 1935. This had a tuned engine with higher compression ratio (8·5 to 1) and a dry sump, a double-plate clutch to transmit the extra power, and a dash mounted Scintilla Vertex magneto driven from the left-hand camshaft. The front axle was articulated in halves with a rotating collar in the centre with appropriate brake torque radius rods, and de Ram shock-absorbers were used. The whole chassis was of lower build, the rear axle passing *through* the rear frame. The prototype seems to have had the normal flat radiator, but the normal production 57S has a handsome V and very low slung radiator.

Type 57, Series 2   At the end of 1936 or early 1937 an important change was made with the introduction of a rubber mounted engine, changes to camshafts and engine timing, a heavier chassis with more cross-bracing, and a different dashboard with twin in place of a single large instrument. The exhaust manifold was also changed, the down pipe being taken off centrally, instead of at the front. About this time too (probably 1937 at about car No. 57450–57500) the crankcase was modified to make provision for a blower drive, on the right side, the drive being blanked off on the normal car.

Type 57C   A compressor fitted to the standard model made the 57C of 1937–8, although the 57SC may, in fact, have preceded it by a few months. There are those who claim that the 57C is the best of the 'touring' 57 models, the supercharger enhancing performance and flexibility.

Type 57SC   In 1937 a supercharger was added to the 57S to produce the sparkling 57SC, a car usually fitted with striking bodywork and certainly with a performance in speed and acceleration quite remarkable in 1937 and even today when other 125 mph cars are available. Both the 57S and 57SC were withdrawn after 1938, probably as they were too expensive to manufacture while the 57 and 57C were selling well.

223. *Atalante on 57.*

224. *Atalante on 57S.*

225 and 226. *Atalante drophead 57S, looking very up to date and capable of 120 mph.*

(photo: R. Oliver)

227 and 228. *Atlantic coupé—perhaps the most bizarre of all Bugatti bodies.*

(photo: Motor)

229. *The 1939 Galibier 4 door saloon. Apart from a strengthened cruciform frame, the big improvement was Lockheed hydraulic brakes, hydraulic telescopic shock absorbers all round and an even quieter engine—really remarkably smooth and silent. All this could be had at a chassis price of £590 in 1939, as against £975 exchange rate in 1936.*

230. *T.57C coupé by James Young of Bromley. Introduced in 1938, the supercharged version of the T.57 was otherwise identical in all respects. The addition of a silent-running, low-boost Bugatti Roots-type blower, driven from the rear end, greatly increased the acceleration and flexibility and gave a maximum speed in saloon form of 105 mph. It cost an extra £155 (in 1939 this chassis cost only £745).*

Type   At the end of 1938 further improvements
57, Series 3   were made to the 57 to refine it. The most
important was the introduction of hydraulic brakes of Bugatti-
Lockheed design, with twin master cylinders, and the substitution of telescopic Allinquant shockabsorbers for the highly
expensive de Rams, which in turn had replaced the cheaper,
but less effective Telecontrol Hartfords of earlier cars. To allow
the front shockabsorbers to be mounted vertically, the wings
were swept up high alongside the radiator and usually were
faired into the lamps.

Contemporary descriptions

One of the early descriptions of Type 57 was given in the
May 1934 issue of *Motor Sport*. This article is no doubt responsible for the error, since repeated, of ascribing nine bearings to
the crankshaft instead of five, or six if the one behind the rear
camshaft gear is counted.

The existence of a new Bugatti sports car, said to have almost the
acceleration of the blown '2·3' up to 80 mph, has for some time been
known in England, and a visit to Molsheim to try the new machine
seemed indicated. When we did get there we found that the Type 57,
as the new model is called, was already in good demand and a
number of chassis were coming through. In fact, with two other
widely differing activities, that is, preparing the racing teams and
building the new rail-cars, the famous factory was very busy indeed.

In appearance the new car is not unlike the previous 3·3 litre model
Type 49, except that it has shutters on the radiator and a built-up
front axle. Rudge Whitworth wire wheels are used instead of the
aluminium type.

The car we were to try was the one usually driven by Costantini,
the first of its type and still used for testing purposes. Réné Dreyfus,
for some years past one of the star performers in the Bugatti racing
team, was at the wheel.

After three minutes of warming up we took our seats, and the
car moved off smoothly. 'Delightful cars, these', said M. Dreyfus,
and thereupon changed from bottom to top gear. In this ratio we
burbled along perfectly smoothly to the factory gates, and so out on
to the fine straight road between Molsheim and Strasbourg.

After a fast run up and down to get the oil circulating, Dreyfus

Fig. 38. *In 1939 hydraulic brakes and telescopic shockabsorbers were introduced.*

Fig. 39. *The right front spring had a special shackle to avoid shocks from the road being transmitted to the steering wheel.*

268

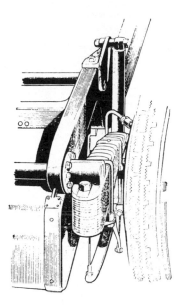

Fig. 40. *The rear end of the 1939 series cars, with traditional springs but telescopic shockabsorbers added. The contraption below the spring is to enable the jack to be slid under the axle.*

(*drawings:* The Motor)

pronounced himself satisfied. 'First of all notice the flexibility', he said, and ran down to 10 mph on top gear. 'Now the smooth pick-up', and proceeded to put his foot down hard. The speedometer needle swung round at an ever-increasing rate without any trace of hesitation. 'All-out speed', and we reached 95 mph. 'Finally the road holding', so we drove down a minor road at 75, slowed to 60 with a gentle application of the brakes, and took a 60 degree bend without any reduction in speed. The car neither rolled, slid nor gave any indication that the manoeuvre was at all unusual. '*Vraiment une voiture fantastique*', a remark with which we could not fail to agree as soon as we could think of an adequate reply.

The brakes were extremely efficient, and from a speed of 40 mph the car came to rest in approximately 53 feet, without any tendency to swing or for the wheels to lock. This test was, in fact, considered too tame, so we tried again, this time from 75 mph. The retardation was equally safe and sure, the distance being about 70 yards.

Instead of the shrill scream which usually comes from third gear on a Bugatti, on the '3·3' there is a complete absence of noise. Constant mesh gears are used for second and third gears, and the change is further simplified by having a single-plate clutch lined with Ferodo in place of the multiple-disc pattern which is usually fitted to Bugatti cars. The exhaust note is subdued and even when all out there is nothing more than a slight rumble.

269

Owing to the limitations of the Works insurance policy, we were not able to drive the car ourselves, but the ease with which it cornered and the accuracy of the steering could not be doubted from what we saw. The suspension was good throughout the range, aided by friction dampers controlled from the dashboard.

After lunch at the famous 'Hostellerie du Pur-Sang', that unique inn-cum-clubhouse which 'M. le Patron' has built to accommodate those who visit the factory, Jean Bugatti came with us instead of Dreyfus, and we went out on to the high-road to obtain a series of acceleration figures.

Without doubt this latest product of the Molsheim factory is *une voiture de pur-sang*, and no one can deny the benefits of racing when they experience the high performance and ease of handling which are directly derived from high-speed international competition.

The maximum speed on the level is about 95 mph with closed bodywork, and would be comfortably over 100 in the case of an open car. 70 to 75 mph can be obtained in third gear, and 50 in second, and at 60 mph on top gear the engine is doing approximately 2,500 rpm. A rev-counter is not fitted as no harm results even if the engine speed reaches 5,500 rpm.

In the course of the timed tests the car several times reached 105 mph on slight down-hill slopes, and a flying kilometre was covered at over 100 mph. The standing kilometre was done in 39 seconds. All this was carried out with hardly a murmur from the engine, and Jean Bugatti finds that a fast average, even of over 60 mph, can be kept up with much less effort in a closed car than an open one.

After completing the tests we had occasion to go to Strasbourg, a drive which was performed with all the verve for which Jean Bugatti is famous. We arrived there too early of course, so the time was spent in driving through the crowded streets of the town at 7 to 10 mph on top gear. Another feature was shown on the return journey, when the driver suddenly executed a series of zig-zags at 60 to demonstrate the absence of rolling, but our new passenger, who had not yet become accustomed to Jean's virtuosity at the wheel, did not seem to appreciate it.

Turning to the technical side of the car, the engine is a straight-eight unit with two overhead camshafts, and gives 140 horse power at 4,800 rpm. The valves are inclined to one another at 90 degrees with the sparking plugs in the centre of the head, and the camshafts are driven by gears at the rear end of the engine. White metal is used in the nine [six] main bearings and for the big-ends. The cylinder head and block are in one unit and the cam-cases are made in that

270

1. Types 57 and 57S, showing the different radiators and the lower chassis of the latter model which is also shorter—9 ft 9½ in. wheelbase—and much stronger, with deeper side members and passing ove and below the rear axle. In all main essentials the two models were very similar, but the 57S had more powerful engine with increased compression ratio of 8·7 to 1, dry sump lubrication with 3½ llon oil tank, Scintilla Vertex, Bugatti's own double carburettor, stronger clutch, higher effective ck axle ratio (larger tyres), divided front axle and de Ram shock-absorbers all round. When first roduced, the chassis price was £1,300, but by 1938 favourable exchange rates had reduced it to 60, which represented remarkable value.

. Earle Howe at the wheel of one of the 1935 Tourist Trophy T.57 cars. They were the fastest in the e and Earle Howe finished 3rd at an average speed of 79·72 mph on the Ards circuit.

271

233. *This handsome Type 57S was originally owned by Sir Malcom Campbell, and has a Corsica bo*

TYPE 57S

234. *Type 57S. The first of the series, introduced in 1935 as the competition model, had the normal T.57 flat-fronted radiator with thermostatically controlled shutters. It was, however, mounted lower in the frame and gave way the following year to the well-known oval and pointed grille with the shutters mounted behind. The first of these had vertical chromium strips, but in 1938 this was replaced by an imitation honeycomb. This bizarre body by Jean Bugatti was shown at the 1936 Paris Salon. The front part of the wings swivelled with the wheels.*

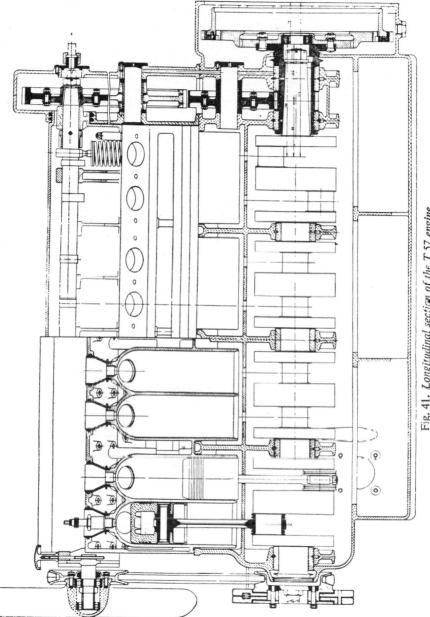

Fig. 41. *Longitudinal section of the T.57 engine.*

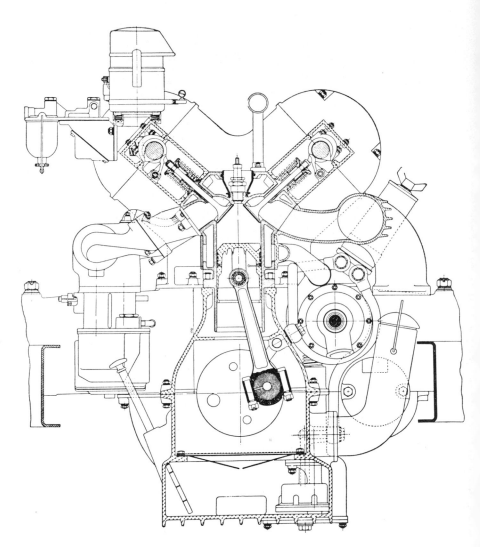

Fig. 42. *Section drawing of T.57 engine.*

hand-polished aluminium which is the joy of every Bugatti owner.

The distributor and petrol pump are driven from the rear end of the offside camshaft, and two coils are mounted at the rear of the dashboard. A single vertical Zenith carburettor is fitted on the offside. Water pump, starter and dynamo are all carried at the near side of the engine. The engine and gearbox unit has a rigid four-point suspension.

An open propeller shaft is used, and the back-axle reaction is taken by the usual long torque member.

The top line of the chassis runs straight as far as the back axle, where the side members are swept up, but from a depth of 10 inches at the rear engine mounting, the side members taper to the size of a normal dumbiron at the front of the chassis. The front axle is built up from two hollow sections with a shouldered shaft in the middle. A large nut with a right- and left-hand thread pulls the two sections up against the shoulder. [This feature was not perpetuated.] The front springs are half-elliptic, while the familiar reversed quarter-elliptic springs are used at the rear.

The brakes are of large diameter, cable-operated, with the cycle-chain compensators which have long been a feature of Bugattis. The engine sump holds 4 gallons of oil and the petrol tank 22 gallons of fuel.

Jean Bugatti has for some years been responsible for Bugatti coachwork, and has designed many striking closed bodies with ultra-sloping windscreens.

Writing in the *Field*, 4 September 1937, Sir Malcolm Campbell, the famous racing driver, had this to say of his new T.57S open two-seater:

If I was asked to give my opinion as to the best all-round super-sports car which is available on the market today, I should, without any hesitation whatever, say it was the 3 3 Bugatti. I grant that it is not the type of car that would necessarily appeal to the majority of drivers who merely indulge in a burst of speed from time to time, but it cannot fail to attract the connoisseur or those who know how to handle the thoroughbred. It is a car in a class by itself.

For many years it has been my privilege to be acquainted with Mr Ettore Bugatti, who, in addition to designing all the cars that bear his name, owns the factory where they are built. I can only say that no more brilliant brain than his exists in the motor industry today.

I have so far covered about 600 miles on my own car, as I have only recently taken delivery, but that brief mileage is sufficient to have made me enamoured with my new steed. It is an absolute joy to handle, and although designed for really fast touring, it is amazingly tractable in London traffic, which is unique for a car of this type. Its chief characteristics are superb road holding, really brilliant acceleration and very powerful brakes.

Bugatti cars have always been noted for their stability and this model certainly is no exception. It is probably the fastest standard sports car on the market today, and without doubt one of the very safest.

Modern Road Impressions

The Type 57 is perhaps the most popular model Bugatti today in France and in the U.S.A., no doubt due to its suitability to the road systems in these two countries. It is a car with comparatively 'long legs', better at cruising over long distances than pottering about, or being thrown about in competition. The engine is smooth and powerful, especially when blown, but feeling a little heavy on the throttle. The clutch is not light and the gear change slow, waiting for the dogs to engage. It is difficult to crash into mesh as on a GP or even the heavier Type 43–44. Road holding is quite good, steering excellent and the later hydraulic brakes first class. The earlier cable brakes have to be applied with care, as they have an unhappy tendency to grab.

On rough road the driver is rather conscious of the twisting of the chassis frame and the racking of the body, and it is probably for this reason that open body work seems the most desirable, if in practice unusual.

235. *Once the property of Colonel Giles, this striking 1938 57SC open 2 seater by Corsica Coachworks, to the design of Eric Giles, was familiar to B.O.C. members and is still winning awards in Concours d'Elegance.*

TYPE 57SC

236. Cockpit.

237. *An Atlantic coupé at a motor show at Nice in 1937.*

TYPE 57 ENGINE

238 *and* 239. *The original 'Three-Three' engine of the early solid engine mounting type. Specification details are: 25·7 hp, 8 cylinder, twin overhead camshafts, driven from the rear and operating 2 valves per cylinder, bore and stroke of 72 × 100 mm, 3,257 cc, 6 plain crankshaft bearings, twin coil ignition, single Stromberg UUR-2 carburettor with A.C. petrol pump, dry clutch and new 4 speed gearbox with silent 2nd, 3rd and top gears, and wheelbase of 10 ft 10½ in. The illustration shows a Schebler carburettor and an unusual rear engine mount detail.*

(*original factory photographs*)

240. *Chassis and engine. The gearbox is integral with the crankcase.*

241. *Front end.*

(*photos: R. Kelly*)

242. *T.57 rear end.*

243. *Gear box.*

(*photos: R. Kelly*)

T.57SC ENGINE
(below)

244. *The 57SC engine develops around 200 bhp and the 57S about 175 or so—with a rev. limit of 5,500 in each case as against the 5,000 safe limit on the normal T.57. This supercharged version of the 57S was introduced at the end of 1937 and the chassis price in 1938 was only £1,015. The Roots-type blower (note the liberal ribbing on both blower and manifold) runs at 1·1 times engine speed, is relatively silent running and boosts at about 3 to 4 lb pressure.*

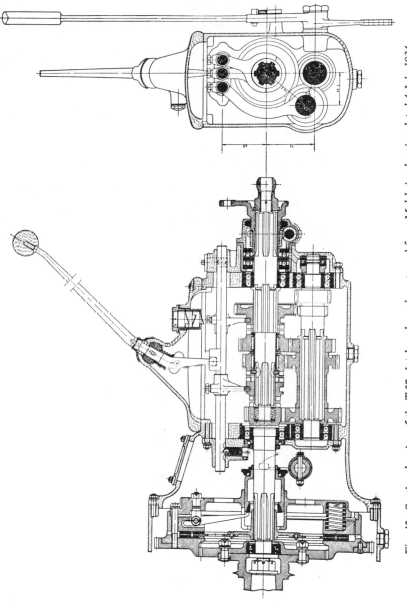

Fig. 43. Section drawing of the T.57 clutch and gearbox, traced from Molsheim drawing dated 4 July 1934.

281

TYPE 59
the last G.P. racing car

THE LAST G.P. CAR THAT BUGATTI PRODUCED IN ANY NUMBERS was the 3·3 litre Type 59, although in fact the single seat works G.P. cars mentioned in the next pages were to follow. The 3·3 litre car was produced as a Molsheim answer to the 1934 G.P. formula (750 kg maximum weight); it appeared initially as a 2·8 litre car (67 mm × 100 mm; 2,821 cc) and ran 4th in the 1933 Spanish Grand Prix in September of that year, having failed to appear for the French G.P. but was seen at practice at the Belgian event. After the Monaco G.P. in 1934 where Dreyfus was 3rd and Nuvolari 5th, the bore was enlarged to 72 mm (as for the T.57) and a works team of three cars, plus three or four spares, ran with fair success. *Motor Sport* quotes the cars as being enlarged to 3·5 litres for the 1934 Belgian G.P., but they were back to 3·3 litres for the Spanish G.P. in that year.

In 1935, one or two cars were retained and driven subsequently by Wimille and Benoist, the other four being sold to England as follows:

(1) Noel Rees (driven by Brian Lewis); subsequently Craig; Clarke; Ludington, New York.
(2) Earl Howe; subsequently Hooper, Durban; Kelfkens, Johannesburg; Hindle, Johannesburg, and now back in Britain.
(3) C. E. C. Martin; subsequently Duke of Grafton (killed himself in it); Arthur Baron; Abecassis; Bear (killed himself in it); now dismantled.
(4) Lindsay Eccles; subsequently Burton; Hindes; Carr; Roberts; Ferranti.

Six cars (four British and two Works) ran in the 1935 Grand Prix of Dieppe; perhaps there was even a seventh car; *Motor Sport* in January 1935 thought nine had been built in 1934.

The Works entry in the 1935 French Grand Prix seems to have been one of the cars retained, with a 4·7 or 3·8 litre T.50B engine. The car was scarcely ready and lost its bonnet on the fourth lap, eventually retiring. It had a cowled radiator and an oil cooler alongside Benoist's left ear – an unusual location.

The Type 59 used a chassis rather similar to the Type 45 and Type 54 assemblies, the rear spring base being full width and the ends projecting outside the pointed tail, unlike the T.35 and T.51 series. Since all known T.59 cars have 54,000 series numbers Molsheim probably rated them as T.54 chassis. The front spring mounting was by a slideblock at the front end, and the rear axle was double reduction. The engine was based on the 57S, having the same six bearing crankshaft arrangement and rear camshaft and blower gear drive. It developed 230 hp. A fuller description is given below.

Racing successes

Eventually outstripped by the Mercedes-Benz and Auto-Union, its performance was better than its race-winning record would lead one to believe. For example:

In 1934:

> 1st, 2nd and 4th Belgian G.P. (Dreyfus, Brivio, Benoist)
> 1st Algiers G.P. (Wimille)
> 3rd and 5th Monaco G.P. (Dreyfus, Nuvolari)
> 3rd Spanish G.P. (Nuvolari); Wimille was 6th, Dreyfus 7th
> 3rd Swiss G.P. (Dreyfus)

In 1935:

> 1st and 2nd Picardy G.P. (Benoist, Earl Howe)
> 1st and 2nd Mannin Moar (Brian Lewis, C. E. C. Martin)
> 2nd Tunis G.P. (Wimille, at an average of 99 mph)
> 2nd Lorraine G.P. (Wimille)
> 2nd and 3rd Donington G.P. (Earl Howe, C. E. C. Martin)

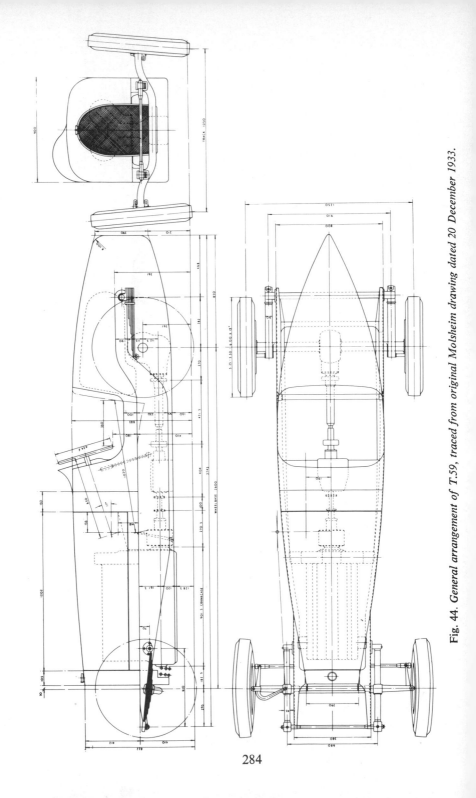

Fig. 44. *General arrangement of T.59, traced from original Molsheim drawing dated 20 December 1933.*

284

245. *The last of the classic racing cars; the stubborn Ettore still feels that a G.P. car should look like a 2 seater even if there is little room for a mechanic.*

TYPE 59

246. *This type had highly original wire wheels, the rim being supported by radial spokes and driven rotationally by dogs or serrations on the brake backplate. The chain compensating gear and tubular oil cooler can be seen.*

247. *The frontal aspect of the T.59 is both pleasing and businesslike.*

248. *The rear view of the T.59 shows how well the typical pointed tail can be blended in to the full width rear chassis and faired spring mounts.*

249. *The unusual Bugatti wheel on the T.59, where the spokes deal with radial loads only, and the drive is taken through splines between rim and back-plate.*

3rd Dieppe G.P. (Wimille)
4th Spanish G.P. (Wimille)
FTD and record at La Turbie (Wimille)

In 1936 Wimille was 1st in the Deauville G.P., 6th at Monaco. Subsequently, he was 3rd at Tunis and 2nd in the South African G.P. – lapping at 103 mph in the latter; he also won the Comminges G.P. in an unsupercharged version. In addition, Earl Howe's 3·3 was 4th fastest car ever to lap the Brooklands Outer Circuit – at 138·34 mph, a Class 'C' record. He covered the standing-start lap at 118 mph. Mr A. H. L. Eccles covered the standing-start kilometre at Brighton Speed Trials at an average of 78·95 mph (28·3 sec). Earl Howe and Brian Lewis finished 3rd in the 1935 500-mile race at Brooklands at an average speed of 115·03 mph, driving in this case an unsupercharged car.

In 1937 Wimille won the Pau, Bona and Marne G.P.s in an unsupercharged version, the latter two with a cowled radiator but presumably the same car. He drove at Tunis with the same car, winning the two heats but running out of fuel when leading in the final. Doors were fitted to the body of this car, probably to comply with sports car regulations. But the finest performance of all was when Wimille won the 400,000 franc prize for lapping Montlhéry at over 91 mph. He lapped this 12-mile road circuit for 162 miles at an average of 91·13 mph – just a fraction below von Brauchitch's Mercedes-Benz record for one lap. In so doing Wimille established a new record at 92·44 mph. The car had no cowl for this event, which was early in the year, and again it was probably the same car.

Contemporary description

A description of the Eccles car appeared in the *Autocar* of 19 April 1935 under the title 'A Modern Grand Prix Car':

The car was designed to obtain the maximum possible speed from a car weighing 750 kilogrammes (corresponding to about 15 cwt) empty and without tyres. The engine size was unlimited; the body had to have a definite minimum frontal area which made it almost the

287

equivalent of a two-seater, but the main difficulty was to bring the car down within the weight limit.

The engine is a 72 mm × 100 mm straight-eight with eight cylinders in line, having integral heads and two valves of equal size in each head placed at an angle so that they can be operated by a pair of overhead camshafts, an arrangement adopted by Bugatti a year or two ago. The crankshaft is arranged with its throws 2–4–2, and this time the roller bearings have been discarded and the crank journals are held in very large plain bearings, plain bearings also being used for the connecting-rods. At the back the crank drives the gear wheel which, through two intermediary gears, drives the two camshaft gears, one of the intermediary gears driving a side shaft on which is the water pump, run at half engine speed. An extra gear on the opposite side drives a big Roots blower at engine speed, the blower nestling between the crankcase and the frame side, where there is only just room for it.

A Vertex-type Scintilla magneto is driven from one end of the camshaft, with its distributor projecting through the instrument board, while the other camshaft drives a normal-size revolution counter. The right-hand camshaft also operates a small air pump, used to maintain pressure above the fuel in the main tank. The camshafts take bearings in the aluminium casing, and are so arranged that they can be detached from the cylinder heads and their driving gears, but without disturbing the other timing gears. Each of the gears on the camshaft ends has a separate cover so that the remeshing of the teeth can be seen plainly when the camshafts have to be retimed. Each camshaft also has three keys for the one key of the driving gear, with the aid of which, and by turning the driving gear round, the equivalent of a vernier adjustment is possible. The valves have detachable guides, three coil springs, and are operated direct by the cams themselves.

The supercharger sucks from two big down-draught Zenith carburettors, and, since the combined effect of the fuel pumps in those carburettors might flood the blower, the safety valves are carried below the blower casing, the stem of each having a ring to allow the valve to be opened by hand for draining.

On the delivery side is a plain inlet pipe of aluminium, with the usual rubber joint stoutly reinforced by numerous metal clips, and there is a wire guard over the carburettor intakes to prevent anything being dropped into the carburettors. The exhaust pipe on the opposite side is of the usual Grand Prix type, eight short leads blending in a single big pipe.

It is an interesting peculiarity of Bugatti design that the plugs,

288

which are in the centre of the cylinder head, screw into bosses in that head, but are within a steel shell. The shell is reduced in diameter at the lower end to be a tight fit on the outside diameter of the plug hole boss, and at the top is much wider, a rubber ring being used to make an effective water-tight joint between this shell and the cylinder block. It is a most unusual arrangement, and presumably adopted in order to allow ample space for removing the core from the head and afterwards inspecting the water passages round the valves.

Oil is delivered to the engine by the smaller of the two spur gear pumps, via a pressure filter, a separate supply being led to the valve gear, each bearing, of course, being fed under pressure. Oil draining into the crankcase is picked up by the larger pump and forced to a big oil tank placed next to the driver's seat and serving as a separate sump. The return pipe from the pump to this tank is of considerable diameter, and connects to the oil cooler, consisting simply of a number of plain copper pipes exposed to the air passing round the car. Behind the engine is a small flywheel, in which is the usual Bugatti multiplate clutch, taking the drive to the gearbox, but fly-wheel, clutch and clutch operation are now enclosed within a casing though the gearbox is still separate.

There is a considerable change in the transmission. The forward universal joint is mechanical; behind that is the sliding end of an extremely robust, very short, tubular propeller-shaft, and behind that again a fabric joint. Then comes the bevel pinion shaft, which drives a crown wheel to which is bolted a massive spur gear machined from solid and containing the four spindles of the differential bevel pinions. Each driving shaft, which is tubular and enormous, is part of a rear wheel hub at one end, connected by splines to the bevel of the differential at the other. The whole construction is massive compared with previous Bugatti practice, and it will be noticed that the crown wheel does not drive the rear wheel direct, but through reduction gearing, the propeller-shaft and bevel being carried quite low in the chassis. [A typical ratio was $20:28 \times 12:33$.]

There is still a torque member bolted through fabric to the gearbox, but the radius rods have been eliminated and the car is now driven through the rear quarter-elliptic springs. These, as usual, are bolted to the rear of the frame, project forward to the axle, and each leaf is securely clipped to its fellow. The shockabsorbers are entirely new, are hydraulic, and at the rear are set within the body, though the adjustment, which is a needle, can be operated from outside. In the front the two shockabsorbers are placed within the frame, close behind the radiator, and their adjustment is on top of the shock-absorber casing.

289

The front axle, like that of the 'four-nine', is in two pieces; it is still made hollow, round in section, and formed as a box passing completely round the front springs; but at the centre each half of the axle is recessed internally as a cone, and the distance piece between the two halves is a double cone, the whole being covered by a short sleeve spun over a rim on one half of the axle, screwed on to the other, and by this means the axle is allowed to move with each front wheel independently, apart from the effect of the tie-rod.

The steering column is now very short, is coupled to the steering gear through a fabric joint, and there is the typical plated drop arm and fore-and-aft rod. In addition to the fact that the brakes are very much more powerful, they also are of Bugatti pattern, the pedal operating a cross-shaft, and the brake cables being linked together by a chain passing round two sprockets on each side of the car. There is no adjustment, because it is deemed easier to change the brake shoes entirely at a pit stop, a process made extremely easy by the fact that the brake drums are changed with the wheel. The aluminium brake shoes are only held in position by their pull-off springs, and so can be detached in a second.

Once more Bugatti has produced an unusual wheel, for this car has wire wheels with straight spokes, and built-up hub, to which is attached the aluminium brake drum and a circumferential circular flange extending right up to the wheel rim, to which it is attached by gear teeth, all torque and drive passing through this flange, not through the spokes. The wheel is held to its hub by the usual quick-acting Rudge-Whitworth nut. The body and bonnet are extremely light, though not very thin and are probably of duralumin. The tank in the tail has twin fillers.

The gear lever is outside the body, and, as in all Bugattis, moves forward for second and top. The instrument board contains only the revolution counter, air pressure gauge, oil pressure gauge, and water thermometer. There is a compound tap which allows the driver to maintain air pressure in the fuel tank either by a hand pump or by the engine pump, to release the pressure in the tank or to turn off the supply pipe altogether. The fuel pipes are much larger than hitherto, probably because the consumption is relatively high with alcohol fuel.

Experience with a Type 59

In *Bugantics*, 6, 1, January 1937, C. E. C. Martin wrote of his experiences, some happy, some unhappy, with a Type 59:

At the beginning of 1934 I toured all over the Continent trying to

50. *Grand Prix de Comminges, 1936; Robert Benoist on the starting line in a T.59. Motor Sport commented that Bugattis discarded their streamlined bodies and came out in their true guise as G.P. cars sans superchargers. The sight of them so infuriated the Delahaye drivers that they threatened to strike and the organizers had a tricky time negotiating a settlement. Wimille won in the other car.*

(photo: T. A. S. O. Mathieson)

251. *Three T.59s at the 1934 French G.P. driven by Nuvolari, Benoist and Dreyfus*

2. *Wimille again, this time San Sebastian the 2.8 litre*

253. *Wimille at Montlhéry in April 1937 competing for a prize offered by the French Government.*

254. *Wimille in a road-equipped T.59 at Pau in 1937.*

255. *The 1935 Frenc Grand Prix saw Benoi with a special T.59 wit partially cowled radiato and either an enlarge 3·8 litre T.59 engine o more probably, a 50B e gine of 4·7 or 4·9 litre (contemporary reports a contradictory). The bo net flew off on the four lap, nearly decapitati Benoist, who continue but retired on lap 34.*

256. *Wimille drove this modified T.59 at Comminges in 1939, fitted with the 4·7litre engine*

TYPE 59 ENGINE

257. *This engine was developed from the 57S engine with 6 crankshaft main bearings and rear camshaft drive.*

(*photo:* Autocar)

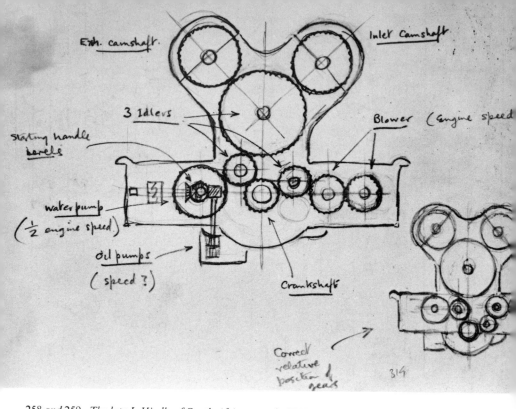

Exh. camshaft.

Inlet Camshaft

3 Idlers

starting handle
levels

Blower (engine speed

water pump
(½ engine speed)

Oil pumps
(speed ?)

Crankshaft

Correct
relative
position of
gears

314

258 and 259. *The late J. Hindle of South Africa owned a T.59. As an engineer he delighted in studying the construction of the car. These unretouched reproductions of two of his sketches illustrate: (above) the gear train arrangement at the rear of the engine, with the starting handle projecting at right angles on the left side; (below) the double reduction rear axle.*

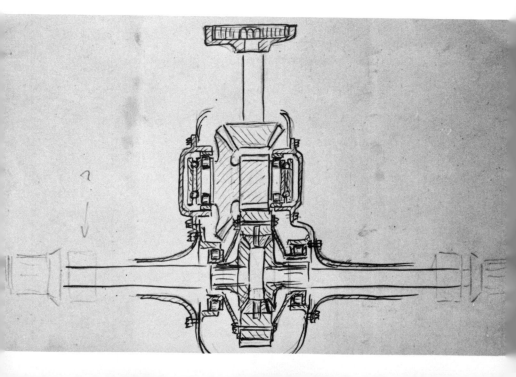

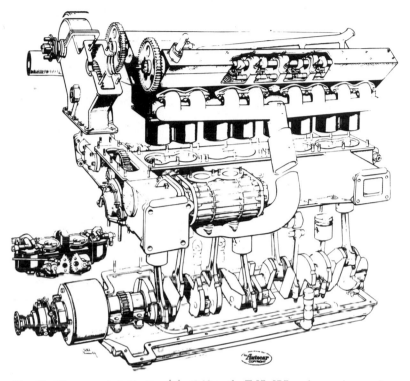

Fig. 45. *The general similarity of the T.59 to the T.57–57S engine can be seen from this Max Millar drawing.*

(Autocar)

find a suitable mount for the coming season, and finally finished up at Molsheim, where I eventually bought a 3,300 Grand Prix.

The delivery of the 3,300 was promised for January, but it was not until April that I finally got the car over to England.

When I finally heard from Molsheim that [it] was ready, I flew over there with Shuttleworth, arriving one Saturday afternoon. Imagine my thrill, when I found the car all ready, waiting for me to drive away.

I packed a small suitcase in the back, borrowed a mackintosh and set off for Strasbourg in the pouring rain with no wings, lamps or windscreen.

Unfortunately, the Works had sent her out with the mixture far too rich, and volumes of black smoke kept pouring out all the time. By the time I reached Strasbourg, practically all the plugs had given out, and I stopped to see what could be done.

295

An enormous crowd collected round me, and got very excited about everything: finally I pulled into a garage to change all the plugs, and, to my horror, in the excitement of the moment, I dropped one of the terminals in the plug hole. I had awful visions of having to get the car back to the Works and having her dismantled, but after frantic efforts with bits of wire and other odds and ends, the garage proprietor finally managed to stab the end of the terminal with the end of a file, and I got it out safely.

I then set off north in the pouring rain, and was very soon soaked through to the skin.

Owing to the very rich mixture, I very soon oiled up a lot more plugs, and we even blanked off part of the radiator to try and overcome the trouble.

I found it extremely difficult trying to pass the average French driver, not having any horn on the car, and I travelled quite a long way in various ditches, trying to get past.

I spent that night in Metz, about half-way to Boulogne and the next morning set off again with some new goggles, and a very smart beret, bought in the town.

I filled up with No. 1 petrol, in an endeavour to lessen the richness, and after persuading some enthusiasts to tow me to start the engine, went off like a flash.

It was still pouring with rain, my face was red and extraordinarily painful. It was extremely difficult to see where I was going in all the mud, and I was absolutely frozen stiff. Another difficulty was that once I stopped, I found it quite impossible to start the engine again, unless I stopped on a hill, or got someone to push me.

After lunch, to my intense joy, the weather cleared and I had a much more enjoyable run to Boulogne, where it turned out to be fine and sunny. Here, with some able assistance, I washed the car off and had her nicely cleaned up, before embarking, and so ended one of the most hectic rides I have ever had.

Then came the [1935] International Trophy, with the disaster to the 3,300s which is probably well known. We all had transmission trouble and the cars went back to Brixton. Jean Bugatti came over from the Works with some of the Works mechanics, and finally the cars were put in running order again.

We then set off for the Isle of Man, and this time Brackenbury took my 2,300 as well. We had an excellent and trouble-free run on the 3,300 and the result was that Brian Lewis was first and I was second.

I then entered the 3,300 at the Whitsun Brooklands Meeting, and after stalling the engine on the line I got away, but after one lap the propeller shaft went again completely locking the back wheels, and tearing away the petrol tank.

After this further set-back, I had the transmission entirely re-designed by Hardy Spicer, after which it never gave any further trouble.

As soon as she was again complete, I set off for the Grand Prix de Marne. The first morning's practice was extremely satisfactory, and we lapped at approximately 97 mph and reached a maximum speed of 154 mph on the long straight leg of the circuit. She was magnificent to handle at this speed, and I was thoroughly enjoying myself, but to my horror the morning before the race the gearbox casing cracked. Brian Lewis very kindly lent me his Type 57 Saloon, and I set off for Molsheim with the gearbox. On arriving I handed over the gearbox and went to bed, and by 8 p.m. they had it repaired, and I collected it and set off again for the scene of the race. I finally got back to Rheims about 2 a.m. and the mechanics spent the rest of the night putting the car together again; and so after the most hectic period I arrived on the starting line on time!

We qualified in the preliminary heat, and finished sixth in the final, just behind Brian Lewis, and on this occasion the car ran extremely well.

The next event for which I entered the 3,300 was Dieppe and again disaster overtook us during practice a connecting rod came through the side of the crankcase and, feeling very gloomy and depressed, I sent the car back once more to Molsheim for repair, and for the time being, lost all interest in cars.

The car was then entered for the Nice Grand Prix and was sent there direct from Molsheim. I flew over there with Shuttleworth in his plane, and during practising everything went off without a hitch.

The day of the race dawned, and in terrific heat we set off, but unfortunately after 29 laps out of the 100, the same thing happened again – a rod came through the side of the engine, and the whole engine was very badly smashed.

This time I decided to take the matter in hand myself, and after carefully examining the engine, it was decided that the connecting rods were far too light. I had some special ones made, and finally the car was re-assembled once more, and prepared for the Donington Grand Prix.

In the meantime, Brackenbury had won the Gold Star at Brooklands at 125 mph on my 2,300, and secured third fastest time at Brighton. The 2,300 also went to Shelsley, when she put up the extremely good time of 42 seconds. I believe this is the fastest time ever recorded at Shelsley by a Bugatti, and definitely the fastest time

297

ever put up by a car with single rear wheels. I had the rev. counter disconnected, so as not to upset my feelings too badly, and did the whole climb on first and second gears only!

Then came the Donington Grand Prix and the 3,300 seemed to be running better than she had ever done before, and practising went off without any hitch.

The morning of the race turned out thoroughly wet and beastly, but it cleared somewhat just before the race began. The result of the race is now, of course, well known. I had an excellent trouble-free run, and with only thirteen laps to go, I had the race absolutely in hand, and all I had to do was to follow Shuttleworth, who was just one lap behind me. What happened at Maclean's Corner I don't know – whether I dropped asleep for a second, or whether I was not thinking of what I was doing, I don't know, but the fact remains that I spun round, ended up backwards off the road, and, of course, the engine stopped.

This car had always been extremely difficult to start on the handle, and after driving all this time, I found it completely impossible. Finally, after trying for a long time, I got a couple of marshals to push me off – the engine started at once, and I drove round to the pits to tell them what had happened. I thought that having had outside assistance, I should automatically be disqualified, but I learnt that marshals were allowed to help, and so I set off on the last few laps, and finally finished third behind Shuttleworth and Lord Howe.

My last event with this car was the Mountain Championship, in which I finished second to Shuttleworth, and so ended my career with that ill-fated 3,300.

She was a magnificent car to handle and a joy to drive when she was running properly, but she gave me endless trouble and cost me a small fortune in repairs, but in spite of all this, I shall always be grateful to her for the unlimited experience she gave me in the handling of a really fast car.

The Cars Today

Of the surviving genuine Type 59 cars, one is in the U.S.A. and no less than three are in England. At least two other chassis which remained in France still exist without engines or with substitute ones. A seventh car delivered to King Leopold of Belgium is still in that country in other hands and splendidly original.

TYPE 57S 45
and other special racing cars

BUGATTI HAD RACED THE TYPE 57 IN THE 1935 T.T. AND A FEW other sports car races: he had produced the small series of 3·3 litre Type 59 racing cars in 1934–35. Thereafter Bugatti's racing programme became involved and very confusing to the humble historian, without accurate factory records. The cars used were special bodied 57S and 57C cars (known at the factory as the 57G) and a special car (or cars) known as the 57S 45 which was basically a modified T.50 engine in a 57S chassis, together with some special single seaters, at least one of which was a Type 59 fitted with a 50B engine.

In 1936 a special ultra-streamlined T.57S sports car created a sensation when three of them first appeared in the French Grand Prix at Montlhéry. Driven by Wimille and Sommer, it won the race, and during that year Wimille also drove it to victory, against strong opposition from the larger 4·5 litre Talbots and 3·5 litre Delahayes, in the Marne G.P. at Reims, Benoist being 2nd, and Veyron 4th in similar cars. During the winter, Wimille, Williams, Benoist and Veyron took a whole string of Class C world records with this unsupercharged car including 'The Hour' at 135·42 mph (Benoist driving) and 24 hours at 123·93 mph (the other three drivers). Success continued in 1937 and perhaps the greatest victory of the year was at Le Mans, where Wimille and Robert Benoist, driving an identical car, won the 24 hour race at the record average speed of 85·13 mph establishing a new distance record; a second entry (Labric – Veyron) ran well until it retired with a fuel leak after many hours.

For 1936 Bugatti had also decided, according to *L'Auto*, 'to

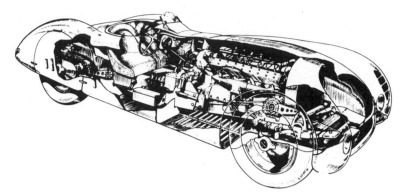

Fig. 46. *The 1936 57G tank car in section by the French artist Gedo. The chassis has front slide blocks to the front springs and de Ram shockabsorbers. The gearbox is T.57, integrally mounted.*

construct six cars with a new engine, and with a capacity of 4·5 litres. The chassis will be on established lines dear to Bugatti. The springing and brakes will remain the same. The gearbox will be new. It is hoped to be able to produce 400 hp' (*Bugantics* 5, 2, March 1936). This car (probably only one was made) was evidently the 57S 45 which used the Type 50B engine; superficially similar to the Type 50 engine, supercharged, with a nine bearing crankshaft and front gear drive to the twin camshafts, the 50B differed in detail and power output (470 hp). The crankcase was a light alloy casting, with steel cylinder liners and valve seats. The bore and stroke were listed as 84 mm × 107 mm (4,739 cc) compared with the 86 mm × 107 mm of the Type 50, but no doubt a 4·5 litre version (bore 81 mm?) was produced, justifying the model designation. It seems only to have been used in this or these cars and later single seaters, the normal T.50 engine being used on Types 53 and 54. The new engine was rather lower in height and had a different, flatter shape to the 'cleavage' between the two camshaft bevel covers. The type 57S 45 was listed by Molsheim along with a smaller engined 4 litre 57S 40 (77 mm × 107 mm). If a few of the former were produced for racing it seems certain that none of the latter was made.

The first appearance of the 57S 45 seems to have been in practice at the 1937 Le Mans race; the car had a good looking streamlined body, T.59 wire wheels and could be distinguished from the earlier 1936 car by the absence of slots in the wings to admit cooling air to the brakes and by the wheel fairing line dropping down between the wheels. It is not clear what events the car took part in subsequently. Although entered in the poorly supported French G.P. of 1937, Bugatti arrived 'late as usual'. According to *Motor Sport* for July 1937, 'Benoist insisted on showing off the paces of a private Bugatti to a prospective customer during a practice period, in face of a direct warning of the officials. For this he was disqualified from taking part in the race, and as the cars were late anyway Bugatti withdrew both his cars'. They were 'tank' models; which ones is not clear, but probably the 57S 45.

The year 1938 seems not to have been a great year for the sports bodied cars, due in part to the racing department being disorganized by mobilization as a result of war scares, but in 1939 a further 'tank' bodied car, this time fitted with the super-charged 57C (not 57SC) engine was successful, including winning at Le Mans. The body was more tank-like than ever, the line between the wings not being faired down below wheel level; front scoops were fitted to admit air to the engine. The Le Mans car was driven to win at 86·5 mph by Wimille and Veyron. Jean Bugatti wrote that the car was standard, except for the axle ratio (14:42) giving 142 mph at 5,000 rpm, increased carburettor size, an oil radiator and that Bugatti wire wheels were used to facilitate brake lining change, although in fact, they did not need changing. The fuel consumption throughout the 24 hours was 10·8 mpg. The engine developed 200 hp at 5,000 rpm and Jean Bugatti felt that 168 mph would be possible. Not a spanner or tool was used during the the whole race, and the bonnet was never raised during this time! Unfortunately, Jean Bugatti met his death in this car in August 1939, testing it prior to the La Baule Grand Prix.

Single seat G.P. racing cars

In 1935 Molsheim produced an experimental Type 59 fitted with the new T.50B engine of 4·7 litres and supercharged, the blower layout being similar to the Type 50 engine from which the modified engine had stemmed; this was the car entered in the 1935 French Grand Prix. At the end of 1935 a streamlined single seater with a bulbous radiator cowling was produced. The car appeared in practice at Monaco in 1936, in supercharged

Fig. 47. *The 1936 single seater with 4·7 litre engine.*

4·7 litre form. The radiator was fully cowled with an integral grille lying behind the front cross tube and an oil cooler below the cowl in front of the radiator. The exhaust was external, and the rear body shell was riveted along the centre line as on the Type 57 Atlantic coupé. The car was a true single seater, with central steering, perhaps for the first time at Molsheim. The same car (or was there a second one?) with no front oil cooler but a fairing behind the driver's head, competed in the Vanderbilt Cup in the U.S.A. and finished second, Wimille driving.

302

260. *The first three tank cars to appear were the streamlined T.57S or 57G racing cars at the 1936 French Grand Prix at Montlhéry. Wimille/Sommer (No. 84) won; Veyron/Williams (No. 86) were 6th and Benoist/P. de Rothschild were 13th.*

TYPE 57S

61. *Wimille in the 1936 French G.P.*

262. *Rear view of the 1936 Tank car.*

263. *Wimille and the T.57S with which he captured so many Class C world records in 1936, including the hour at 135·42 mph. Note Le Patron's signature.*

264. *Wimille and Veyron in the winning Le Mans car, 1939.*

265   *One Tank has survived.*
(*photo:* **The Motor**)

266. *The T.57S 45 tank car with 50B engine which appeared in practice but did not run at Le Mans 1937. This car is less tank-like than the earlier or later, and successful, cars.*

(*photo: The Motor*)

(right). *Wimille driving the 3 litre ~le seater G.P. car at Cork in 1938, ~re it made its début. It was timed on ~ quarter mile straight at 147·2 mph ~le missing on one cylinder. He retired ~wo-thirds distance.*

268 (left). *The engine of the 3 litre car.*

(*photo: H. Hastings from* The Motor)

269. *Wimille walking alongside the 3 litre car at Reims 1938.*

270. *The final 1939 single seater: Wimille in the 4·7 litre.*

271. **The cylinder block of the 50B engine as used in the Wimille single-seater is a magnificent production.**

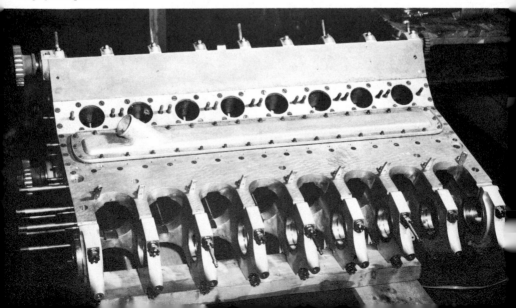

The car was, of course, in 4·7 litre form ror this race. In 1937 the single seater, still with the fairing but with the oil cooler on once more, competed in the million-franc prize, offered for the fastest time achieved by 1 September 1937 over 200 km of the Montlhéry road course. Wimille failed to beat Dreyfus on a Delahaye, retiring with mechanical trouble.

In 1938 a new car was produced on the same chassis, fitted with a supercharged 3 litre version of the T.50B engine, the bore and stroke evidently being 78 mm × 78 mm (2,985 cc). The car

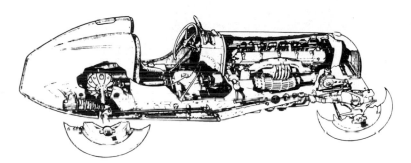

Fig. 48. *The single seater 3 litre G.P. car with 50B engine. A fine section drawing by Gedo, originally published in the now defunct* Speed.

was first seen at the Cork race in April 1938, being timed over a kilometre at 147·2 mph, but was unplaced. The *Autocar* reported: 'Cork also marked the first appearance of the G.P. Formula Bugatti, which is not strikingly new in conception as far as one could ascertain. The engine is a twin-camshaft straight-eight with the supercharger and low-slung carburettor on the off side of the power unit. The chassis reminds one of that used on the 3·3 litre with deep drilled side-members, half-elliptic springs fore and reversed quarter-elliptics with de Ram shockabsorbers aft. The front axle is split. In appearance, however, Bugatti has followed the inevitable rounded contour of the modern racing

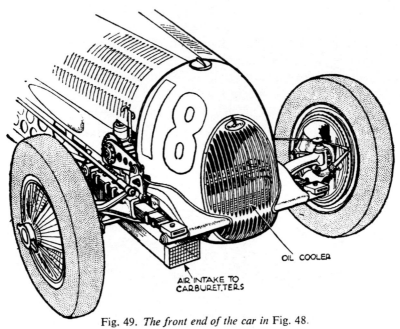

Fig. 49. *The front end of the car in* Fig. 48.

(*drawing:* Autocar)

car with a Mercedes-like radiator cowl and flowing tail. The mechanical braking arrangement and wheels integral with the drums are as before. The car was the fastest machine at Cork, and will no doubt make an excellent showing'. This car differed from the earlier one in having the radiator cowl elongated to lie forward of the front cross tube, but it may have had the same chassis.

In 1939 another similar single seat car was produced, with faired-in sides to the body, hydraulic brakes and the supercharged 4·7 litre Type 50B engine. Wimille again was the driver, being 2nd fastest at the La Turbie Hill-Climb, then winning the Coupe de Paris at Montlhéry at 85·3 mph, and making 2nd Fastest Time at Prescott in July (the first and only appearance of a Molsheim entry at the Bugatti Owners' Club hill). He had also competed in, and won, the Grand Prix at Luxembourg in a

308

SHROUDED MAGNETO

CONCEALED FILLER CAP

Fig. 50 *The rear end of the 3 litre car.*

(*drawing:* Autocar)

4·7 litre car, probably a T.59 chassis 'equipée en sport', in June. The single seater car was preserved during the war and is still in existence. Wimille also won the very first post-war race with it – the Coupe des Prisonniers in the Bois de Boulogne in Paris on 9 September 1945, averaging 71 mph. The serial number of the car is 50180.

TYPES 60 - 252
twilight - the war and after

BY 1939 THE SHADOWS OF IMPENDING WAR FELL OVER EUROPE, and nowhere more than in a border town such as Molsheim. Ettore, past his prime as a racing car maker and saddened by the labour unrest in France in the 1930s, spent much of his time on an aeroplane design and on the Bugatti railcar; his son Jean had found his feet as an engineer and was mainly occupied with improving the Type 57. The 57S model had been dropped in 1938, but other new cars were planned.

Type 60 This was a 1938 project for an aeroengine, 8 cylinder, 4·1 litre, 86 mm × 88 mm, with four valves per cylinder; it may also have been intended to replace the Wimille 3 litre single seater.

Type 64 In 1939 a prototype was built to replace the Type 57. This had a similar if strengthened chassis, but in light alloy with the flanges outwards, still with the classic leaf spring suspension, and a new twin chain-driven camshaft engine of 4·5 litres (no doubt derived from the T.57 engine); double downdraught carburettors were used, and a Cotal gearbox. The radiator was of a new V-shape. Another chassis with what seems to be a normal Type 57 engine was prepared for the October 1939 salon, which never took place; this chassis was stored and is still in existence.

Tragedy overtook Bugatti, just before war came, with the death of Jean Bugatti on a road near Molsheim on 11 August 1939. He had been testing a 57C tank-bodied car prepared for the La Baule races, and ran off the road at high speed, when swerving to avoid 'a bloody-minded local on a bicycle who rode out of a side turning ignoring all caution on this stretch of a

310

272 and 273. *The last pre-war model and prototype of what would have been the 1940/41 successor to the famous T.57 with 4·5 litre twin overhead chain-driven camshaft engine, double downdraught carburettors, Cotal gearbox and hydraulic brakes. This car would have been a certain success.*

TYPE 64

274. *The wartime 370 cc Baby Bugatti.*

(photo: F. Schlumpf)

TYPE 68

275. *T.73 single-cam and T.73C twin-cam 1·5 litre engines.* (*photo: W. Turnbull*)

TYPE 73 AND 73C ENGINES

276. *T.73C racing engine.*

(*photo:* The Motor)

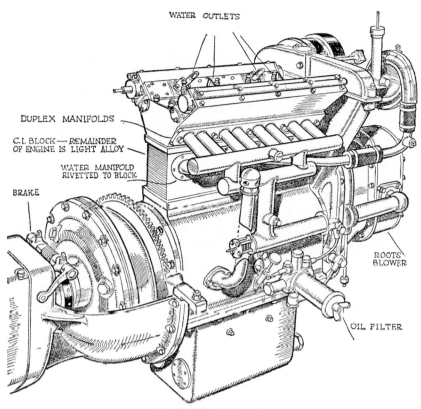

WATER OUTLETS

DUPLEX MANIFOLDS

C.I. BLOCK — REMAINDER
OF ENGINE IS LIGHT ALLOY

WATER MANIFOLD
RIVETTED TO BLOCK

BRAKE

ROOTS
BLOWER

OIL FILTER

Fig. 51. *The T.68 engine.*

(*drawing:* The Motor)

road which was "policed" by Molsheim mechanics'. Ettore moved to Paris and then Bordeaux during the war and, judging by his war-time patent specifications, was still designing cars, along with boats and machine tools.

The post-war programme, on which he was working at the time of his death at the age of 66 on 21 August 1947, included the Type 68, 370 cc supercharged baby car and the Type 73, 1·5 litre touring and racing cars. After his death the Type 101 (virtually a Type 57) was produced at Molsheim under the direction of M. Pierre Marco.

Type was a small two seater roadster with a 370 cc (48·5 mm
68 × 50 mm) engine, with twin overhead camshafts and

313

16 valves. It was produced at a time when all France was clamouring for cheap motor transport with negligible fuel consumption, but no production materialized. The design of the racing Type 73 was under way in Paris as early as the beginning of 1946, Ettore now being assisted by the younger son Roland. Production was slow, however, no doubt due to the prevailing conditions. The work was being carried out in the old factory of the La Licorne car at Levallois, a suburb of Paris, Bugatti owning this factory. A batch of twenty cars was reported at the time to be under construction. A Type 73 chassis was shown at the 1947 Paris Salon a few weeks after the death of 'le Patron', together with the racing engine (T.73C). A brief typewritten sheet handed out on the Bugatti Stand at the 1947 Show, stated that the bodywork would be a 2 door, 4 seat aerodynamic coach.

Type The chassis was conventional Bugatti with a solid **73A** front axle and usual reversed quarter-elliptic rear springs. The engine had 4 cylinders and a single overhead camshaft and blower driven off the front of the crankshaft. The engine construction was slab-like with a detachable block and a cambox rather like a Type 40. The carburettor was a downdraught mounted on an elbow on the blower, which fed the manifold by a long pipe. The exhaust manifold, as Mr J. L. Burton put it, was 'no longer a bunch of bananas, but a product of cast iron'.

Oh dear! Large coverplates on the sides of the crankcase proclaim the name of the maker. So Ettore, who started at Molsheim with his signature on the valve cover of the 8 valve car, finished with his imprint in enormous lettering on the ill-fated T.73 – an epitaph perhaps, poor man.

Type According to Mr Gene Cesari the explanation of the **73C** suffix letters on the T.73 is as follows: 'Originally he envisioned a single-cam four cylinder 1·5 litre sports machine to replace the Type 55. Before the prototype engine was tested he decided that wet liners were imperative. While the draughtsmen altered blue prints, Bugatti decreed that the engine must become a twin-cam unit to allow the basic design to achieve its full potential. Hence, the T.73, the T.73A and the T.73B'. In

314

any event, the T.73C (the C could stand for 'Course') was the racing single seater version with chain-driven twin cams and, as Mr J. L. Burton has put it, 'with detachable head – after forty years of success with the other sort. The blower is mounted on the nose, but is larger than the 73A, and the carburettor hangs below. The delivery pipe which is huge rises from the top of the blower and finds its way in a respectable swerve to the centre of the induction manifold. A technical note, possibly a sign of 1947, those expensive little nuts (so dear to us) are not so evident, but the ordinary hexagon type with separate washer were *de rigueur*'.

At least one other 73C was made, in this case with the blower alongside the engine in a more normal Bugatti arrangement.

These cars, if not to be ignored because of their parentage, are not 'pur-sang'. Even the Master is allowed his mistakes.

Type The car as produced (only a few were made) differed **101** from the pre-war T.57 only in a few details, although the engine had chain-driven camshafts as on T.64. The use of 17 in. wheels with 6·00 × 17 tyres was a worthwhile improvement; manifolding was different with a downdraught carburettor and a Cotal gearbox was used. There was also a 101C with blower.

In the French motoring paper *L'Auto Journal*, 1 September 1951, there appeared front page headlines stating that 'The heir to the 57 will cost over three million francs', followed by an article describing the new model and illustrations of the complete car as it would appear at the Paris Salon. All this was, of course, most exciting as being the first solid confirmation of actual production activity since the many rumours and speculations of the previous few years.

The article started thus:

The famous iron curtain is being raised at Molsheim in Alsace and it is more likely to become a paper curtain capable of being torn aside by hand. Snow has given way to sunshine, silence to the noise of the machines and the air of sadness to smiles. Walls have been erected, roofs covered and machine tools installed. During the last six months the Bugatti Works have been rebuilt and a festive air pervades every brick, and every piece of metal plate, in fact, everything.

The General Manager, M. Marco, triumphantly announced that the Bugatti is at last ready to resume its place on the world automobile market. For the first time since the war, following a careful investigation, and with the will to continue, we shall be exhibiting the Works' latest offspring at the 1951 Salon.

The engine was a typical straight eight with a double chain-driven overhead camshaft, and had a cylinder capacity of 3,257 cc. Of monobloc construction, this engine had a non-detachable cylinder head with hemispherical head and central sparking plugs. There were still two valves per cylinder. Ignition was by Delco unit and a double Weber carburettor with pump was fitted. It was supplied with and without a supercharger, the 26 hp engine developing 135 hp at 5,500 rpm without the supercharger, and 188 hp at 5,200 rpm with a 3 psi boost. With a $4\frac{1}{2}$ psi supercharger pressure, more than 200 hp could be obtained. A 5-speed mechanical or Cotal gearbox was originally listed. It was claimed that this new gearbox, of Bugatti design, giving four speeds with a fifth overdrive speed, would be silent on all except first gear.

The Lockheed hydraulic brakes incorporated eight positive shoes, two on each wheel, each of these shoes being operated by an independent circuit. Accordingly, the risk of the car being without brakes in the event of a broken pipe was eliminated. Allinquant special telescopic shockabsorbers were used. Thus equipped, the weight of the chassis was in the neighbourhood of 2,300 lb and with coachwork it was expected not to exceed 3,200 lb. Coachwork was by Gangloff of Colmar. The design of the cabriolet and of the coupé followed the contemporary line, being low and wide, and provided for four comfortably.

Types 251 and 252 Towards the end in 1956, Molsheim, but not Bugatti, produced an 8 cylinder racing car designed by the Italian engineer, Colombo, as Type 251. The engine was 76 × 68·5 mm, 2,486 cc. It was not successful. Type 252 was a prototype sports car of 1·5 litres.

316

277. *Coupé.*

TYPE 101

278. *Drophead.*

279. *Chassis.*

280. The Type 101 engine was very similar to that of the T.57C except for the manifold and carburettor. (*photo: Bucher Molsheim*)

TYPE 251

281. The T.251 post-war single seater racing car, engine athwartships, with Pierre Marco standing behind. Ill-fated and unsuccessful, it had better be mentioned because it had a Bugatti nameplate.

282. There have been more rumours of new Molsheim products than actual cars. This impression of an impending production is from the Auto-Journal *of Paris (1960) and shows the T.252 prototype.*

PART II

HISTORICAL INFORMATION

Chronology of early Bugatti designs*

FOR MORE THAN FIFTY YEARS THE AUTOMOBILE DESIGNS OF ETTORE Bugatti have aroused interest and controversy among car enthusiasts and engineers. An enthusiastic Club and a wide circle of owners of his cars have made the history of his racing successes and his designs in the 1920s and 1930s widely known and well documented. But there is a notable absence of accurate information on early car designs, particularly those before the first world war. The following notes review contemporary and more recent published information in an attempt to get to the facts.

Car No. 1 According to Bradley (1948), Bugatti produced
1898 a tricycle with two engines, winning races in Italy when he was 18 (he was born on 15 September 1881). He entered it in the Paris–Bordeaux race on 24 May 1899, but retired about half-way following an accident with a dog. At this time Bugatti was working at Prinetti and Stucchi in Milan; according to Grégoire (1953) he was 16, the tricycle was of their manufacture and Bugatti bought and modified it, and this is believed to be correct.

Bonneville (1949) (page 173 *et seq.* 'Bugatti Beginnings') gives some details of Ettore Bugatti's early successes in 1899 as a race driver at the age of 18, culled from contemporary journals:

1 March: Reference to Bugatti in Nice–Castelanne race, No. 72 on De Dion Bouton tricycle of 1·25 hp.
12 March: Verona–Mantua 161 km race; 18 tricycles start. Bugatti wins on Prinetti tricycle with De Dion Bouton engine; Count Biscaretti 2nd; Fraschini 3rd. Agnelli of Fiat won the car class.

---

* This chapter is an amplification of some notes originally published in the *Autocar*, 3 June 1960; a brief bibliography is given on page 343.

8 May: Pignerol–Turin 90 km race; 42 entries in Tricycle class. Bugatti wins on machine with De Dion 1¾ hp engine at record speed.

14 May: Padua–Trevise and back 175 km race. Quadricycle class, Bugatti takes 4 h 35 min and makes best time of *all* vehicles. (This may have been on Car No. 2 – see below.)

11 September: Brescia–Verona and back 223 km. Bugatti 2nd in Tricycle class.

28 September: Trevise 3 km speed event. Bugatti 3rd in Handicap class.

28 September: Trevise 80 km event. Bugatti is non-finisher due to petrol blockage.

Car No. 2
1898   According to Bradley and Grégoire, Bugatti designed a small 4 engined car, one engine at each wheel, but it was not successful. Bugatti himself in a 1929 Works publication indicates that the engine had 4 cylinders and was mounted on the back axle. A 4 wheel car, with two single cylinder engines in the Turin Auto Museum is labelled as Bugatti's design and this may be car No. 2.

Car No. 3
1900   The third car was more conventional and was financed by the Count Gulinelli. It had 4 cylinders, 90 mm × 120 mm bore and stroke, 4 speeds and chain drive. This car won a gold medal at the International Breeding and Sport Exhibition, Milan, in May–June 1901 and is stated to have received an award from the Automobile Club of France in 1899; this may have been incorrect as the car seems only to have been completed in 1900 or 1901 (see page 321). Pozzoli (1961) gives this car as Type 1.

La Gazetta dello Sport, Milan, 22 May 1901, had this to say about the exhibit:

On the Ricordi stand there figures, by his kind permission, the sensational novelty of the Exhibition: The Bugatti–Gulinelli carriage. The engaging dare-devil of Italian motorcycling conceived the idea of producing a kind of light vehicle which was not at the time on the market. It would not be the minute and very fragile vehicle too similar to the bicycle, nor yet the complicated, useless and costly mastodon, and this first attempt made a very good job of it, a

ETTORE BUGATTI'S CAR
(Translated from *Gazzetta dello Sport*, Milan, 10 May 1901)

As a passionate follower of automobilism, this new sport which occupies more and more minds in a search for perfection, I have for some time been following the feverish development of innovation and improvements in motor construction. Yesterday was a great day for me, for I was able to observe the complete success of my good friend Ettore Bugatti, who by himself, unaided, has built a vehicle which is quite magnificent. Having followed Bugatti in his patient research for 10 months I am delighted to report his triumphant success.

In the motorcar field Bugatti is very well known; son of an artist, he is himself an artist at heart. He has served his motoring apprenticeship racing a motorcycle. He loved his machine; there were modifications every day in the workshop until the tricycle carried him victorious to the finishing line in the many road races in which he took part. But his dream was of a car, a fast car. He studied all the various types of motor, analysed them, observed their faults, thought up modifications and foresaw in his imagination a perfect car.

However, he lacked the material means to put his ideas and studies into practice. His own nature, cheerful and waggish, was little encouragement to others to take him seriously and associate themselves with him in a programme of construction, and most of them abandoned him. Then he started to make sketches of the multitude of ideas which crowded his brain. His father's studio was full of vast rolls of paper – Bugatti spent whole days designing the vehicle in pencil and crayon in all its details.

How often the worthy Bugatti took me to his studio, showing me and explaining on a score of sheets of paper the functioning of his car! His enthusiasm in describing it was such that it seemed to be already on the road at 60 km/h; indeed I feared it might turn his mind. Among his many friends, it was the brothers Count Gulinelli di Ferrara who recognized in Bugatti a hidden brilliance and helped him realize his project. It was thus that in October of last year Bugatti began to reproduce from his drawings the wooden patterns for the foundry; then the construction of the chassis, the making of the large cast parts and practically all the small delicate parts which go to make up a car.

A month ago, on my return from the Circuit of Italy trials I went to visit Bugatti in his workshop in company with Cav. Ricordi and my good friend Georges Berteaux. The car was under construction. Berteaux was most enthusiastic and told Bugatti that it would be an undoubted success even abroad. So sure was he of its success that he undertook to buy the first one of the type.

The day before yesterday Bugatti fitted the wheels, installed the provisional ignition system and drove out of the workshop for the first test. The car went superbly and can at present do 60 km/hr, but the power of the engine is such that it can without any effort pull a higher gear ratio.

It is a light car not to be confused with a cycle car. The motor has four vertical cylinders with electric ignition tubes; valve housings and cylinders are contained in a single casting. Completely new is the system for closing the inlet valves, the removal of a single nut being sufficient to dismantle each pair of valves without removing any tube. The engine, the gear change and all the rest of the machinery are fixed on a double frame of rectangular steel of very great rigidity. The chassis with all the mechanical parts is completely adaptable to any type of coachwork.

Yesterday the courageous and enterprising young man received the enthusiastic compliments of the most competent automobilists. Yesterday's boy – he is only 19 – has disappeared: today he is the esteemed constructor of a model which has reached a high degree of perfection.

The car now built is the welcome result of the anxieties, the difficulties and the efforts of the past. Now Bugatti, teamed up with the brothers Count Gulinelli will start a vast establishment in Milan for the building of motorcars.   E. V.

323

triumph in fact: a small carriage, simple and most potent with a 12 hp, 4 cylinder motor, capable of exacting daily service and of very great speed if necessary.

We shall not dwell here on the most interesting characteristics of the vehicle with which we are already occupying ourselves and shall continue to do so with pleasure: on this occasion we shall only state that it rounded off the Ricordi Stand to perfection.

It is obvious that a reception such as this to a first design must have had a great effect on young Bugatti's estimation of his own abilities and must have conditioned much of his future activity.

Car No. 4 In 1902, at the age of 21, Bugatti was designing for 1902 the de Dietrich Company at Niederbronn; they had acquired a licence for Car No. 3. Possibly the first English reference to Bugatti's design is in the now defunct *Automotor Journal*, 18 April 1903, which illustrates and describes a 4 cylinder, 114 mm × 130 mm car, rated as 24 hp, which Pozzoli claims is Type 2. This car had a 4 speed gearbox and chain rear drive. According to the description the overhead valves were operated from a pair of camshafts by what appear to be pull, as opposed to push, rods. The cylinders were cast in pairs, each pair being surrounded by a cylindrical aluminium casing acting as a water jacket. Plate 286 illustrates the chassis, and 288 a complete car. This is undoubtedly the production version of the car that Bradley illustrates – a large 4 cylinder chain driven car with the driver sitting over the rear axle. He wrongly labels it 1901 (so did the original *Bugatti Book*). This is understandable as the 1929 Works brochure gives this date.

The German motor journal *Der Motorwagen* refers to Ettore Bugatti in its issue of 15 September 1902, describing the Frankfurt race meeting held on 31 August. Race No. 6 was a handicap event for gentlemen drivers, the cars carrying a total of four persons, and the distance being 12·87 kilometres. Goebel won in an 8 hp Bergmann from a 3·75 km handicap, Bugatti 2nd from 250 metres, in a 20 hp de Dietrich, and Emil Mathis from scratch being 3rd in a 24 hp de Dietrich. In the next scratch

283. *A Prinetti and Stucchi quadricycle Bugatti, now in the Turin Auto Museum and probably similar to the tricycle Bugatti first worked on and with which he made a name for himself as a race rider.*

284. *The 4 wheel, two-engined car in the Turin Auto Museum which may have been of Bugatti origin. The Museum catalogue states that Ettore Bugatti contributed towards this project. Bore and stroke are 68 × 71 mm, cubic capacity 516 cc, alleged bhp 4 at 1,500 rpm. It had two speed transmission with belt drive, and the weight is given as 210 kg.*

(photos: Turin Auto Museum)

285. *Ettore Bugatti's first car design, built in 1900 when he was* **19.**

DIETRICH-BUGATTI

286. *The chassis*

287. *The 4 cylinde 114 × 130 mn 24 hp engine.*

288. *With the brand new car, Ettore Bugatti arrived from Niederbronn at Vienna for the 1903 Motor Show. His passenger is J. Y. von Ritsch, the de Dietrich importer.*

289. *Bugatti and Mathis at Niederbronn, 1902. Bugatti reproduced this photograph, but with Mathis touched out, in a 1929 Works brochure, claiming to have built the car in 1901; it seems undoubtedly to be a version, perhaps the prototype, of the Dietrich-Bugatti car.*

290. *Bugatti's Paris-Madrid car of 1903, after the seating had been modified to give better visibility, having been refused permission to start in its original form.*

291. *The chassis of the Burlington-Bugatti.*

(*photo* : Autocar)

292. *A smart 4-seat body on the Dietrich-Bugatti.*

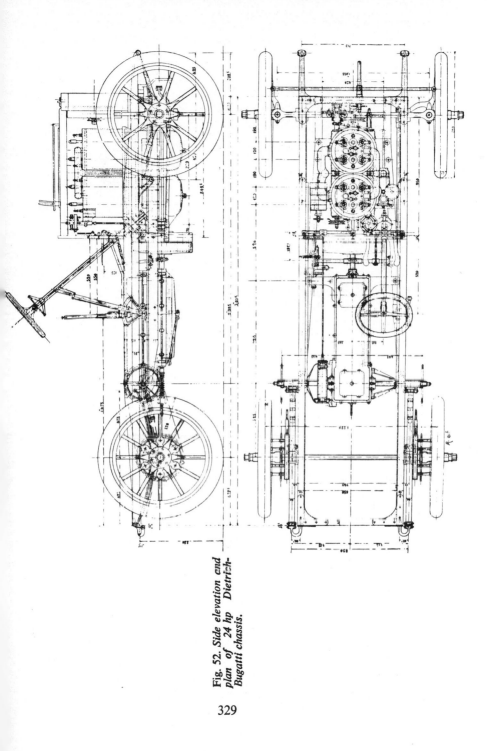

Fig. 52. Side elevation and plan of 24 hp Dietrich-Bugatti chassis.

329

race over 16 km Bugatti was again 2nd, this time to a 40 hp Mercedes. But the journal had this to say:

In the case of Race 7, in which a Mercedes Simplex of 40 hp was competing against a Panhard & Levassor and a de Dietrich of 16 hp and a de Dietrich of 20 hp, every spectator had the feeling that such a race was an absurdity, for here the victory was decided at the start. It must go to the Mercedes car of 40 hp, providing no accident occurred. But the result appears quite different, if the speeds of the four cars in this race are calculated; we then get the following:

	hp	km/h
Mercedes-Simplex car	40	68.48
de Dietrich-Bugatti car	20	63.83
Panhard & Levassor car	16	58.15
de Dietrich-Turcat-Méry car	16	55.16

and then the real winner is the new Dietrich-Bugatti car, with a 20 hp engine, which achieved almost the same performance as the Mercedes-Simplex with 40 hp!

Curiously enough, the spectators during the race had the right idea all along, and greeted Mr Bugatti, who proved himself to be a driver of the very first rank, every time he drove past the Grand Stand. Even the officials who were present left their places in order to get as close as possible to the bends, where one could see exactly in what masterly fashion Mr Bugatti took them every time.

This is the first reference found to Bugatti in a racing car, and indeed with a car bearing his name. He celebrated his twenty-first birthday two weeks after the races, on 15 September.

Car No. 5 *The Automotor Journal* quotes Bugatti as designing
1903 a 50 hp car for the 1903 Paris–Madrid race, and states that the frame was made from large diameter tubes, serving to carry cooling water. Bugatti himself stated that this car, as originally intended for the race, had the driver sitting over the rear axle (along the lines of the car shown in Plate 289); Pozzoli quotes Type 3 for this car. Bugatti was refused permission to race due to the lack of visibility for the driver. He drove it, however, in the 1903 Frankfurt races in August. Later he modified the chassis, the modified version being shown in Plate 290.

Car No. 6
1904   The Show number of the *Autocar*, 6 February 1904, records a 24 to 28 hp and a 30 to 35 hp 'de Dietrich (Burgatti)' (*sic*) with 4 cylinders, 4 speeds and chain drive, and handled by the Burlington Carriage Co. These were offered in addition to the de Dietrich (Turcat-Méry) cars. The *Autocar*, 27 February 1904 describes the 24 to 28 hp car under the title Burlington, and the illustrations (see Plates 291, 292) show that it is similar to Car No. 4, except that the latter has a proper radiator shell, while the Burlington had an exposed film-radiator. The smaller Burlington car had an engine 130 mm × 140 mm, with cylinders in pairs and again boxed in by twin copper water jackets, the 30 to 35 hp presumably being similar but larger in scale. Pozzoli allocates Types 4, 5 and 6 to these cars.

Car No. 7
1904–5   The de Dietrich arrangement ended and in 1904 and 1905 Bugatti designed the Hermes car for Emil Mathis at Strasbourg, the car being built close by at Graffenstaden. Mr L. T. Delaney arranged to import the car into Britain and raced one at Blackpool (*Autocar*, 5 August 1905) but did not manage to make any sales and turned elsewhere. Bugatti himself appears to have driven a Mathis (or Hermes) in the Herkomer Cup of August 1905. In the *Autocar*, 19 August 1905, there is a brief report of the Bleichroder Race which more or less occurred at the same time as the Herkomer Cup. Entries included Mr Mathis with a Fiat and 'Mr Bugatti with a Bugatti' – perhaps the first known reference to a Bugatti car in its own unqualified right. One of these cars still exists in the Montlhéry Motor Museum (Plate 293). Mr J. Rousseau writes regarding the model:

Several types of Hermes Mathis were built, differing mainly in engine capacity. They were listed as 40, 98 and a lighter 28 hp models. The last and the more common '40' were touring chassis, as the '98' was intended for racing purposes.
There was a great family similarity between the three models called either Mathis, or Hermes Simplex. All were fitted with an in-line, twin-block, 4 cylinder engine. The cylinder walls were heavily

331

jacketed with big water jackets. Overhead inlet valves were mechanically operated by push rods from a camshaft located in the sump and also actuating side exhaust valves. The camshaft drive pinion was made of fibre while the ignition was by means of a H.T. magneto.

Cooling was by pump, the carburettor was automatic, and spark adjustment was made by moving slightly the camshaft. The clutch was of usual Bugatti multi-plate type. The Mercedes-like gearbox was entirely ball bearing mounted. The car had three brakes: one on the gearbox shaft, one on the differential and one on the rear wheels. Needless to say, the car was chain-driven. The balance of the car was rather classical, but well proportioned.

Some details of the car can be culled from *La Vie Automobile*, 4 March 1905, pp. 136–7; there are illustrations of the chassis and engine, and a section drawing of the inlet valve operation by means of a pull rod. The chassis is also described and illustrated in the *Handbuch des Automobilbaues* by Thomas Lehmbeck, 1909; he quotes 50, 60 and 90 hp models. Pozzoli allocates Types 7 and 8 to these cars.

Car No. 8 In 1906 Bugatti parted with Mathis and became an
1906–7 independent consulting engineer. He designed at least two cars for the Deutz Company at Cologne; the first was a 4 cylinder, 50 to 60 hp, 150 mm × 150 mm (or 145 × 150 as Bradley has it), with overhead valves driven by curved tappets from an overhead camshaft; the construction was similar to the later Type 13 and Brescia design except that the curved tappets had rollers at their ends. The clutch was of the pure Bugatti multiplate toggle operated type and the car had a 4 speed gearbox and chain drive. The engine is illustrated in *The Motor*, 24 August 1955, but the whole chassis is well illustrated by Heller in the *Z.V.D.I.*, June 1908, page 919 *et seq*. (Fig. 53). Pozzoli uses Type 9 for the model but a contemporary reference book quotes Deutz Type 8.

Car No. 9 Although details are meagre, it appears that a
1908 racing car with engine dimensions and layout similar to car 10 was designed for Isotta Fraschini, and three cars were built for the 1908 Coupe des Voiturettes at Dieppe. *The Motor*, 28 July 1908, has an illustration of the car, showing

332

293. *The 1905 Bugatti-designed Mathis or Hermes car as it was known in Britain. The chassis number on the plate is 15. Chassis 30 still exists.*

BUGATTI'S MATHIS-HERMES

294. *Bugatti at the wheel of one of his cars at the Kaiserpreis at Taunus, June 13–14, 1907. In the first edition of this book the copy reproduced had 'Mathis' on the radiator and was a souvenir from E. Mathis to his friend Friderich, dated 10th October, 1948. This original copy from the Fiat library has the word Bugatti scraped off the radiator.* Left to right in the photograph: *Scarfiotti, President of Fiat, Friderich, E. B., P. Marchal, Felice Nazzaro, Vincenzo Lancia, Rembrandt Bugatti, Mathis, Louis Wagner, G. Agnelli.*

295. *Was it designed by Ettore Bugatti? No!*

THE ISOTTA-FRASCHINI LIGHT G.P. CAR

296. *The engine; undoubtedly similar to later Bugatti designs in general layout if not in detail.*

297a *The original 'pur-sang' Bugatti.*

THE ORIGINAL 'PUR-SANG' BUGATTI

297b. *The original engine, with overhead camshaft and exposed valves, operated by curved tappets.*

298. *Ettore Bugatti in the original Baby Peugeot which had reverse quarter-elliptic springs at the rear and an oval radiator. This is probably at the end of 1911.*

299. *A 1913 Baby Peugeot owned by C. W. P. Hampton. It still provides 35 mph and over 50 miles/gallon.*

300. *The second Deutz design with the unusual skew drive for the waterpump.*

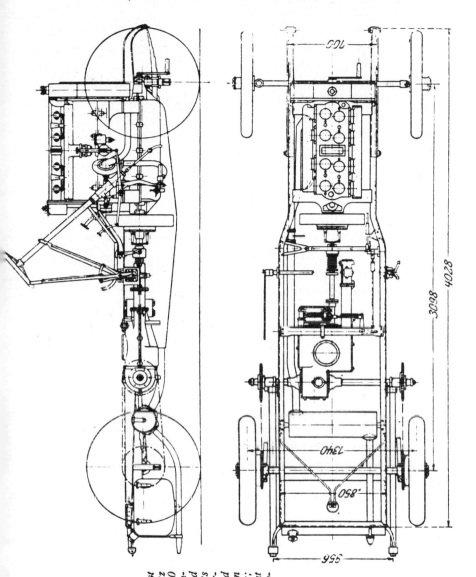

Fig. 53. The first Bugatti - Deutz chassis, 150 × 150 mm, 4 cylinder, chain-driven. This car had arc-shaped tappets between the over-head camshaft and the valves, as on the later 8 valve car; rollers were used at the ends of the tappets.

337

clearly its resemblance to the later car 10 (below), and refers to Isotta Fraschini of Milan being a subsidiary of Lorraine-de Dietrich of Lunéville; in this event Bugatti, who may conceivably have had something to do with the design, must have gone back to work for de Dietrich. From data communicated by the Turin Automobile Museum, it appears that in 1907 an agreement was reached between Isotta Fraschini and Lorraine-de Dietrich, to the effect that the former would design the engines (the designer being Cattaneo), while the French Company would take care of the chassis and sales.

The agreement ended in 1910–11. It is thus possible that Bugatti was mainly engaged on the chassis. One of these cars still exists in Australia, fully restored; illustrated in the *Autocar*, 25 February 1911 was another, then belonging to Colonel C. Dawson of Lowestoft, who is thought to have been the owner of the Hampton 1910 Type 13. This reference quotes the engine as 62 mm × 100 mm, with a bevel-driven overhead camshaft and the crankshaft carried on two ball bearings. The wheelbase was 6 ft 10 in. and the track 4 ft 1 in.

Mr Cattaneo has recently denied that Bugatti was concerned in any way; while it is possible that he had a finger in the Isotta-pie, as he was the last person not to seek credit where credit was due, the fact that he never mentioned Isotta Fraschini in any subsequent publicity that has come to light is significant. To the engineer, only the *layout* of the Isotta and the later 'petit pur-sang' engine is similar – the detail is quite different. The conclusion is inescapable. Ettore Bugatti must have seen the Isotta Fraschini cars and as a result was stimulated to abandon the monster cars he had been designing and try something smaller – and what a success his attempt was to be.

Car No. 10 The first *Pur-Sang* Bugatti was the prototype 1908–9   Type 13, 4 cylinder 8 valve, 62 mm × 100 mm car with half-elliptic springs at the rear, built in 1908–9 in the cellar of Bugatti's house at Cologne while he was acting as Works Manager for Deutz (Plate 297). Bugatti himself stated that he built the car in 1907; he probably began designing it then. It is sometimes claimed that this car ran at Gaillon 1908 but this is certainly not confirmed. Pozzoli and the Author agree on the allocation of Type 10 for this car! This car was in the possession of the Bugatti family up to the war, and has turned up again recently. It is stated to be marked Type 10, and has exposed, curved cam followers as on the Deutz design.

Car No. 11 This is the second Deutz design fully described and
1909   illustrated in the *Z.V.D.I.*, 11 June 1910 (Fig. 54).
This car dating from about 1909, was 13 to 25 hp, 4 cylinder, 95 mm × 120 mm, 3·2 litre, with 4 speed box, Bugatti clutch, propellor shaft and torque rod, normal rear axle and rear half-elliptic springs. This article does not show the engine in section, but the general layout is pure Bugatti – front cross-mounted magneto and water pump, front bevel drive to overhead camshaft, steering box mounted above engine bearer (as on Black Bess) and so on. Pozzoli quotes Type 11 but a contemporary reference gives Type 9C for a 110 × 130 mm shaft-drive model.

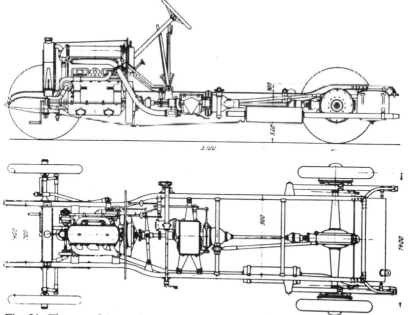

Fig. 54. *The second Deutz design; 3·2 litre, Bugatti toggle clutch, cross-mounted gearbox, normal rear axle replacing the chain drive.*

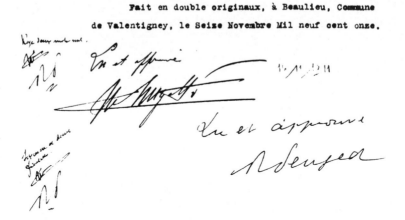

-bution de juridiction au cas de contestation .

Fait en double originaux, à Beaulieu, Commune
de Valentigney, le Seize Novembre Mil neuf cent onze.

Fig. 55. *Facsimile of the licence agreement between Bugatti and Robert Peugeot,
signed at Beaulieu on 16 November 1911.*

**Car No. 12
1910** Bugatti broke his ties with Deutz at the end of
1909 and in January 1910 he and Friderich opened
at Molsheim. Production began of the first series Type 13
similar to the prototype, with half-elliptic rear springs, and
evidently 65 mm × 100 mm, in place of 62 mm × 100 mm.

It would have been agreeable but not, unfortunately, neces-
sarily accurate to describe the thirteenth car as the real 8 valve
Type 13 which certainly was the car which established the
Bugatti reputation.

**Car No. 13
1911** Bugatti produced another design in 1911 which he
sold to Peugeot; this became the famous side
valve Baby-Peugeot and may have preceded the Bugatti
model (i.e. being Type 12). This had an engine 55 mm × 90 mm
(855 cc) with side valves; it had a cone clutch, two speeds
(although Bugatti's prototype had four or five speeds and
Peugeot eventually added a third), and reversed quarter elliptics
at the rear which tends to date it *after* the larger car. This car

340

301. *This used two 8 valve engines in series. For another version of this car see Plate 309, page 349.*

THE 8 CYLINDER CAR

302. *100 × 180 mm. This car had a normal rear axle. Friderich at the wheel.*

THE 1914 INDIANAPOLIS CAR

303. *Although this photograph of Bugatti by the 1909 car has been reproduced before, the original print has the flag pole rising across the front wheel touched out—but not the shadows! The inscription on the original is very interesting: 'En souvenir de la Prince Henri 1909 E. Mathis'. The car was a Deutz; Mathis drove a Fiat.*

THE 1909 PRINCE HENRI CUP CAR

304. *Bugatti at the start of the event.*

is described in *The Motor*, 8 October 1912, and also, with chassis drawings, in the *Autocar*, 11 November 1912 (Figs. 56 and 57).

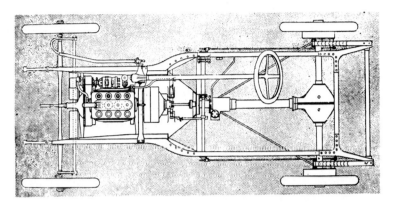

Fig. 56. *The Baby Peugeot of 1911 and the invention of the reversed quarter-elliptic springs, from then on standard Bugatti practice.*

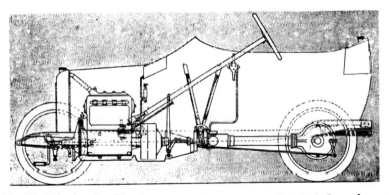

Fig. 57. *Side elevation. The clutch was of the leather cone type. Only 2 speeds were available there being two concentric propellor shafts continuously driving bevels, the selection of either ratio being by means of a sliding dog clutch at the forward end of the propellor shaft. Reverse was selected by engaging a separate gear train through the lever and remote control seen in the drawing.* (drawings: Autocar)

Car No. 14 In 1911 and 1912 Bugatti produced the chain-
1911–12   driven 5 litre 100 mm × 160 mm racing car, two of which are in existence (the famous Black Bess described on page 47). Pozzoli claims this is Type 16.

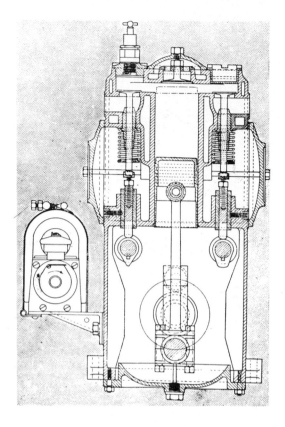

Fig. 58. *The Tee-head Baby Peugeot in section. Note the method of sealing the cylinder head.*

(*drawing:* Autocar)

Car No. 15 This was a special racing car with two Type 13
? 1913   engines in tandem. It was fast, but not very successful in racing, but was the first 8 cylinder Bugatti (see page 75). Two versions appear to have been produced. This model could not be Type 15 which is known to be a long wheelbase T.13; Pozzoli allocates Type 14 to it.

Car No. 16 An anonymous correspondent from Molsheim in
? 1912   the *Autocar*, 5 November 1937, in answer to a query about a mysterious 1,500 cc, 4 cylinder side valve car with three speeds and a cone clutch, states that six such cars were built by Bugatti in 1911. A copy of the original licence agreement between Bugatti and Robert Peugeot has been examined and it is

clear that Bugatti contracted to build a larger car for Peugeot, in addition to the smaller vehicle. It seems more than likely therefore that he did produce (in 1912) a 1,500 cc car resembling the 855 cc car in its side valves and cone clutch. An unusual Peugeot car conforming to the description and with certain Bugatti-like features has recently turned up in Germany and may be one of the cars referred to.

Car No. 17 A special version of the larger racing car was pre-
1914   pared with a lengthened stroke, 100 mm × 180 mm, for the 1914 Indianapolis race; Friderich drove it until a rear axle failure occurred. This car had a conventional rear axle in place of the chain drive of the 5 litre car (Plate 302).

This appears to complete the list of pre-war Bugatti designs as far as they are known to the present author. The car shown in Plates 303, 304, the 1909 Prince Henri Cup car, is given in the 1929 Works brochure as a Bugatti, but it was a Deutz car; Pozzoli claims it was a Type 11. It is probably the same car that Bugatti illustrated in a 1910–11 catalogue with the first of his pear-shaped radiators.

The 16 valve Type 22 and 23 cars which became well known in the early 1920s were first produced just before the 1914–18 war. If it were not for this we might use a little licence to indulge in a numerical fancy of allotting the missing serial numbers. But we soon run into difficulties in conjecturing and it would be wiser not to! Mr Pozzoli has been less timid.

BIBLIOGRAPHY

BONNEVILLE, L. *Le Moteur Roi* (*Origines de l'Automobile*), Paris, 1949
BUGATTI, E. Portfolio of Bugatti designs, issued about 1929 by the factory
BRADLEY, W. F., *Ettore Bugatti*, Motor Racing Publications, London, 1948
GRÉGOIRE, J. A., *L'Aventure Automobile*, Flammarion, Paris, 1953
POZZOLI, S., *L'Auto Journal*, May 4 1961
HELLER, A. *Zeitschrift des Vereines Deutscher Ingenieure*, 52, 23, 6 June 1908
    pp. 919–925, and 54, 24, 11, June 1910, pp. 971–974
The Horseless Age, 14, 24 June 1908, p. 739 etc.
La Gazetta dello Sport, Milan
Die Motorwagen und Fahrzeugmaschinen, Berlin, 1912
Early issues of various motor journals:
    English: *Autocar, The Motor, Automotor Journal*
    German: *Der Motorwagen, Allgemeine Automobile-Zeitung*
    French: *Omnia, La Vie Automobile*

How the Firm of Bugatti was born *

MY DÉBUT WITH MONSIEUR BUGATTI BEGAN IMMEDIATELY AFTER THE famous Paris–Madrid race, which, as all keen followers of early motor racing know, was stopped by the authorities at Bordeaux owing to the fact that it had already caused a large number of fatal accidents.

I set up in 1904 in Strasbourg as a mechanic with Monsieur Mathis, who at that time was carrying on an export and import business under the name of E. E. C. Mathis. Monsieur Mathis was, moreover, the agent for the de Dietrich cars of Lunéville and Niederbronn, and also Fiat of Turin. My work consisted of tuning cars which we received from these various firms and delivering them to customers. Our garage comprised a shed capable of holding 6 cars, while alongside it was a stable for horses belonging to M. Hyllé, of 54 Faubourg de Pierre, Strasbourg. Later on, when the building of cars by Dietrich at Niederbronn was stopped, Monsieur Bugatti entered into partnership with Monsieur Emile Mathis for the construction of an entirely new car.

The Chief took up his quarters in the attics of the Hotel de Paris, rue de la Nuée Bleue, which was converted into a drawing office; the building itself belonging to Monsieur Mathis senior.

The car was built at Illkirch Graffenstaden, and was given the name of Hermes. In order to reach the Works, which were 5 miles from Strasbourg, I went by tramcar and Monsieur Bugatti on horseback. Subsequently, when I became fully employed by Monsieur Bugatti, I built 25 chassis which were stored out in the yard. The American General, Costry Butt, bought one of them, and I drove him to the great German manœuvres and also to the great French manœuvres.

It was also in one of these cars that, in 1905 [1907?], I took part as mechanic to the Chief, who was the driver, in the Kaiserpreis at Homburg, and later in the Prince Henri Cup. Following these trials, Bugatti and Mathis parted company, and at Monsieur Bugatti's request I went with him in a new venture. We took up our quarters 1 km from Graffenstaden in a shed in the centre of a large garden,

---

* This article was written by the late E. Friderich in 1949 for the Bugatti Owners' Club and published in *Bugantics* 12, 2 and 3.

HOW THE FIRM OF BUGATTI WAS BORN

305/306. *These 1911–12 photographs show Bugatti's first workshop at Molsheim.* *The chassis on the right* (top) *seems to be a Deutz, the remainder 8-valve.*

307. *Friderich at the start of the Grand Prix. The car is an 8 valve Type 13. Note the bolster tank and wire wheels instead of the more usual wooden ones.*

FRENCH GRAND PRIX, 1911

308. *In the 'petite cylindrée' class, Friderich was winner.*

309. *Single-seater Bugatti of 1913. This 8 cylinder, 2·8 litre car comprises two T.13 engines, one behind the other. Note the two separate bonnets and early attempt at reducing wind resistance. At least one other car of this type was produced (see page 344).*

310. *The start of the Le Mans Grand Prix in 1920—a far cry from today's event.*

311. *The 1920 Bugatti équipe at Le Mans, with a very happy Ettore behind the centre car, No. 12, driven by Baccoli. Friderich, the winner, is in No. 23 (right) and de Vizcaya is in No. 1.*

THE BUGATTI TEAM AFTER THE KAISER WAR

312. *From left to right: top row, de Casa Maury, Friderich, de Vizcaya; bottom row, Baccoli and Marco.*

backed by the Darmstadt Bank, who advanced the money which enabled the Chief to purchase the necessary machines for building a new car. The shed and workshop adjoined the drawing office in which three draughtsmen started getting out the rough drawings to the Chief's instructions. There were also three of us in the workshop, one turner, one fitter and myself. This was in 1906 and 1907.

In July of the last mentioned year the car was completed and the tests proved very satisfactory. After a few trips to Cologne Deutz, to the Deutz Gas Engine Works, the latter firm acquired a manufacturing licence. Monsieur Bugatti became the Manager of the car-building department and lived in a Villa inside the Works. This was at the end of August, and the beginning of September 1907, and my last job was to dismantle the car, part by part, and deliver the latter to the drawing office. I then joined my regiment at Lunéville in October 1907, and spent two years with the Horse Artillery. On completion of my service I found the Chief just as I had left him, although his family had been increased by a new baby. In the interval, Monsieur le Patron had built the first Pur-Sang Bugatti in the cellar of his villa.

There I met Monsieur Blériot (the famous aviator) who had been invited by the Chief. He came every day to the aviation meeting at Cologne on board the famous Pur-Sang. I in turn made a trip to Eastern Prussia and Russia in one of the cars produced by the Works, accompanied by the General Manager of the Gas Engine Works. On my return the Chief told me that he had resigned his position with this firm and that he intended returning to Alsace; I followed him, and in December 1909 we left Strasbourg in the small Bugatti car, which was known as the 'bath' because of its peculiar carosserie. We stopped at the Bank of Darmstadt where an appointment had been made with Monsieur de Vizcaya, senior. The latter took us to inspect, at Molsheim, an old dyeing works which had ceased to function. It was in that old factory which was rented from the Fraulcins Gcisscr for 5,000 marks per annum, that we installed our new plant.

This occurred at Christmas 1909. The Chief had gone to Paris and Cologne, and I was left alone at the future Bugatti Works with the job of whitewashing the walls and having a general clear-up. About 25 January 1910, the first machine tools arrived, and continued arriving at the rate of two to three per week. It was also my job to find a nucleus of workers, turners, millers, fitters, smiths etc. The equipping of the Factory was completed and the draughtsmen who had been with us at Deutz also rejoined us. In 1910 five cars were produced and delivered to customers, and it was in that year, that is to say, 39 years ago, that I started racing, although of course on a small scale.

351

Thence forward my job was the finishing, final adjustment and testing of the chassis. At the beginning of 1911 the Works were already rapidly increasing in size. We employed 65 workers, and the Chief, always on the alert, had installed himself in a completely separate workshop with three workers and myself. There we assembled a new 7 hp car which I subsequently presented to the Wander Works at Chemnitz in Saxony, and Peugeot at Beaulieu, in the department of the Doubs. The latter firm having acquired the licence, I left for Aix-les-Bains to show the car to Monsieur Gudorge, the General Manager at Peugeot. I left it with him and returned to Molsheim by rail; it was essential to lose as little time as possible as production could not be allowed to suffer as the result of this considerable travelling. Production gradually increased and amounted to three chassis in February 1911, and then to four chassis in each of March and April; May and June six chassis each month, whilst for the third quarter our production had risen to eight chassis per month, and I remember that in December the Chief wanted nine chassis in order to obtain a total of seventy-five for the year 1911. By good will, hard work and perseverance we succeeded.

In the meantime, Monsieur le Patron, always on the look out for new and better ideas, had secretly designed a new car, totally different from the preceding cars, since this time it concerned a large car of 5 litre capacity, with a 100 mm bore and 160 mm stroke. Manufacture was pushed forward, and the car saw the light of day at the beginning of 1912; it was with one of these cars that Monsieur Hyllé, a great friend of the Chief, took part in the Herkomer Fahr (a race reserved to car owners) and I was his mechanic. This road race through Germany and Alsace passed through Molsheim where, at the gates of Monsieur Bugatti's estate, a buffet was installed by Madame Bugatti for the competitors, and it was a great joy to us to be able to pull up there. We enjoyed an excellent glass of champagne and splendid sandwiches. At the end of the race we were declared the winner on points. That was one more victory and it was only the start.

But let us go back to 1911, when, at the suggestion of Monsieur Huet, the Bugatti agent in Paris, I took part in the Grand Prix at Le Mans, for Class 1·4 litre cars. My car was, of course, the 65 mm bore and 100 mm stroke eight valve model of 1,327 cc. Engaged in both classes, large and small, I won the small car race and obtained the 2nd place in the general classification. Hémery in a 6 litre Fiat, gained the 1st place. During the year we constructed a test car with a view to reducing the forward wind resistance. This car was equipped with two of the normal 1·4 litre engines coupled in tandem by means of a

352

rubberized leather flywheel. Proud, and overcome with emotion, I was the happy driver. This car reached a speed of 86 miles per hour, whereas the car used in the Grand Prix at Le Mans did not exceed 66 mph. With the same 2 engined car, I took part in the hill-climb at Gaillon in October 1912 in which I failed to complete the course, the third gear change having broken in the middle of the hill. At the Whitsun Meeting at Le Sarthe, both Monsieur Bugatti and I were engaged, Monsieur Bugatti in the 100 × 160 model, whilst I was driving a 1·4 litre. We won the three races which were held at Sillé le Guillaume, Flèche and Laval in that order.

[At the Gaillon event, however, a 65 × 100 Bugatti won its class (under 1·4 litre, racing) in 53⅔ sec. Erle on a 200 hp Benz of 200 × 250 made Fastest Time with 22 sec. Another Bugatti driven by Tonello won the under 1·4 litre Touring class in 58 sec, the fastest Touring-class competitor being an Hispano-Suiza of 80 × 180, in 43 sec. This course was on the Grand Route from Paris to Dieppe, between Vernon and Rouen. At the Mont Ventoux Hill-Climb (also in 1912) Monsieur le Patron drove one of the new 100 × 160 5 litre chain drive cars and made 4th Fastest Time of Day in 19 min 16⅔ sec for this 13¼ mile course. Fastest Time, and a new record in 17 min 46 sec, was made by Boillot on a Grand Prix Peugeot, an average of 45 mph for the ascent. Friderich drove a 65 × 100 Bugatti and climbed in 27 min 14 sec. At the same event the previous year, the small Bugatti won its class on formula. – C. W. P. Hampton.]

In 1913 the works acquired even greater importance, and Monsieur Bugatti engaged a Works Manager named Wolfram, a very capable man. Production was increasing; orders were flowing in. It was essential to keep customers satisfied as well as the Office of Monsieur Pracht, Monsieur le Patron's representative, who often came to worry me to get chassis completed and delivered, because at that time we were not building bodies.

The name of Bugatti was becoming known, but not so much as we desired. To enhance our reputation, therefore, I took part in numerous races: on the Côte du Val-Suzon, Limonest to Lyons, Ventoux to Avignon, Nancy, La Baraque, Toul etc., in which I invariably gained the first place. All this travelling had to be undertaken between Saturday and Monday morning, as I had to be present at the Works during the normal working hours of the week, where the task of carrying out trials and the final adjustment of chassis absorbed the whole of my time, often till very late in the evening. The monthly output at the beginning of 1913 was 12 chassis. It increased monthly, until, in December, 19 chassis were turned out, that is to say 175 for the year.

At the beginning of 1914, our work was increasing, and the rate of output reached 27 chassis in March, to say nothing of the preparations of a 100 × 180 racing car which I was to drive in the Grand Prix at Indianapolis (500 miles), on 30 May 1914, in which I was 3rd place after covering 425 miles. I had every hope of success, but a misfortune put me out of the race, the ball bearings on the driving pinion having broken.

[The race was won at 82·47 mph by Thomas on a Delage of 6,165 cc. Duray on a Peugeot, Guyot on a Delage and Goux on a Peugeot finished next in order. During practice, Boillot on a Peugeot did a lap at 99·9 mph. – C. W. P. Hampton.]

I returned to Molsheim without glory, and resumed my work and the testing of cars until, a month later, on about 15 July, rumours of war began to circulate. During the French mobilization in August, I left Molsheim and regained France via Switzerland, and was mobilized with the 8th Artillery at Lunéville. Monsieur Bugatti and his family also left Molsheim on the same day, or the next day, by rail, Madame Friderich having met them at the station. A few days later Monsieur Bugatti returned to Molsheim and left again with two racing cars by road in the different direction of Italy! Three similar cars were left at Molsheim where the camshafts were buried, which we recovered at the end of the war, in January 1919, and raced and won at Le Mans in 1920. These cars were the Type 13, twin-ignition model with 65·6 mm bore, 100 mm stroke, giving a swept piston volume of 1·4 litre, the formula for the light cars for the Coupe de L'Auto which would have taken place had it not been for the war. One fact worthy of mention is that the cars which were taken to Milan by the Chief sustained damage. Hidden in a cave, they were flooded out and were subsequently brought to Paris in 1915.

Monsieur Bugatti left Italy, and went to Paris, where he and his family spent the whole of the war years, to design and supervise the making of aeroengines. I took part in the fighting at Grand Couronné, Nancy, followed by the fighting towards the sea to the north of Arras, and was awarded the Croix de Guerre on 9 May 1915. In September I was recalled behind the front and sent to work with Monsieur le Patron at Puteaux, on the building of an aircraft engine with 8 cylinders in line, and subsequently in designing a 16 cylinder engine with two rows of 8 cylinders. This engine developed 524 hp. The 50 hour bench tests were successful and, a licence having been granted to the French, American and Italian Governments, I left for the United States in charge of the manufacture of the engine. A works was built at Elizabeth in New Jersey, which was to be managed by the Duesenberg brothers.

The end of the war came and I returned to France about 20 December 1918. I rejoined the Chief in Paris, and from there we went to Molsheim where the Works was at a standstill, and the workers were not very reliable. Accordingly, the Chief decided to dismiss the whole of the staff and to start again with reliable workers. Manufacture

354

and research were resumed, and the chassis were turned out at a rate of 10 in March 1919, the building of light racing cars of 1·4 litre, 16 valves being carried on, side by side with the normal production, with a view to winning the light car Cup at Le Mans in August 1920, which I won with car No. 23. I also won several other races of lesser importance. During the same period our great Chief, Monsieur Bugatti, untiringly continued his efforts to improve our famous car. He decided to mount the crankshaft in ball bearings. It was after a few successful innovations of the same kind that I won the Grand Prix at Brescia, Italy, in 1921; this, therefore, was the reason for the name the 'Brescia' type.

[At Le Mans, Friderich averaged 57·6 mph for 256·5 miles, the best lap being covered in 9 min 43 sec, an average of over 66 mph. At the end of the first lap, the three Bugattis of de Vizcaya, Friderich and Baccoli were respectively 1st, 2nd and 4th. At half distance Baccoli led the race with de Vizcaya and Friderich next in order, and with only four laps to go, de Vizcaya, lying 2nd, called at his pit for oil, and as he was moving off again Monsieur Bugatti, suspecting over-heating, started unscrewing the radiator cap. This caused de Vizcaya's instant disqualification, and was a most unpopular decision on the part of the stewards, especially since, according to the rules, Monsieur Bugatti should have been given the opportunity of taking over the car henceforth. He was given no such oppor-tunity, and accepted this harsh blow without comment.* Baccoli thus moved up to 2nd place, but was slowed by plug trouble just before the end, and finished 5th. Friderich, too, nearly came to grief due to a stone penetrating several tubes in his radiator. The winning car was subsequently purchased by Major H. O. D. Segrave and brought to England. These cars developed 29·5 hp at 2,750 rpm, weighed less than 13 cwt, had a wheelbase of 6 ft 5 in., single Zenith carburettor, 3·25 to 1 top gear ratio and 710 × 90 tyres, and 4 sparking plugs each side of the cylinder block with a single double spark magneto mounted forward by the radiator (see the *Autocar*, 26 February 1921, pp. 365–8). Their performance and roadholding were outstanding, the *Autocar* race report commenting '. . . they held the road in a most remarkable manner, and seemed to be giving their drivers no trouble whatsoever . . . in the matter of holding the road the Bugattis were equal in every respect to the best ever built by Peugeot, Delage or Ballot'.

The cars which swept the board at Brescia in September 1921 had an increased bore of 68 mm, giving a capacity of 1,453 cc, roller bearing big ends, 3 to 1 top gear ratio and 710 × 90 tyres, a weight of 1,088 lb, and developed maxi-mum power at 3,350 rpm. The eight sparking plugs were now coupled to two Bosch magnetos mounted on the dash and driven from the rear end of the over-head camshaft. The race was over 20 laps, each of 10⅜ miles, and Friderich's winning time was 2 h 59 min 17 sec, an average of 72 mph. This time established a record for the fastest-ever light car race in the world. De Vizcaya led on the first lap, and at half-distance he had again retaken the lead from Friderich, who had burst a tyre, with Marco 3rd and Baccoli 5th. Gradually the Bugattis wore down all Italian opposition, and finished with Friderich, de Vizcaya, Baccoli and Marco filling the first four places, and only 78 seconds between 1st and 2nd. Minoia, who drove for Bugatti in later years, drove an O.M., the first Italian car to finish, and 14 min behind the winner. – C. W. P. Hampton.]

The year 1922 saw the construction of this marvellous type accent-uated; but a new car was laid down, a 2 litre Type 30, one short

---

* This popular story is in fact incorrect; see page 358.

chassis and one long. Three racing cars were also built for the Grand Prix at Monza, but only one car, driven by Pierre de Vizcaya, took part in the race, as the Works lacked the tyres for the other two cars. In 1923, short wheelbase, tank-type racing cars with the straight eight 2 litre engine, were built for the Grand Prix of the A.C.F. at Tours, in which I finished 3rd behind Segrave and Divo.

The building of the so-called Grand Prix cars with aluminium wheels was undertaken in 1924, and they were delivered to customers who desired to take part in racing. During the same year, 1924, I went to Nice to establish the Bugatti agency for the Côte d'Azur, whilst the Chief asked me to take part in the Grand Prix of the A.C.F. at Lyons, together with Costantini, Vizcaya and Marco. Unfortunately, we had continuous tyre trouble through which we lost the race.

Subsequently, I took part in numerous competitions in the Côte d'Azur district on my own account and there were many victories, always with Bugatti. For that purpose, I opened a school for racing drivers: Dreyfus, Czaykowski, Chiron, Wimille, Toselli and many others who have long since gained their spurs after having written their name on the annals of victory, always with Bugatti. Now I am entitled to retire, but I still keep a jealous eye on the overhauls and final adjustments of all these marvellous Bugatti cars with which I am happy to associate my name, side by side with that of our great designer and master, Ettore Bugatti.

Racing activity from 1920

BEFORE QUOTING FROM AUTHORITATIVE REFERENCES TO THE brilliant racing period beginning in 1920, the facts on the disqualification of de Vizcaya in the 1920 Le Mans race, as mentioned earlier, should be given. This story resulted from a casual conversation with E. Mischall in 1959, who volunteered the first hand information given below; the story was subsequently confirmed by Madame Friderich. The truth of this incident, so often retold by Bradley and others, had been a well-kept Molsheim secret! The story lends interesting colour to the subsequent development of roller bearing crankshafts – it seems certain that these were introduced by Bugatti to cure bearing trouble which other engine designers avoided by proper pressure lubricated bearing design.

Mischall's story originally appeared in *Bugantics* 1958, 21, 4, and is worth reproducing in full.

FLASH BACK – LE MANS 1920

The story of the 1920 Le Mans race, won by a 1·4 litre Bugatti, has been told before, but not perhaps by one of the mechanics in the Bugatti team. The truth behind the famous incident when Ettore Bugatti 'inadvertently' caused the disqualification of the leading car may be of interest; I know the facts because I was the mechanic to de Vizcaya in that car.

I joined the Bugatti works as an apprentice at the age of 14 in 1917. I saw the return of the Patron, the resurrection of a number of chassis and parts, hidden from the Germans, and eventually was lucky enough to be chosen as one of the mechanics for the Coupe Internationale des Voiturettes to be run on 29 August 1920. The race was for cars of up to 1,400 cc, 500 kilos weight and over a distance of 410 kilometres. Our drivers were Pierre de Vizcaya with me as

357

mechanic, Ernest Friderich with Etien, and Baccoli with another lad Lutz.

The cars were of course 16 valve models with plain bearings on the crankshaft: the bore and stroke were 66 × 100 (1,368 cc), and the engines had a single magneto. I have in front of me as I write a copy of *L'Auto* dated Monday 30 August 1920 with an account of the race by Mr Charles Faroux. This article quotes the winning car (Friderich) as having two plugs per cylinder, and my car as having one only: as far as I can recall this is correct.

During practice de Vizcaya and I had trouble on our car with overheating of the rear main bearing, and it was decided to remove the engine to examine all bearings. I had done this and was about to replace the connecting rod bearings and sump, when I was told by a certain senior member of the team to do another job and that he would finish off my engine job. Now thereby hangs a tale, as you will presently see.

De Vizcaya had been ordered to drive in a particular way but he and I had discussed this and he had decided to go out to win. We believed, however, that we had been overheard in this conversation by him who had decided to finish off the assembly of my engine.

We started and led the race almost to the end; according to the account in *L'Auto* and often repeated since that day what happened was the following (translated):

Great dismay was caused at the elimination of de Vizcaya, who had driven a remarkably successful race. Three laps from the end, de Vizcaya stopped 100 metres beyond the pits. Bugatti himself ran forward, and with understandable emotion, unscrewed the radiator cap to see if the car needed water. But the regulations had been broken: the car must be disqualified.

But this is not what really happened! We had had bearing trouble again and a connecting rod had broken! We stopped beyond the pits and opened the bonnet for Bugatti who had arrived on the scene. One glance was enough – and at a quick sign from him we closed the bonnet, while he walked round to the front of the car and started to unscrew the radiator cap. No wonder he was reported to have accepted disqualification without comment!

But when the engine was removed later to inspect the damage I found that one big end had become unbolted. I could find no trace of split pins. Did my helpful colleague of the night before forget them?

My Bugatti days were happy ones, however. A year or two later I was sent to London with Mr Marco to open the Bugatti station in Brixton Road, and Friderich went off to Nice. I remained at Brixton Road with Colonel Sorel until 1940.

13. *De Vizcaya and Mischall at scrutineering at Le Mans, 1920.*

14. *Baccoli at the pits during the Voiturette Grand Prix on the south circuit, Le Mans, 1920. Ettore, ?een standing on the right, 'unwittingly' caused Vizcaya's disqualification at a pit stop by unscrewing ?e radiator cap.*

315. *The team of four 16 valve, 1,453 cc Bugattis swept the board at Brescia, finishing 1st, 2nd, 3rd, 4th, and establishing a record for the fastest-ever Voiturette race average. Friderich was the winner, in 2 hr 59 min 18 sec, an average of 72 mph. It was after this great victory that the model was named the 'Brescia' Bugatti.*

BRESCIA, 1921

316. *This photograph, dated 8 September 1921. has been signed by Pierre Marco, who finished 4th at Brescia.*

317. *Friderich in the 1922 Strasbourg G.P. 8 cylinder unblown Type 30. P. de Vizcaya finished 2nd (at 69·2 mph) and Marco 3rd with similar cars. De Vizcaya also finished 3rd in the Italian Grand Prix at Monza the same year.*

318. *The 2 litre Bugatti team at the Grand Prix de l'A.C.F. at Tours, 1923. Left to right: de Vizcaya, Friderich, Prince Cystria, Marco.*

319. *Prince Cystria in No. 18, Marco in No. 16 and de Vizcaya at Tours. The fourth car was driven into 3rd place by Friderich.*

320. *Marco in No 16.*

321. *A view of the pits i* *the 1924 race. Even th* *large number of wheels wa* *insufficient to avoid th* *tyre disasters.*
(*photo: Autocar*)

BUGATTI RACING HISTORY 1922–24

by C. W. P. Hampton

[The article by the late M. Ernest Friderich on page 346, dealt in detail with the early successes of the marque, and only touched briefly on the first straight eight racing cars. The following is therefore an attempt to complete the story up to the time of the introduction of the 1924 G.P. cars.]

The French Grand Prix at Strasbourg in July 1922, over 60 laps of 8·3 miles, was won by the famous Felice Nazarro, driving a 65 mm × 100 mm 6 cylinder Fiat, at an average of 79·2 mph for the 499 miles. Four of the brand new, hastily prepared and untested 2 litre, Type 30 Bugattis were entered, fitted with a bulbous front end and pointed tail containing the large exhaust outlet. At the end of lap one, Friderich's Bugatti was barely a length behind the leader, Nazarro, and took the lead on the third lap with Segrave 4th on the Sunbeam. But this success was short-lived, as both his Bosch magnetos packed up, a trouble which afflicted all the team cars in this race, causing incessant misfiring. Another weakness was the inefficient four wheel brakes. However, Pierre de Vizcaya finished 2nd, a long way behind Nazarro, at 69·2 mph, with Marco 3rd at 63·8 mph. The only other survivor in the race was Mones Maury, on the third Bugatti, who had three laps to do at the end of the race. The *Autocar* reported that 'Ettore sat cross-legged on his pit counter and smiled broadly to encourage each driver, never turning a hair or showing any trace of emotion, whether success or disaster was his portion'!

The Italian Grand Prix, two months later, was held on the 'new' race track at Monza, near Milan, and was won by Pietro Bordino, Fiat, at 86·89 mph for the 497 miles. Felice Nazarro on the Strasbourg-winning Fiat was 2nd, and P. de Vizcaya 3rd on the Bugatti which ran this time without its streamlined bulbous front end. Vizcaya was lying 2nd at the end of the first lap, but the gear ratio was unsuitable and caused a loss of 1,000 rpm. Plug trouble also slowed the car towards the close.

At Indianapolis, on 30 May 1923, much slimmer Type 30 Bugattis were driven by Count Zborowski, Pierre de Vizcaya, Prince de Cystria, Alzaga and Riganti. The two last mentioned retired early with broken conrods and badly leaking petrol tank respectively. The cars were reported as being much slower than the American cars and the Mercedes, but very good on the turns and possessing marked acceleration. Count Zborowski and de Vizcaya drove wheel-to-wheel in line-ahead formation and impressed everyone by their masterly driving. This partnership ended when the former broke a conrod.

363

Vizcaya was 6th at half-distance, and 5th at 450 miles when he, too, suffered a broken rod. Prince de Cystria ran right through without relief and finished 9th. The winner's average speed was 91·44 mph.

Subsequently, George Duller, driving one of the single-seater Indianapolis Bugattis, broke several class B records at Brooklands including one mile standing start at 75·86 mph, one mile flying start at 105·55 mph, and 10 miles at 104·89 mph. Fair enough for a Type 30!

The 1923 French Grand Prix was held at Tours, and the Bugatti team cars were the 6 ft 6 in. wheel base tank-bodied 2 litres of 60 mm × 88 mm, with hydraulic front brakes, a track of 3 ft 4 in. and overall height of only 2 ft 7 in. Their appearance created a sensation, as did the rather similarly bodied Voisins. These Bugattis, which weighed between 1,678 and 1,737 lb, had special chassis, underslung at the rear (very unusual for Bugatti), very short steering column, close-up engine and cock-pit and centre gear change – also unusual at that early date. In the race itself, which was won by Segrave at 75·3 mph in a 67 mm × 94 mm 6 cylinder Sunbeam with Albert Divo 2nd, at 71·8 mph on a similar car, Friderich's Bug. ran extremely well to finish 3rd at 70·8 mph, and thus separate the Sunbeam team, as K. Lee Guinness's Sunbeam was 4th at 70·5 mph. The Sunbeams could pull out about 115 mph maximum, the Bugattis 117 and the new 8 cylinder and sensationally supercharged Fiats were faster still, the champion Bordino being timed at 122·3 mph, and creating a lap record at an average of 87 mph. Bordino led the race for eight laps before a stone punctured his crankcase; the Fiats were, in fact, hot favourites for the race but suffered misfortune. P. de Vizcaya had a tremendous crash in his Bugatti at the La Membrolle hairpin on the first lap while following in the dust cloud set up by the cluster of cars just ahead of him.

In this day and age of streamlined, dishcover Cisitalias, Maseratis, Ferraris, Coopers and the like, it is interesting to record a motor press comment of this 1923 Grand Prix, remembering that we are often told that the racing cars of today are the sports cars of to-morrow. Quote: 'one particularly pleasing feature of the British success is the fact that the three cars representing this country, which finished 1st, 2nd and 4th, more nearly approximate in general layout to a touring car than any of the remaining contestants, some of which had weird bodies almost enveloping the chassis and wheels, to reduce wind resistance. A touring car developed on the lines of the victorious Sunbeam is a distinct probability of the future.' Apart from the fact that Bugatti, as a concern, outlived Sunbeam and that its subsequent touring cars more nearly approximated its racing cars than did the latter, this is another clear example of how far in advance of current design was Ettore Bugatti. Though he subsequently shelved the streamline form for thirteen years, he produced it again in basically similar outline in 1936, and again caused a sensation by sweeping the board in the 1936 French G.P. From then on, the classic 'Le Mans' styling was outmoded and all, repeat all, the latest English, Italian, German etc., sports car streamlining owes its origin entirely to the 1923 Bugs. in the first instance and, more particularly to the 1936 3·3 litre cars, which really set in motion this present-day fashion.

If the 1923 Bugattis caused a stir, the factory's cars for the 1924 French Grand Prix at Lyon created a much bigger commotion. They were entirely new, and were really designed for the job in hand. Monsieur le Patron was in earnest this time, and produced the most lovely little racers that were to be the hall mark of racing cars for the next decade, cars on which in one form or another, nearly every driver in Europe was at sometime to learn the game or earn fame and fortune. They were, of course, the Type 35 8 cylinder, unblown model with full roller bearing crankshaft, and still built to the 2 litre formula, and had the new aluminium alloy wheels. Quote: 'The most uncommon feature of the Bugatti cars is the wheels, which are aluminium and composed of a special alloy, which is a secret of the Bugatti factory. Brake drums are cast in one piece with the wheels [in fact, pressed in], which are nearly 7 lb lighter than a wire wheel of similar dimensions, but quite as strong. A great deal of this weight reduction has been obtained in the rims, the peculiar form of which enables them to grip the tyre in such a way that the cover may be said to become practically solid with the rim.' In the race, using specially made tyres, the Bugatti team had endless tyre trouble, lap after lap the five cars tearing up their covers and ruining any chance of success. But not once did the covers leave the rim, and the new wheels stood up manfully and confounded all critics. The cars were probably faster than their rivals (most of which were using superchargers for the first time) and possessed remarkable acceleration. The Sunbeam team, headed again by Segrave, had twin-camshaft 6 cylinder super-charged cars, the Fiats and Alfa Romeos used 8 cylinder engines, and were also supercharged, and Campari was the winner on an Alfa Romeo, with 12 cylinder twin camshaft, unblown Delages 2nd and 3rd. In view of their tyre trouble, the little unblown Bugs. did remarkably well to gain 7th and 8th places, driven respectively by Jean Chassagne and Friderich. But it was a big disappointment to the Bugatti équipe, who had to wait till 1925 before success with the new cars came their way. And then it came and multiplied exceed-ingly – but that is another story.

365

THE GRAND PRIX OF EUROPE AND OF THE A.C.F.—LYON CIRCUIT 1924
ETTORE BUGATTI'S OWN STORY

(A translation of a circular letter issued by Bugatti to his agents and customers after the race)

Dear Sir,

Very disturbed by the results of the European Grand Prix I had decided not to dwell on my defeat and not to draw the attention of my customers to the vicissitudes of this race.

Being daily consoled by people both friends and clients and wishing to do justice to those persons who have shown their loyalty by letter or article or who have made other personal gestures, I am obliged to explain as exactly as possible the circumstances of the event in order to demonstrate that the confidence which has been shown might easily have been justified.

First of all I would like to draw the attention of my friends and customers to a few extracts from testimonials which have been lavished on me:

M. Delage, the famous constructor, after himself driving the G.P. Bugatti sent me the following message on a visiting card:

'You have given me a great deal of pleasure in allowing me to try out your racing car and you ask my opinion. It is, with all the brilliant qualities of a racing car, the most perfect touring car that the amateur could dream of.

'I am happy to tell you this voluntarily. Cordially, Louis Delage.'

Mr Rapson, the celebrated English maker of racing car tyres, has written in an article published in the Autocar, *1 August 1924.*

'I supplied tyres only to the Sunbeams and the Miller of Count Zborowski, although I was warned that in not supplying Bugatti I probably missed the possible winner of the European Grand Prix.'

On 15 August last Mr Rapson wrote me a personal letter from which the following is an extract:

'I had like you many regrets for the bad luck that you had with your tyres in the European G.P. Without these misfortunes your car would have won or have finished in the first three. The tyre faults showed up the efficiency of your aluminium wheel which was very satisfactory. I was very favourably impressed by all the improvements that you have so judiciously made to your wheel, and I think that one of the large wheel makers in the U.S.A. would be ready to pay you substantial royalties for the manufacturing rights for that country.'

I made the greatest effort to produce, for the first European Grand Prix run in France, five cars and one reserve all identical, with irreproachable finish, fine appearance and perfectly developed. These six cars were ready well before the first practice on the circuit.

The six cars arrived the day before the first practice day with the circuit closed, no work was necessary and the drivers, out of pride, washed and polished their cars so that they could arrive at the start in impeccable condition. Next morning at 5 o'clock everyone was ready on the circuit and each had carried out the predetermined test programme on the lines of what he was expected to do on the day itself. No incident occurred during practice and all tests were carried out similarly without even having to lift a bonnet either at the pits or on the circuit.

I had brought to Lyons a camping installation and to give an idea to those who have not seen it, it suffices for me to say that the transport of the camping equipment was made in three railway wagons and two road trucks with trailers. The racing cars went to Lyons under their own power and the supporting supply vehicles carried a total load of 30 tons.

Everything was provided: a wooden floor under a large tent, real beds for 45 people, a shower installation, running water in each cabin, plenty of electricity. Cooking was carried out in a solid wooden hut with everything necessary to feed the personnel properly for almost a month. At the side, ditches were dug for drainage. There were two ice-boxes, one of very large size, the other smaller. There was also a caravan for my own family.

The tyre shape I had adopted after making many tests, first of all on protected roads near my factory and then on the circuit itself, had given the best possible results. The construction of the cover itself and of the wheel allowed running with a deflated tyre, and I thought it better to risk loss of time due to a flat tyre than to carry a spare wheel which would certainly cause the loss of five minutes on the total time for the event.

Everything was thus prepared for the best.

Well prepared, more than satisfied with my drivers, happy with the choice of circuit, I believed my car the most suitable for this race. All the qualities of the 'thoroughbred' should come out in an event such as this: rapid starting, good acceleration, more than adequate speed on the straight, progressive and powerful brakes. Everything was well determined, well chosen and ready. Accordingly I arrived proudly at the start. I drove the reserve car and my five drivers followed with their handsome 'thoroughbreds'. The starting flag fell. The car driven by Mr Chassagne, carrying Number 7, lay third at Broken Bridge. The first ten laps were expected to be completed calmly and when I heard this news I thought to myself that I might be hopeful of the outcome of this race.

The first arrivals on completing the first lap included Mr de Viscaya with a deflated tyre, after completing part of the lap on the flat tyre. I wasn't worried; I was very pleased to see that my specially built wheels complied with one of the first conditions I imposed in their design, namely to operate without air pressure.

All went well, but then on the third lap Mr de Viscaya came in again with a tread off a tyre. Not a bit of rubber. The adhesive that joined the carcase to the tread was soft and could be rolled into balls, which confirmed the bad state of vulcanization of these two.

At this moment I realized that the race was lost as far as I was concerned. In succession Mr Chassagne on the fourth lap and then two cars at the same time came in to change rear wheels. I reminded my drivers that they should be careful, since in certain tests made previously with other tyres, the throwing of a tread had endangered the life of the driver. If a tyre lost a tread, pieces could wrap round the steering gear (this had happened to Mr Chassagne) and cause a serious accident. Happily no front tyre lost a tread during the Grand Prix and all drivers drove in the race without trouble due to this.

Car No. 22 driven by Mr Costantini had its gear change lever torn by a tread from a right-hand rear tyre. He had to complete several laps with the gear lever completely bent and unable to select 2nd and 4th, damaging the gears in the box also as they could not engage over their full width. He had therefore to retire. I might remark that this car came into the pits, and completed its last lap sufficiently fast, which shows that no other accident occurred to the car, which was driven in front of the Stand and left under its own power at the end of the race for our encampment.

Mr de Viscaya's car was put out of action due to tyres. Taking a corner, a tread failed, the car skidded unforseenly and demolished a barrier, running into the front of a house on the first corner at Givors. Heartbroken, the driver had to abandon the car which had the rear axle completely bent back and the chassis broken.

Once again I told my drivers to be careful, explaining why the two cars had been eliminated. It is for all these reasons that it was not possible to demonstrate what the cars could really do.

My greatest regret is that I could not demonstrate my new wheel, nor could I show the real speed of my cars.

The features of the new wheel are as follows:

a) good cooling of the tyre, due to the rim in aluminium, which has a much greater thermal conductivity than steel;

b) fixation of the cover to the rim by a safety ring preventing the cover being detached and all relative movement of rim and cover;

c) perfect cooling of the wheel including the brake drum.

There are some who thought that my wheel was the cause of the tyre trouble. It is sufficient for me to say that the tyres on the front wheels never budged, so that it was not a question of the wheel, nor of heat, but only a lack of adhesion of the tread to the ply which caused the tread-

368

throwing, probably because the tyres were of too recent manufacture.

Some said also: the cars are not fast. This I will demonstrate on another occasion, but it suffices to know that when Mr Chassagne was told that he did a lap in 20 seconds longer time than the car that made the record lap, he was astonished with the result, and if he had been advised during the event of this small difference he would have made an attempt at the record, for at no time had he pressed his car to the limit. On several occasions in the climb through the zig-zag up to Givors my cars had passed every other competitor. It must not be deduced that my cars were faster than my competitors, this would not be sportsmanlike, but what I can claim is that my cars were the fastest in the climb between Givors and Broken Bridge.

The public in the Stand were able to note the following: first of all the continual stops for tyre changing, the speed with which wheels were changed, the speed of refuelling, and the restart of the cars with a quarter turn of the starting handle. Everyone was surprised to see that my cars had no need to be pushed to start them. The mechanic had only to make a single twist and the engine started, which showed the good tune of the cars and the potentiality for normal use of these racing cars.

Ten of these cars have been built. They are almost all sold to customers. Some are already delivered and are a joy to their owners. One can use them as easily in town as in any race. I hope on the next occasion to make a better demonstration of the quality of my construction.

I will finish by saying that this car must not be considered a racing car. It has been built on the same principle as all the others, since I do not propose ever to race with a machine that is not strictly that that the customer can buy. The engine has only one change, namely roller bearings on the connecting rods and crankshaft, as well as a special extra light front axle, round and hollow. All other parts are similar to those of production cars.

The total weight of the car is only 1,450 lb. Great speed is obtained for the least weight, due to the good shape of the body and particularly by the road holding, since speed depends often on the way the car behaves on the road.

I would hope that after having studied the reasons which prevented me from confirming the confidence that has been accorded me in hoping for my success, you will be assured that although it will not be possible to make a new effort on this scale, I will always do my best to enter in a race with the maximum chance of showing my customers the excellence of my construction.

Yours truly

(Signed) **Ettore Bugatti**
MOLSHEIM

369

Racing activity after 1925

The success of the Type 35 in the period after 1924 has been well documented, for example by Laurence Pomeroy in *The Grand Prix Car*, vol I (Motor Racing Publications, 1954) or earlier articles in *The Motor* of 16 and 30 December 1942. It has also been described in detail in the Author's book *Grand Prix Bugatti*.

In 1925 Bugatti was outclassed without a blower but the Type 35 managed to win:

Targa Florio	.. Costantini	
Rome G.P.	.. Masetti	
French G.P. (Tourisme)	.. Costantini (1·5 litre, possibly plain bearing engine)	
Italian G.P. (Voiturette)	.. Costantini (1·5 litre, possibly plain bearing engine)	

In the most important French Grand Prix the outclassed Bugattis ran with commendable regularity but could only finish 4th to 8th (Costantini, Goux, F. de Vizcaya, P. de Vizcaya and Foresti). *The Motor* reported, in the description of the race:

The night before the race a dispute arose and Mr Bugatti considering himself unjustly treated, withdrew all his entries, and only after the A.C.F. had implored him almost on bended knees did he finally consent to let his cars run. The cause of the dispute was a trifling one. Apparently a few months ago the Alfa-Romeo and Delage concerns wrote to ask whether, as mechanics were not being carried, they would be allowed to cover over the mechanic's seat with the streamlining of the body. Although there was nothing in the regulations to debar them from doing this, the Club replied that they did not approve of the scheme. Bugatti, on the other hand, seeing that there was nothing against it in the regulations asked no questions and built his body to his own requirement. When M. Delage saw the Bugatti cowling over the mechanics seat he was greatly incensed, so much so that he immediately entered a protest, on the strength of which Bugatti was told to remove his cowling.

In the Spanish Grand Prix again he could do no better than 4th to 7th (P. de Vizcaya, F. de Vizcaya, Goux, Lehoux). The following year the car found its feet.

In 1926 the official formula was 1·5 litre; the Type 35 now

370

blown, sometimes 2 litre, then evidently 1·5 litres with reduced bore 52 mm × 88 mm, in some races although it is not always clear which, soon became the 60 mm × 66 mm T.39 for the works entered cars in the French and Spanish G.Ps. Successes were many:

Provence G.P.	Williams (T.35)
Rome G.P.	Maggi (T.35)
Targa Florio	Costantini (T.35T)
Alsace G.P.	Dubonnet (1,100 cc)
French G.P.	Goux (52 × 88 mm S)
European G.P. (San Sebastian)	Goux (T.39A)
Spanish G.P.	Costantini (2 litre)
Boulogne G.P.	Eyston (52 × 88 mm)
Italian G.P.	'Sabipa' (T.39A)
Milan G.P.	Costantini (T.35C)

In 1927 Bugatti was a non-starter in the French and European Grand Prix, and failed narrowly in the Spanish Grand Prix. Successes included:

Targa Florio	Materassi (T.35C)
San Sebastian G.P.	Materassi (T.35B)
Tripoli G.P.	Materassi (T.35)
Marne G.P.	Etancelin

In 1928 Fiat, Talbot and Delage withdrew from G.P. racing and Bugatti had things his own way (so did Chiron):

Targa Florio	Divo (T.35B)
Rome G.P.	Chiron (T.35B)
Marne G.P.	Chiron (T.35B)
Spanish G.P. (San Sebastian)	Chiron (T.35C)
Italian G.P.	Chiron (T.35C)
French G.P. (Sports cars) ..	Williams (T.35B)

In 1929 there were a few significant results:

Monaco G.P.	Williams (T.35B)
Targa Florio	Divo (T.35C)
French G.P.	Williams (T.35B)
Marne G.P.	Etancelin (T.35C)
German G.P.	Chiron (T.35C)

1929 was the last year before the introduction of the twin-cam Type 51, and the gradual eclipse of Bugatti as the dominant car in European racing. Successes in 1930 included:

Monaco G.P. ..	..	..	..	Dreyfus (T.35B)
Marne G.P. ..	..	..	..	Dreyfus (T.35C)
French G.P. ..	..	..	..	Etancelin (T.35C)
European G.P.	..	..	..	Chiron (T.35C)
Algerian G.P. ..	..	..	..	Etancelin (T.35B)

If the 1920s were the golden decade for official works entered Bugattis the next decade up to the beginning of the war saw the Bugatti as the amateur's car, sought after and beloved by many who raced for the fun of it at Brooklands and Donington and in smaller local road races in Europe.

Aeroengines and aircraft

Engines of the first world war

THERE IS A GOOD GENERAL ACCOUNT OF THE ORIGIN AND DEVELOPment of the Bugatti aeroengines during the 1914–18 war in Bradley's book on Ettore Bugatti, although the rather rosy and optimistic tale there is not borne out in detail by the other references consulted. For example, Bradley implies that many aircraft flew with Bugatti engines but in fact it has only been possible to confirm positively that one engine flew on one occasion. It is unreasonable to assume that no other did but nevertheless some confirmation would have been expected.

Bradley indicates that an 8 cylinder 250 hp design was produced early in the war and licenced to Delaunay-Belleville in Paris and Diatto in Italy (Plate 324). This engine evidently did not go into production, the Hispano Suiza equivalent being preferred. Bugatti then produced the better known 16 cylinder double-bank 500 hp design, which did not go into production in France but was purchased by the American Government and produced in the U.S.A. There is some evidence (British Patent 101534 of 21 September 1915) that Bugatti had begun to think of parallel double-banked engines geared directly together without a reduction gear, as early as 1915.

Bugatti had conceived the new engine layout as a means of allowing the firing of a cannon through the propeller boss. In fact there is his British Patent No. 131652 on file dated 11 June 1917 and claiming this idea. Interestingly enough this patent was never granted as a few months earlier a certain Marc Birkigt (the designer of the Hispano engine) had filed, on 27 January, the identical idea, but using a V-engine. Birkigt has always been known as the inventor of the 'moteur-cannon'; did Bugatti conceive the idea quite independently, or was his idea started off by some suggestion or rumour not consciously absorbed?

In 1917 the need for aeroengines in the U.S.A. became acute and many designs, domestic and foreign were adopted. A commission visited Paris and chose the Hispano Suiza and the Bugatti, notwithstanding that the French themselves had not adopted the latter. The American authorities chose Mr Charles B. King of the U.S. Signal Corps to father this engine, to redesign it for American production methods and to arrange production by the Duesenberg Motors Corporation of Elizabeth, New Jersey. The engine became known as the Bugatti-King. Some interesting background information has become available through the kindness of the late Mrs Ernest Friderich and her son Paul. Mr Ernest Friderich was sent by Bugatti to collaborate with the Duesenberg Company and Mr King, and to test a pair of French engines (one 16 cylinder, one 8 cylinder) in the U.S.A. The file of information includes Friderich's original instructions from the A.E.F. in Paris, signed by Colonel R. C. Bolling, 29 November 1917, to act as a civilian employee of the U.S. Government at a salary of 15 dollars a day; an instruction dated 5 January 1918 to proceed from Dayton, Ohio, to Elizabeth, New Jersey, the Duesenberg plant location; an instruction from King, dated 22 February, to test a French-built engine; a further note on the same lines dated 22 June; and then, after the Armistice, instructions dated 6 December 1918 to proceed back to Paris for demobilization, details of the boat to be taken on 10 December and a final discharge dated 19 December – home for Christmas!

More important perhaps than these interesting sidelights on dates is a note prepared by Friderich on the test on the 16 cylinder engine of French manufacture. It was run up first on 19 February 1918 and then the test started as instructed on 22 February. However, severe vibration occurred and eventually the test was discontinued when a noise was heard. On dismantling, it was found that two bearings had gone, one wrecking the rod and piston and cracking the crankcase. Friderich's conclusion reads:

Herewith my conclusion on breaking of motor. Motor running without propellor was not being cooled in any way, thus causing the crankcase to attain a high temperature in a very short time, thus causing oil to lose its density and not giving proper lubrication. The white metal of the connecting rod melted away, thus causing the connecting rod to grip crankshaft and this breaking cylinder and piston No. 3 and consequently these broken parts caused the breaking of the cylinder block, crankcase and piston.

Then we see a pen-written letter of 25 February from Dr Espanet at Detroit (he was over preparing to fly the engine in a Packard aeroplane), which starts off:

I have been asked to ask you some details of the little [sic] damage which occurred during the engine test. It was, it appears, a piston pin which again broke. If this was so you can ask directly to Mr King to have a complete set of 16 made up. Also we would ask you earnestly not to let this influence you to push the motor to its limit; we have no need to break it before flying and this would certainly not be in the interests of our common 'patron', don't you think; just what is needed to establish a power curve in the shortest possible time.

A typical letter from a test pilot who had not seen the damage, of course!

A second letter, dated 14 March, from Espanet reads:

I am happy to learn what happened to the engine and that it was due to a simple failure of lubrication due to a blockage of an orifice in the crankshaft; all is thus well and the remedy is easy.

This explanation of the failure hardly agrees with the official report made by Friderich!

There is a letter from Ettore, dated 12 February, telling Friderich that he is very disturbed not to have heard from him since 3 January, and mentioning that it is very disagreeable not to have heard from Dr Espanet, and a further letter of 22 February saying he had still not heard. He 'recommended' Friderich to keep him informed. Poor Friderich was probably wondering how to put it!

There is no further reference to the French engine tests until 24 June when a power curve is published presumably following a successful test. The engine gave 460 hp at 2,190 rpm. There is a copy of a fascinating letter from Ettore to the 'Director' of the Duesenberg Company, dated 11 April, which starts off:

As far as changes made to my engine are concerned I regret that these have been made without me being warned beforehand. I have no intention of questioning the competence of the engineers who are concerned with the transformation, and I will content myself simply with giving my advice.

He deals with the various changes, disagreeing with all of them. His jet-controlled centrifugal lubrication is *more certain* than pressure lubrication; he had thought of eliminating the detachable cover plates to the cylinder walls three years previously and had abandoned it. The use of an integral cylinder head and cylinder block had been used on his cars for ten years; the water circulation changes were not so good as the original. The rounding of the cylinder block had been something he used to do on his cars, and he included a photograph (presumably of the 8 valve type) to show this: but for reasons which he does not make clear, he had gone over to the square-cut design which Quesenberg (i.e. King) wanted to change. The rectangular cylinder blocks persisted of course into his later engine designs. He objects to the rounding of the inlet and exhaust passages and says he believes in square ports, adding that the efficiency of this engine in terms of output per cylinder size is superior to any other engine, even racing car engines. He also objects to the inlet manifold being water cooled since the water may leak into the engine. One notes, however, that he later adopted this idea on his car engines! He indicates that both 8 and 16 cylinder engines had successfully passed 50 hour type tests (in France?), the latter giving 494 hp at 2,200 rpm driving a test fan-dynamometer and 520 hp at this speed with a propellor during a supplementary test. He feels that any change made should be based on test results obtained first with the original design. Bugatti's advice was evidently not taken. An American engine (No. 4) started test on 26 June, and completed 30 hours running up to 28 August when one crankshaft broke. *This crankshaft was one of the old style shafts cut from a billet and made of poor material,* explains the official report.

There is a note by Friderich that the production programme was scheduled to be 15 engines by October 1918, 50 in November and 2,000 by April 1919. He felt that the output could not begin until November and that the 2,000 mark would be reached by June 1919. The file is completed with the official report from Mr King on a 50 hour endurance test in the U.S. Bugatti completed on 4 October 1918. A supplement to this report was attached containing the comments by Mr J. R. Harbeck, President of the Duesenberg Motors Corporation:

The following is submitted as matter supplementary to the formal report of the fifty hour endurance test on Bugatti engine finished 4 October 1918 which test was under observation of Government engineers and was reported upon fully and formally by Charles B. King, Engineer-in-Charge.

GENERAL DESIGN: The motor conforms in general design to the French Bugatti motor, but has had incorporated into it several changes, the most important of which are as follows:

1. Substitution of a high pressure oiling system for the splash system incorporated in the original motor. This change was made in conformity with the best current aeronautical engine practice and has been justified by the performance of the motor under test, and from the further fact that the original Bugatti motor failed to lubricate satisfactorily on tests in this country.

2. Change in the water-jacketing of the cylinder blocks by the substitution of an integral cast plate over the cylinder heads and the application of cast aluminium plate jackets as a substitute for the gasketed sheet aluminium top plate and sheet steel side jackets, as applied to the original motor. These changes have had no effect whatsoever on the function of the motor and were made in the interests of production.

3. General change in the circulating water system, resulting in the elimination of many pipes and connections. This change has worked out in a perfectly satisfactory manner, and the cooling of the motor being correct in every way.

4. Re-design of the front end by substitution of series of Hess-Bright compound annular and radial thrust bearings in place of the very complicated double bearings used on the original French model. These re-designed parts have given perfect satisfaction, having stood up for eighty hours of heavy running without defect or appreciable wear on the bearings or the closely associated gears.

The specific design of the motor has been changed in other minor particulars, but aside from the points above enumerated is substantially the same as the original Bugatti.

The outstanding features of the design of the motor lies in the general arrangement of cylinders whereby two series of vertical cylinders arranged in parallel groups of eight on each side are each coupled to an independent crankshaft, each crank being geared to the central propellor shaft. The motor, therefore, consists substantially of two eight cylinder motors arranged side by side driving a common propellor shaft. Owing to the small size of the cylinders

377

and the compact grouping the area of the vertical cross-section of the assembled group is exceedingly small resulting in a very low head resistance when housed. The overall length of the motor is also exceedingly short, and the general bulk of the design is such that the motor as a whole in its overall dimensions lies within the dimensions of any aviation motor of 300 hp or over. Into this concentrated package is incorporated a motor conservatively rated at 420 hp and actually capable of delivering 500 hp at approximately 1,550 revolutions per minute, propellor speed.

Further advantages of this design are as follows:

1. Carburetion and ignition are arranged in groups of four cylinders thus avoiding complicated and uneven gas distribution and difficulties in ignition incident to the ordinary six and twelve cylinder grouping.

2. The use of forked or articulated connecting rods is entirely avoided, thus eliminating a source of trouble common to 'V' type motors.

3. The use of parallel crankshafts and the central propellor shaft and housing running laterally the full length of the case results in an enormously stiff crankcase and an even and divided distribution of stresses. This motor has probably the most substantial crankcase found in any aviation motor.

4. The gear drive is so arranged that the total load is absorbed at *two* points on the periphery of the driven gear. Gears are of comparatively small diameter and, because of the fact that the whole gear load is not carried at one point, gears are materially smaller and lighter than would be necessary to transmit the same amount of power through a single spur. The enormous difficulty heretofore encountered in building gear drive motors of ordinary or 'V' type construction have been entirely overcome in the Bugatti motor. Sets of these gears have been operated for eighty hours without the least trouble, and during such period have transmitted from 400 to a maximum of 500 hp.

5. The use of sixteen comparatively small cylinders results in a perfectly balanced running condition and perfect synchronization. The size of the cylinders permits operation with safety at high engine speeds, and the skilled adoption of the gear principle permits the use of these engine speeds at *useful* propellor speeds. The motor at its rated horse power (420) operates at an engine speed of 1,996 revolutions and a propellor speed of 1,330. At its maximum of 500 hp it operates at an engine speed of approximately 2,300. The maximum power of the motor as developed on the stand may, therefore, be made useful in flight, which is *not* true of the non-geared type of

378

motor which develops an unusual amount of power developed at 1,700 revolutions. This condition represents the outstanding advantage of the Bugatti motor over any motor approaching it in power, and is made possible by the successful working out of its unique gear system.

6. The unique design makes possible the introduction of a cannon mounted within the propellor shaft housing and firing through the hollow shaft and centre of the propellor hub. This arm is adapted to use 37 mm ammunition, and when used in connection with a synchronized machine gun of the same ballistic energy, can be discharged automatically six successive times as the instant range and alignment are determined by the flight of the tracer bullet fired from the synchronized machine gun, which is also attached to the motor. This peculiar advantage is of use only in connection with combat planes. It is an incident to the design of the motor increasing its usefulness in the combat field, but in no way impairing its usefulness in other types of planes.

7. The great power, compactness, flexibility and *reliability* of the motor permits its use in a variety of planes covering a range from the very high-powered combat plane to the heaviest type of bombing and sea plane.

8. The motor in weight, per hp, compares favourably with the Liberty and is much lighter per horse power than the Rolls-Royce or other reliable foreign motors. On the base of its rated horse power (420) the weight is two and one-half pounds per horse power, and upon the base of its maximum useful horse power approximately two pounds per horse power.

In conclusion, it may be stated that the Bugatti motor is to be regarded as a fully developed product subject to possible small refinements as production progresses, but at the present moment suitable for general use. It is a significant fact that in spite of the changes in design the third motor submitted to the fifty-hour endurance test went through this test successfully. It may be noted that the motor as at present built is essentially a low compression engine, and that as need develops there is every reasonable expectation of securing very much greater powers, by the increase in compression. Particular attention is again called to the fact that the power developed by this motor is a *useful* one, and that the rating of the motor at 420 hp less than the amount of real power that can be taken from it in flight.

The above is respectfully submitted.

Even allowing for the optimism of a Company anxious to be allowed to proceed further, it is to be regretted that work on this engine was not allowed to continue when the Armistice came a few days later. The now defunct U.S. journal *Aerial Age Weekly*, 9 December 1918, refers to Bugatti engine production up to 22 November 1918 as 11 engines. By June 1918 orders had been placed for 2,000 engines, but *Automotive Industries*, 24 April 1919, quotes the production by the time the Armistice was signed as 40 engines, and illustrates a line of about this number. This same journal has a comprehensive description of the engine in the issues of 24 April and 1 May 1919.

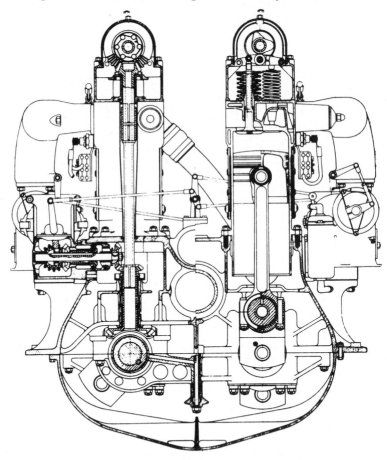

Fig. 59. *Cross section of aeroengine. The propellor was geared down in the ratio 2 : 3. Valve timing compares interestingly with car engines: inlet opens tdc, exhaust closes tdc, inlet closes 45 deg. after, and exhaust opens 45 deg. before bdc.*

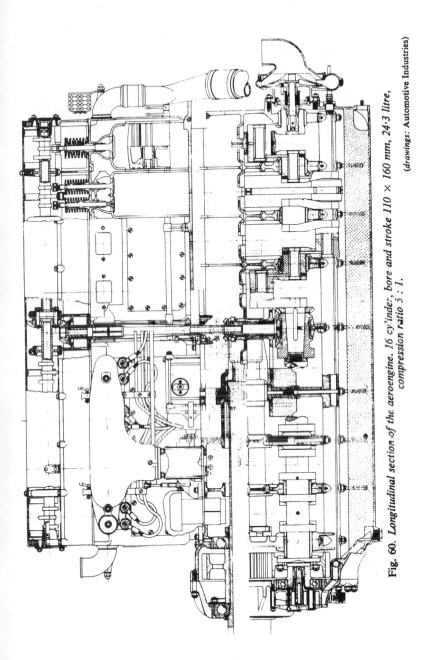

Fig. 60. *Longitudinal section of the aeroengine. 16 cylinder, bore and stroke 110 × 160 mm, 24·3 litre, compression ratio 5 : 1.*

(drawings: Automotive Industries)

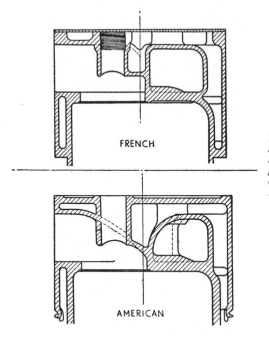

FRENCH

AMERICAN

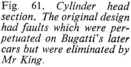

Fig. 61. *Cylinder head section. The original design had faults which were perpetuated on Bugatti's later cars but were eliminated by Mr King.*

Aerial Age Weekly also had an interesting series of articles on the construction of the engine, with full details of the changes made by Mr King. Many of the changes seem to the present Author to have been fully justified and merely underline some of the bad detail design for which Bugatti was, and continued to be, famous even if he did manage to succeed in spite of it! Quoting from *Aerial Age Weekly*:

Because of its unique type of design the Bugatti, when it was first brought over from France, and it was determined to put it into manufacture in this country, aroused a very great deal of interest in automotive circles, the interest being second only to that evidenced in the Liberty. The Bugatti was of the geared type possessing certain features not embodied in the Liberty, and with the special feature of being able to mount a 37 millimetre cannon firing through the propellor shaft.

The engine in fact was rated at 410 hp at 2,000 rpm rather than the 500 hp originally suggested (and 520 hp sometimes mentioned), but as the power : weight ratio seems to have been better than the famous Liberty engine, no doubt this was not a

322. The 16 cylinder Bugatti aeroengine. This example is an American-built engine now in the Smithsonian Institution.

323. *A Duesenberg-built engine on test. King is on the right, Friderich second from the left.*

matter of consequence. Undoubtedly later engines would have been uprated as the design was developed. To quote once more:

One of the points that required special study was the pressure oiling system due to cross interference of oil in the crankcase. The non-pressure system as used in the French type of Bugatti was considered unsafe owing to the many long leads and on the uncertainty of outside temperature, and it was consequently abandoned. The pressure system developed by Mr King has worked out very satisfactorily, as was proved by the fine condition of the bearings and running parts after the fifty-hour test.

This extract underlines the basic weakness of all or at any rate of most of Bugatti engines up to 1928 or so. Bugatti insisted on relying on splash or drip lubrication of the type seen on the Types 13, Brescia, 30, 35 and early Type 40 etc, and indeed on the pre-1914 Deutz design.

The oiling system as applied to the French Bugatti engine can be considered an open system non-pressure type, the pressure being determined by the diameters of the open orifices. In other words, with heavy or cold oil the oil will take the path of least resistance and will not travel to the remote ends of oil leads. The small openings in bearings become clogged with sediment, waste or coagulated oil. Owing to the pressure not being sufficient to clear these passages, trouble can be expected. Such trouble has already been experienced in engines built in this country The fundamental principle in the American Bugatti engine was to obtain a true pressure system on all bearings, including camshafts. The oil to be controlled by a relief valve. This can be regulated and the proper pressure obtained.

These remarks might be echoed as a criticism of the Type 35 G.P. engine; one can't help wondering whether the roller-bearing crank on the G.P. engine was really introduced as a means of making the Bugatti non-pressure system work! Certainly his racing car engines might have been the better for adopting the King improvements, but Bugatti was unusually conservative for all his brilliance.

In the course of a very interesting report, *Aerial Age Weekly* continues:

Mr King offers definite data concerning the specific changes made in the Bugatti design and reason therefor. Owing to the fact that the French engine which was sent over to this country had had a limited test in Paris of 37 hours and had not been in flight, all of the points in the design were very carefully considered. It was soon discovered that if the job was to be made a production one, numerous changes would have to be made.

It was evident that difficulties were experienced in cooling the valve seats of the French Bugatti, as cylinders and sample sections of used cylinders showed cracks between the exhaust and the inlets. In the American design, centres of the valves were increased in both directions from centre of line. The drawing shows the deep unjacketed section of the cylinder in which the strain was set up, causing the cracked valve seats. To obviate this difficulty, the shape of the intake passage and exhaust passages were improved.

The exhaust valve stems were not properly taken care of as to heat transference to the water jacket. The depth of water around valve stem guides is shown in the diagram where the French Bugatti and American Bugatti are contrasted. Owing to poor conductivity through threaded portions of valve guides, the threading was eliminated and cast iron valve guides were pressed into place, thus making a much more uniformly cooled stem. The bronze guides taken from the French Bugatti showed evidence of high heat.

An astonishing snag with the original water pump is referred to:

The French Bugatti pump as mounted on the engine permits water leakage to enter the sump and mix with the lubricating oil. This will lead to difficulties in the operation of the engine. In the American model the pump was moved back, a better support added and an opening was arranged so that the leakage could pass to the outside of engine sump.

The overhead camshaft valve gear is the familiar Bugatti design, much like the later G.P. engines except that the cams bear on rollers on the rocker arm; the valve caps have the familiar button caps for adjustment. The exhaust valve design has the drilled hole oil mist pumping system (found later on the G.P. engines), as the following quotation will indicate:

The exhaust valve stem is hollow from the head to within a short distance of the necked portion at the upper end. The hole is closed at the head end by a short threaded plug screwed in below the surface of the valve, the recess then being filled level with the surface of the valve by welding. This closes the hole tightly and locks the plug in position. The lower end of the exhaust valve stem is of larger dia-

386

meter than the upper end. Both the large and small diameters take a bearing in the valve guide. At the shoulder formed by the junction of the two sizes of stem three $\frac{3}{32}$ in. holes are drilled at an angle of 30 degrees with the axis of the stem sloping towards the head of the valve and connection with the drilled hole in the stem. At the upper end of the stem just below the necked portion a $\frac{5}{32}$ in. hole is drilled through the wall of the stem. The movement of the valve up and down in the guide causes a pumping action, the transfer of air within the valve stem being thought to cool the stem to a certain extent. This drilling also lightens the valve.

The magneto driving gear has an interesting advance and retard mechanism seen later on the G.P. cars.

The gear has four internal spiral grooves sliding over splines on the sleeve which is keyed to the driving shaft, but may be moved along the shaft by lever. The movement of this sleeve revolves the magneto driving gear in relation to the shaft driving gear, thus advancing or retarding the magnetos.

The 8 cylinder engine

Some details have come to light on the 8 cylinder aeroengine licenced in 1916 to Diatto at Turin (from *Motori Aero Cicli et Sports*, November 1916). This engine, which according to Bradley was also licenced to Delaunay-Belleville, preceded the 16 cylinder engine licenced to Duesenberg. Neither the article referred to nor an advertisement of Diatto in the same issue gives any details of the engine, except that it was of 200 hp. The photographs however show it to be of exceptionally clean appearance with a rear camshaft drive (the 16 cylinder engine had a central drive to each bank), and cross-located magnetos and water pump, all similar to the Type 13 or Black Bess. At the front is a propellor reduction gear and an oil pump in the centre appears to be driven by spur gears from a gear on the mid-point of the split (?) crankshaft. It has not been possible to find out what happened to this engine, but no doubt the war situation in Italy who joined the Allies in 1916, did not permit production. It is known that French made 8 cylinder engines were taken to the U.S.A., and at least a few were produced by Duesenberg, one still being in existence.

387

Museum engines

A visit to Paris can afford an opportunity to examine one of the original engines, perhaps the only one remaining other than one in Alsace; there are also two Breguet-Bugatti engines and a 1·5 litre engine. These engines are in the Musée de l'Air in a hangar at the wind tunnel site at Chalais-Meudon, 2 rue des Vertuajadins, Meudon, just outside the Paris boundaries in the south-west direction.

The 16 cylinder Bugatti engine is part sectioned and is a genuine French made one, as can be identified by the cylinder and cambox construction – the American built engines had not got screwed in valve guides.

There are two other particularly interesting engines in the hangar, both Breguet-Bugatti. After the first world war, while Bugatti concentrated on cars, the Breguet Company took over the further development of the aeroengine, producing first of all a number of 16 cylinder engines derived directly from the wartime units. Little seems to have been done with this engine in this form and it was adapted into a 4 bank, 32 cylinder engine for a large Breguet aeroplane built about this time. The first solution was to couple two 16 cylinder power plants together in line. To quote from an early issue of *Jane's All the World's Aircraft* (Samson Low, 1920 ed.):

Two Bugatti units are set in line, turned end for end, with the crank-shafts of one unit at a lower line than the other, and all four shafts gear into a common spur wheel, which drives a single airscrew shaft carried on special bearings under the crankcase of the upper of the two units. But instead of the pinion of each crankshaft being firmly keyed to its crankshaft, an automatic clutch is interposed between each crankshaft and its gear.

The details of the clutch gear are not discoverable, but each clutch is operated by a short length of quick-thread screw on the crankshaft end, in such wise that if any one crankshaft is being driven by its cylinders at a speed less than that corresponding to the speed of the screw-shaft, the clutch is automatically withdrawn, and if it again picks-up a speed unloaded in excess of that corresponding to the main shaft, it automatically re-clutches itself.

Thus the arrangement provides the equivalent of four eight-cylinder engines complete with driving gears.

As compared with the German multiple unit power plants for driving a common airscrew there is a marked saving in space, and one imagines in weight.

The unit is of 800 hp and the space occupied is about three metres long by one metre wide by 1·5 m high – including gears, clutches and starting motor.

Judging from the illustration in *Jane's* the engine was nearer 6 m long than 3 and it is no wonder that Breguet soon produced another version in the form of an H, although several of the tandem types were produced and fitted and flight tested in the Breguet Type 20 'Leviathan' in 1922. One of these much more compact engines is still at Meudon. This was claimed to produce 1,000 hp and was fitted and tested to a later version of the Leviathan, Type 21. However, a 1,000 hp engine at that time was an ambitious target even for a large and experienced aero-engine maker and Breguet was probably not up to the task. Nothing became of the engines or the Leviathan itself. But what grand power plant for a Bugatti-Breguet–Brighton special!

American engines

A sample American-made engine No. J46, dated 14 January 1919, is in the hands of the National Air Museum of the Smithsonian Institution in Washington D.C. (Plate 322). Another is in the U.S.A.F. Museum at the Wright-Patterson A.F. Base, Fairborn, Ohio. What happened to most of the remaining engines is not known but Mr O. A. Phillips writes:

In the late 20s and early 30s, I had considerable experience with these engines, as a close friend of mine had two, which he used as wind machines for both the movies and for blowing away flames in oil-well fires. They were also used occasionally to defrost orange groves, by circulating the air over large areas. Unfortunately my friend was killed in 1937 when he lost his footing and fell into the propellor blades of one of these wind machines during a motion picture. I do not know what became of his engines, but believe they were scrapped during World War II.

The Type 34 engine of 1925

No details of Bugatti's interest or activity in the aeroengine field after the war are known other than that he produced a design for a large 16 cylinder engine, 125 mm × 180 mm, very similar in general outline to the wartime unit. The original drawing is dated 2 September 1925. The design is perhaps of

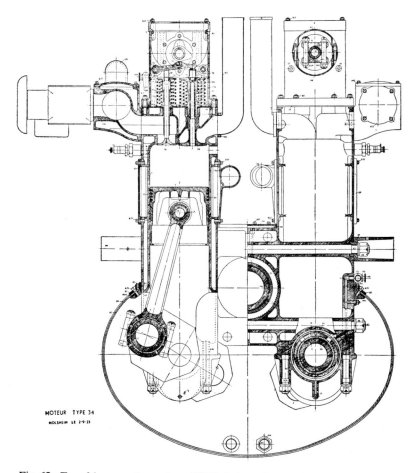

MOTEUR TYPE 34
MOLSHEIM LE 2-9-25

Fig. 62. *Type 34 aeroengine project of 1925. It is not known if this engine was built but its cylinder blocks formed the basis of the Royale engine.*

interest as illustrating the system of suspension of the crankshaft directly from the cylinder block, as used on the Royale, T.50 etc. The main bearings also seem to be water cooled, as on the Royale. The crankshaft appears to have proper pressure lubrication at last – perhaps Ettore had decided that Mr King was right after all.

Type 50B aeroengine

In 1938–39, Ettore was designing and building a 16 cylinder engined fighter aeroplane! The power plant consisted of two Type 50B racing engines coupled in tandem. They should have been capable of producing 850 to 900 hp, which would have been adequate at that time; the 50B was a light weight engine basically very suitable for aeroengine work if a suitable reduction gear had been used.

The Bugatti aeroplane

In 1938 Bugatti set up a special design office in the rue du Debarcadère, Paris, and began to build an aeroplane intended to become a high speed fighter but in the first place to be entered in the Coupe Deutsch. The pilot was to be Maurice Arnoux, later lost in combat flying for his country in 1940. The aircraft was a single seat monoplane, in wood, with a butterfly tail. The contra-rotating propellors in front of the pilot were driven by a pair of shafts from two 50B supercharged engines of about 450 hp each. These engines were slightly sloping and handed so that the exhausts came out each side of the fuselage, the blowers being inboard. The radiator was in the rear fuselage fed by reverse flow from air entering the leading edge of the tail plane and exhausting forward on the fuselage side.

At the time of writing the aircraft is still in existence (just!) in the U.S.A. engineless.

Bugatti boats

IN 1927 BUGATTI BEGAN TO DREAM OF BUILDING A BOAT THAT would cross the Atlantic, Brest to New York, in 15 hours. The boat was to be 35 metres long and 2·5 metres in width, with very low water drag; side elevators were to be used to assist the boat to plane. Eight engines each of 300 hp (Royale type) were to be used, two with reverse gear. A ninth auxiliary engine looked after cooling air supply when the boat was at rest. The crew of eight could remain below deck, navigating from the bottom of the conning tower or in fine weather the captain could climb on to the bridge. The cruising speed was calculated to be 140 km/h (90 mph).

Nothing came of the design, but in 1939 Bugatti tried again with a shipyard at Deauville and when war came was building in Paris a torpedo boat driven by 8 Type 50B engines giving a total horse power of 3,000 and intended to be launched at Deauville. It was launched in 1940, taken by road to Le Havre as the Germans advanced and spent the war years in England. Although returned to France in 1945, Bugatti's death came too soon for it to be completed. He had, prior to this, fitted engines to several racing boats and had won two world records for 6 litre boats (pilot Vasseur) and one for boats not exceeding 800 kg in weight, the latter believed to be the boat *Niniette** in the hands of the Italian Prince Ruspoli. Later Ettore purchased the shipyard Chantiers Naval de Maison-Laffitte but although he worked away during and after the war nothing became of this yard's boat. One was catalogued under the name 'You-You' (believed to be Type 75), an open boat for 6 to 10 people, single cylinder engine forward, and available in lengths 10, 12 and 14 feet.

* After Lidia Bugatti's family nickname.

392

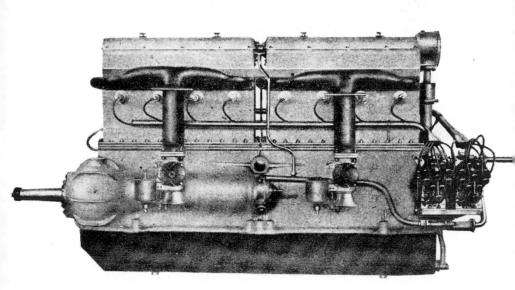

324. *The 8 cylinder Diatto-built Bugatti aeroengine.* (see page 373)

325. *A model of the Bugatti boat of 1927.*

326.

BUGATTI RAILCARS

Bugatti railcars

BUGATTI CONCENTRATED FROM ABOUT 1930 ON RAILCAR DESIGN, producing three basic types, using the Royale engines as motive power. The first railcar was put into service in the summer of 1933 on the Paris–Deauville run, and ran regularly at a cruising speed of 70 mph. Later Jean Bugatti drove an autorail on the Paris–Strasbourg run of 320 miles, at an average of 90 mph and shortly afterwards gained a world record for a railway by completing 70 kilometres at an average speed of 196 km/h (122 mph). Three types of autorail were produced; a light type of 400 hp (two engines), a double type of 800 hp (four engines) with a single trailer and a triple version with a trailer front and back.

The design made use of centrally mounted engines driving the bogie wheels through hydraulic fluid-flywheel clutches, and propellor shafts. A reverse gear was included in the bevel boxes on the driving axles. The bogies themselves were fully sprung and so mounted as to give safety and an excellent ride, far removed from the normal British railway bogie. The wheels were insulated from the steel tyre rims by a rubber layer. Brakes were mechanical, fully compensated and cable operated from a pneumatic cylinder.

BUGATTI RAILCARS
(From information provided by the S.N.C.F.)

Type	Years of Service		No. in Service	Engines	Seats	Speed kmh/	Remarks
	Entered	Withdrawn					
idential	1933	1954	8	4	48+62	140	trailer
ble	1934	1953	3	4	83	150	articulated
t	1935	1947	13	2	36	150	no trailer
gated	1935	1956	27	2	54	140	no trailer
le	1936	1953	2	4	144	140	articulated
a Long	1937	1958	25	2	78	140	no trailer
le	1939	1953	1	4	96	150	articulated

Bugatti Steam Engine[*]

A STEAM ENGINE WAS DESIGNED BY ETTORE BUGATTI IN THE SPRING OF 1934, but I suppose it had been in his head for some time previously. I myself did the project layout work under his direction in May of that year.
In fact it was intended to build:

(i) a locomotive of 1,000 hp with a 4 engined bogie, and a 4 axle trailing bogie, for the State National Railway (Director General: Mr R. Dautry).

(ii) a locomotive of 2,000 hp with two 4 engined bogies for the P.L.M. Railway (Director General: Mr E. Muginot).

These two locomotives were intended to draw several passenger coaches, also to be built.

The project design of the engine and 1,000 hp locomotive was shown to Mr Raoul Dautry when he visited Molsheim at Whitsun 1934.

As a result of this Mr Bugatti obtained two orders, one from the State (1,000 hp steam train) and one from P.L.M. (2,000 hp steam train).

The prototype engine (now in the Schlumpf collection) ran in 1935 or 1936. Intended to be fed with steam at 700 p.s.i., it ran first on steam at 200 p.s.i. derived from the factory boiler. The two illustrations show the engine in the boiler house, close by to the car repair shop well known to many of you.

The features of the engine were as follows:

Eight cylinders in line (I cannot recall the bore and stroke).

Crankshaft carried on nine roller bearings, attached to the cylinder block.

Twin camshafts in the cylinder head. Cams with progressive profiles allowing the duration of operation (or angle of opening) of inlet and exhaust to be varied by moving the axial position of the camshafts. (The control wheels can be seen in the illustrations.) The cams were double and were symmetrical with respect to the central position with the valves shut, allowing the direction of rotation of the engine to be reversed merely by shifting the axial position of the camshafts.

Valve operating gear with vertical rockers (as can be seen in the photographs). The rockers had a ball of 1 inch diameter rolling on the surface of the corresponding cam. The ball was retained in position by others, smaller in diameter, in the cavity or pocket in the rocker.

Inlet valves, arranged horizontally, with two heads, one being flexible (Bugatti patent). This arrangement of two heads (double beat) is indispensable in the case of a steam engine, to compensate for the action of the pressure prevailing in the admission manifold which tends to open the valve.

* From Bugantics 30, 3, 1967.

328. *The prototype Bugatti steam engine on test at Molsheim.*

329. *The steam engine had no type-number, all drawings being numbered in the Autorail series · 'WG'*

Exhaust valves, also arranged horizontally. The two illustrations show the return springs.

Pistons of great height, with two sets of piston rings, one set for sealing, and the other in the centre of the skirt to prevent condensed water from leaking down into the crankcase, the water being led away by bleed holes in the cylinder wall.

A fuller description of the engine would get us deeply involved and would require research in the Drawing Office records.

Apart from the engine, Mr Bugatti undertook the construction of:

A boiler giving 7½ tons of steam per hour at 700 p.s.i. (and in parallel ordered a similar boiler from Babcock and Wilcox, to the same specification).

Fuel oil burners, 8 to a boiler.

Fuel pumps.

High pressure water feed pumps.

Layout of the various parts to permit automatic control of the boilers.

Valves and articulated pipes to connect the boilers to the engines.

The conception of the driving bogies was based on the same layout as on the 4 axle bogies of the Autorails. The crankcase of each of the four engines formed a beam and, joined to the body of the bogie by the suspension springs, played the role of an axle.

The crankshaft of each engine drove the two corresponding wheels by two short interconnecting cardan shafts.

Mr Bugatti undertook the completion of the whole assembly of the two locomotives, chassis, bogies, wheels, brakes, engines, boilers and accessories, bodywork, as well as the passenger coaches.

For a variety of reasons these two trains could not be finished and delivered to the S.N.C.F. which in the meantime had been formed by the amalgamation of the State railway and the P.L.M.

On the eve of the last war, Jean Bugatti took up once more the completion of the work and pressed on with it with his characteristic energy.

In the month of August 1939 along with many other things came the cancellation of the two orders, and the liquidation of the work in agreement with the S.N.C.F.

Mr Bugatti's projects relating to Steam Engines gave rise to many researches, studies, tests, etc. The 1939 war prevented him from developing his inventions in this sphere in the normal way, which was regrettable, because the many new ideas which were found in his designs were of such a nature as to have an impact on railway traction.

N. Domboy, June 1966

(Formerly Technical Director at Bugatti works)

399

The End of the Line—

(This was the notice put in the last pay packet of all Molsheim employees before the firm was handed over to Hispano-Suiza at the end of July 1963.)

PARIS. JULY 22nd, 1963.

To all personnel at the Bugatti factory, to all workmen past and present, we address this farewell full of great sadness.

Since the death of Ettore Bugatti on August 21st, 1947, we have struggled to maintain and re-establish this factory to whose creation your devoted and conscientious work has so contributed, overcoming many and crippling difficulties. Difficulties to which alas you had often heard the echo.

We have always rejoiced at heart in every improvement in the situation, as we had rejoiced in the old days at the successes of the firm. We have together tried to prepare a new Bugatti car.

Meanwhile insuperable financial difficulties made it impossible for us to continue this enormous effort. We were forced to hand over to Hispano-Suiza the responsibility of running the factory. We keep the thought in mind, always, of two generations of Bugatti that passed among you, sustained by your great moral, professional and technical qualities, and of the support given to the Patron, and to dear Jean in difficult times.

It is with emotion that we think of Christmas, of the celebration of the older employees last year, of the unforgettable and moving welcome that the town of Molsheim, bedecked with flags, gave to the International Bugatti Rally in July 1961, of the marvellous proceedings during the generous reception organized at the Town Hall by Mr Meck, President of the General Council of Bas-Rhin and Mayor of our town, whom we thank particularly.

Nevertheless the impossible brings its inevitable consequences. It is with great sadness that we send you these words of farewell, but also wish you good luck for the future.

The Bugatti Family.

PART III

BUGATTI MISCELLANY

LE PUR-SANG BUGATTI

Self-caricature from about 1913.

330. *A recently discovered photograph of Ettore Bugatti taken in 1902.*

331. *The young Bugatti at the wheel about 1908.*

332. *In his workshop about 1903.*

Bugatti, the man

ETTORE ARCO ISIDORO BUGATTI WAS BORN ON 15 SEPTEMBER 1881 at Milan; he died on 21 August 1947; he married Barbara Mascherpa from Milan in 1902 and had four children, two daughters, L'Ebé (named from his initials) and Lidia, and two sons, Jean and Roland*. He remarried in October 1946 after the death of his first wife in July 1946 and had a further son and daughter. Mr W. F. Bradley has ably described his life in his biography *Ettore Bugatti*. The book by his daughter, L'Ebé, *L'Epopee Bugatti*, Paris 1966, is full of personal detail. J. A. Grégoire, *L'Aventure Automobile*, Paris, 1953 writes:

Loud in voice, high in colour, overflowing with life, a brown bowler sitting on the back of his head, he looked more like a horseman strayed among motor-cars. Nevertheless his brilliant life was interspersed with difficulties and catastrophies and came to an end amid material and mental problems. . . .

Bugatti was pure artist; his only scientific knowledge resulted from experience which increased with the years, and a natural mechanical ability aided by a gift of observation. He did not believe in calculations, formulae or principles. He joked about pages of mathematical figures and about integration signs which he called violin holes. He had happily the wisdom to surround himself with talented engineers whom he paid generously, but demanded from them total anonymity.

Others have written of Bugatti as a man. Many English-speaking enthusiasts and drivers knew him but few well – he could speak no English. Charles Faroux, the doyen of French automobile correspondents effused over him. Maurice Phillipe and Roger Labric have described him in more sober terms. Genial and generous he dominated his factory in the best tradition of the English squire. Until the middle 1930s when France, even Molsheim, passed into the grip of labour unrest, communist inspired or fuelled, he knew his men, each of them personally, and concerned himself with their wellbeing in and out of the factory.

* L'Ebé 1905–   , Lidia 1907–72, Jean 1909–39, Roland 1921–

He loved horses and dogs and was surrounded with both. The whole conception of 'pur-sang' seems to stem from the thoroughbred horse – from the handsome, functional line with the wheels at the corners, where they should be, to the horse-shoe radiator. But his stubbornness was a fault and his own belief in his engineering skill masked for him the defects in his designs. Success in his youth had undoubtedly influenced his judgment of his own abilities – his fee from de Dietrich in 1901 was reputed to have been £3,000 and he was then under 21. He refused to fit front wheel brakes in the early 1920s and was furious with Friderich when the latter had a car fitted up secretly, refusing even to try the car. His reluctance to super-charge is well known. 'He was like a big stallion you couldn't ride' (L. d'E.).

If he loved horses, he loved racing and racing drivers too. A daredevil in his teens, he drove his own cars up to 1914, but seems to have given it up after the war, although he had intimate driving knowledge of all his cars. He believed that you should drive with the seat-of-your-pants, and although he would demonstrate top-gear starts, his advice was 'Toujours un metre en premier'.

He was a man of considerable perception and imagination, and had the knack of being able to visualize two dimensional engineering drawings in three dimensional reality. Two examples which have been recalled by close associates will illustrate his imaginative critical ability. At some early race at Monza he asked to see the car driven by Segrave. After several minutes of gazing at the mechanism he turned to Segrave and said: 'This engine bearer will break during the race—and your front axle seems to be unsafe.' Segrave was not pleased, feeling that Bugatti was trying to put him off as a competitor. Bugatti urged his own drivers to be careful not to follow Segrave too closely. The crankcase arm in question broke during the race and Segrave withdrew. In another case, Bugatti was considering a new American machine tool being offered by a salesman from the factory; he asked to see an arrangement drawing, which he studied silently for several minutes. Then he pointed to a weak-

333. *In his favourite garb, riding clothes and a brown bowler, on the favourite Brouillard.*

334. *Father and son Jean about 1936.*

335. *L'Ebé on the right, with Lidia and Roland in the 1920s.*

334. *A fine portrait of Ettore Bugatti in middle life.*

ness, and suggested a possible solution, and left the room; the salesman, astonished, turned to one of Bugatti's colleagues and said, 'We knew the machine had this fault, but no one else did; Bugatti's suggested cure is one we have not thought of, and we will certainly try it'.

History will judge him perhaps as the last of the artist-engineers who could build a business around himself. Engineering is full of artists – men of vision and natural creative talent – but the march of industrial events and technical progress call now for sound theoretical bases for engineering productions – and this is something Bugatti never was able to give his cars.

BUGATTI, THE INVENTOR

(Extract from 'The Automotive Inventions of Ettore Bugatti' by H. G. Conway, *Trans. Newcomen Society*, 31, 1959.)

Ettore Bugatti – mad inventor or mechanical genius? Viewed from the point of view of his car designs and productions, he was certainly a mechanical genius although few engineers would doubt that he had a streak of eccentricity or stubbornness which made him persist with bad design features long after their faults had become obvious to his customers.

But viewed after a study of his inventions it is not so easy to form an opinion. Many of his patents are unbelievably odd, and impracticable, examined thirty years after they were filed. Considered in total and attempting to put them in perspective, they are fascinating.

Bradley in his biography gives the number of Bugatti's inventions as over 1,000. A search in the Patent Office in London shows that there are 340 listed in French files (together with another 32 in the name of his son Jean), and that the number in Britain is 176 (25 being in the name of Jean and one Roland – this one filed after the father's death).

Many of the inventions described appear impracticable and indeed some are ridiculous; but even without allowing for the crudeness of some of the specification drawings they do show considerable mechanical creative ability.

Few of the inventions could be judged as fundamentally important. The patent structure which Bugatti built up around himself seems frail and a little like a house of cards. It may have had more value for prestige than commercial protection.

Bugatti's car engines were characterized throughout the whole of his design experience up until about 1930 with two major defects. Firstly we may note his almost complete inability or stubborn reluctance to design an engine with pressure fed hydrodynamically lubricated bearings, and secondly his retention of a valve layout which if it gave plenty of area for the incoming and outgoing gases did not allow for adequate valve seat cooling, and was thermodynamically inefficient.

The aeroengines of the first world war and the fine results achieved after it, during the Schneider Trophy races in the 1920s showed that engine design had reached a high degree of perfection at the time when Bugatti was winning races by the hundreds with engines which to the engine expert were twenty years out of date. But for sheer artistry and interest the Bugatti engine and car had few peers. Character, even if occasionally bad, is seen at every corner.

But few of the published inventions give the key to his engineering design quality which was based upon simple and straightforward forms which could be machined on the centre lathe or the horizontal boring machine without involving complex angles, and yet could be multiplied into multi-cylinder engines of slab like appearance. And coupled to this was an atmosphere in the factory, dominated by the Patron, of good workmanship, cleanliness and 'doing the job properly'.

Carlo Bugatti (1855-1940)

CARLO'S OWN FATHER WAS AN ARTIST AND ARCHITECT, BUT LITTLE is known about Carlo's own early history. By the end of the last century he had however established himself as a designer and maker of an astonishing output of highly decorated, often bizarre, but beautifully executed furniture, almost Moorish, or Egyptian in style, owing something to Japan and far removed from functional design. There are examples of his work in the Victoria and Albert Museum (at Bethnal Green) and in the Museum of Modern Art in New York, and the quality of workmanship these display is exceptional.

Carlo ran a small furniture factory in Milan until he sold it to De Vecchi and moved to Paris in the early years of this century; always the experimenter, he spent the remaining years of his life dabbling in silversmithing, sculpture and painting, although he produced much fine furniture in his first years in the Paris Studio. In 1910 he left Paris for Pierrefonds, then joining his son in Alsace for the last few years. He died peacefully at Molsheim in April 1940.

Rembrandt Bugatti (1884-1915)

CARLO'S SECOND SON SHOWED THE ARTISTIC TALENT THAT HIS BROTHER had turned from. It is said that his father noticed this when he came across a beautifully modelled clay which his son had produced, unbeknown to the father, from a lump of material left around in the family studio. In any event he was soon studying in Paris and being noted. He became absorbed with animals, and a frequenter of zoological gardens, specially at Antwerp where his best work was done.

In a comparatively short life he seems to have managed a substantial output mostly of animals in natural positions, catching the sense of motion perhaps, or in another work capturing the fatigue of tired horses. A few figure studies – the flowerseller at the corner of his street in Paris, a girl figure – show that the talent went beyond animals.

In recent years his work has been much appreciated and values are high. There are examples in several museums including the Victoria and Albert, and many in private collections.

Rembrandt was not a happy man and ended his own life in January 1915 in a wartime gloom of an unhappy love affair.

La Bugatti en Rodage

WHEN BUGATTI DELIVERS A NEW CAR, HE DOES NOT STICK ON THE windscreen a label exhorting you not to use your car normally for 1,800 to 2,000 km. Twenty-five years of experience of racing and success has taught Bugatti that it is the maker's job to determine the clearances necessary for proper functioning; that when tolerances are judiciously chosen, they remain so during the life of the car which does not wear out. And that it is not for the customer to be asked to wear the new vehicle prematurely under the pretext of running-in. Bugatti says to you: Here is a new car. It is in perfect tune, you may run it fast. You can run as fast as you like when leaving the factory! Bugatti does not restrict speed during the guarantee period. (*From a Bugatti advertisement of 1930.*)

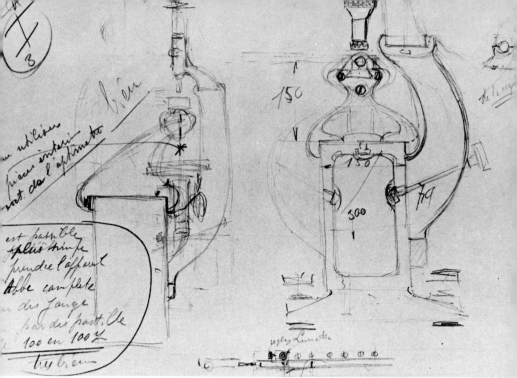

Sketch of a machine.

BUGATTI, THE DRAUGHTSMAN

Sketch of axle detail

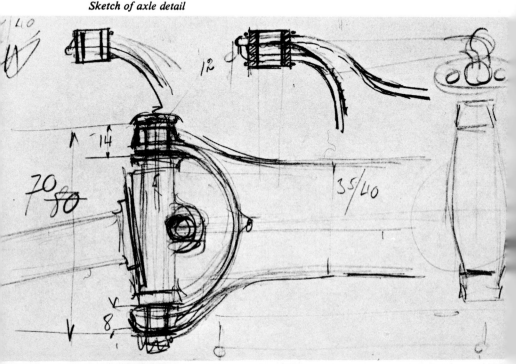

How many Bugattis were made?

SOME FACTORY RECORDS REMAIN TO INDICATE HOW MANY Bugattis were made. Completion of the Bugatti Register also makes it possible to conjecture on gaps in the available information based on serial numbers. Numbers were allotted in numerical order, with occasional gaps in a few cases, from a starting number such as 100, 120 or 150.

The following totals are accordingly fairly accurate in most cases:

8 valve	435
16 valve..	2,000
T.30	600
T.35, 39	340
T.37	290
T.38	385
T.40	830
T.43	160
T.44	1,095
T.46	400 (about)
T.49	470
T.50	65
T.51	40
T.55	38
T.57	710
Total approx.	7,850

A safe figure to assume for total of all production models is 7,800.

How fast is a Bugatti?

IF YOU DROVE A BUGATTI IN GOOD AND STANDARD TUNE TODAY, on a few miles of decent flat highway, how fast would it go? A Brescia would do about 70 mph; so would a Type 40. You might wind a Type 30 up to 75 mph if you have the nerve. With a Type 44 or 49 you should reach 80 mph. A good Type 43 should reach 95 mph without much trouble. At least two Type 43s can still exceed 100 mph with the screen down. The Type 50 was reputed to have reached 115 to 120 mph, but probably today 100 mph if reached would seem a bit hazardous. An ordinary Type 57 should touch 95 mph, a 57C the genuine 100 mph, and a 57S or 57SC at least 110 mph.

Racing models in all cases must have been able to exceed 100 mph. Today a typical 35B will reach 5,500 rpm in top at Silverstone (115 mph), and an unblown 2 litre 35 just about the hundred mark. The Type 59, 3·3 litre was reputed to have been capable of 180 mph which may well have been true. A Type 35B belonging to Lehrfeld in Portugal (Car No. 4952) did a standing kilometre in August 1930 in 30·4 second and a flying kilometre a month later at 124·4 mph. However, if Bugattis get older, tuning methods and perhaps fuels do not: Mr P. Stubberfield's famous single seat, Type 35B, Bugatti did the kilometre at Brighton, post-war, in 26·96 sec, crossing the line with rather unsuitable hill-climb gearing at 120 mph at 6,000 rpm. Another T.35B recently did a standing quarter mile in just over 15 sec.

Some known acceleration data may be of interest. A good Type 43 (new in 1928, and at Brighton in 1959) did the standing start kilometre in just under 35 sec; this is the equivalent of 0 to 60 mph in about 12 seconds. A Type 55 was timed accurately on 12 August 1932 and gave the following figures:

0 – 60 mph	9·5 sec
0 – 80 mph	24·55 sec
0 – 90 mph	27·7 sec
0 – 112 mph	53·0 sec

These are as impressive for a 2·3 litre car in 1962 as in 1932.

In 1928 a T.35B secured the world record for the standing start kilometre in 29·3 sec. In 1930 a T.35C managed 26·9 sec. for the same distance. In 1933 a T.51 obtained world (Class D) records at 27·1 sec for the standing kilometre, which is rather slower than the smaller single-cam car. In 1930 Prince Lichenstein broke the world's Class E record for the standing mile in 38·29 sec (94·01 mph) in a T.35C, a record which stood until 1961 when beaten by the Thompson dragster, fitted with a blown 420 bhp modified Tempest engine.

Mr W. Boddy has dug out the fastest Bugatti lap speeds at Brooklands including the following:

1914: 8 valve, Lambert, 72·7 mph
1921: (1920 Le Mans car?) 16 valve T.13, Segrave, 75·69 mph
1923: Brescia, Marshall, 89·41 mph
1925: T.30 Indianapolis single seater, Duller, 111·17 mph
1927: T.35B, Eyston, 120·59 mph
1929: T.37A, Staniland, 122·07 mph
1931: T.35B, Penn Hughes, 127·97 mph
1934: T.54, Froy, 134·97 mph
1935: T.51, Staniland, 133·16 mph
1936: T.59, Howe, 138·34 mph
1938: T.51C, Brackenbury, 127·05 mph

These speeds will represent very nearly the maximum speeds of the cars.

La Vie Française*

A BROAD, STRAIGHT HIGHWAY, DOTTED WITH AN OCCASIONAL ALSATIAN village, leads to picturesque Molsheim. Lying in the plains, with the Vosges mountains as a distant background and Mount Odile dominating the range of hills, there is nothing in this village to suggest a motor manufacturing centre. It is agricultural, rustic and old-world.

The car swings through double gates into a gravelled courtyard having a country residence and park on the left, high gabled out-houses on the right, and just beyond a stream of water and a water wheel, buildings which are evidently stables and harness rooms. It is the introduction to the Bugatti motor factory. Ettore Bugatti has built his factory around his country estate, or, it would be more correct to say, his factory is a country estate. There is no dividing line between the two; there is no point where one can say 'This is the extremity of the park, and beyond are the works'. Our host opens a polished oak brassbound door and ushers us into a heated harness room where a green-aproned groom has made brass look like gold and nickel like silver. Another and similar door is thrown open and we are amongst some fifteen thoroughbred horses, of which any sportsman might be proud. The double doors of a long, low building brings us into a carriage room with unique contents; a Rolls-Royce, a cheap French car, a straight eight Bugatti, a popular American automobile, a mail coach, an American buggy, an elaborately carved and painted Sicilian's peasant cart, a model motor car, a sleigh, a horse-drawn coupé, and several racing cars. The yapping of dogs instinctively arrests us, and when we have admired the wire-haired terriers, looked in at the riding school, tried to discover whether the solemn one-legged stork standing alone in the garden is a product of nature or the work of man, another brass-bound and polished door is opened by the master key, and we hear the hum of machinery.

It is an entirely modern factory in which we find ourselves. The machinery is the best America, England, Germany and France can provide. An American production expert would be delighted at the high standard, although, having a mind steeped in figures and effi-ciency, he might be puzzled at the setting – at the uniform one-storey buildings surrounded by gardens, at the proximity of all which is

* (W. F. Bradley, *Autocar*, 15 March, 1929).

416

usually associated with a well-kept English country estate rather than with a factory organized on modern lines. M. Ettore Bugatti is one of the most interesting figures in the world's motor movement. As he has himself stated, he is an artist; but when he has compared himself to his father, Carlo Bugatti, and to his brother, Rembrandt Bugatti, the animal sculptor, he realized that he was not fit to follow in their footsteps, and, having a taste for mechanics, he left the art schools and apprenticed himself to a firm of engineers in his native town of Milan. He is an unusual combination of artist, engineer and sportsman. If any other works manager had conducted us round his factory in riding breeches, top boots, a red waistcoat and yellow coat, we might have been tempted to smile at the incongruity. M. Bugatti swings from the saddle of his favourite Irish hunter, gets astride a bicycle built specially for his use, and pedals his way through the grounds of his estate into the various shops, taking a versatile interest in the varied things brought to his attention.

Whether it be factory, house, horses, dogs, cattle or land, the same high standard of efficiency is maintained, and every branch of this factory and country estate appears to receive the same careful consideration. There is something extraordinarily fascinating in an Italian family reflecting the French atmosphere, living in and being the most prominent members of an Alsatian village which for more than forty years was under German domination. M. Ettore Bugatti is generally looked upon as a Frenchman, although he has retained the nationality of his birth; Madame Bugatti is vivaciously Italian; the two daughters are sports-loving young ladies; the elder son has been trained to the father's business, and the baby, a son of $5\frac{1}{2}$ years old, has been an expert motorist for more than $2\frac{1}{2}$ years. It was entirely for the use of the 'baby' that M. Bugatti built a model racing car, exactly to scale, with pneumatic tyres, detachable wheels, four-wheel brakes, worm and sector steering, but with an electric instead of a petrol motor. The child learned to drive it in the corridors, but one of the most delightful exhibitions is to see him racing in the courtyard. Corner work à la Costantini; sudden application of the brakes to avoid an obstacle in the form of father's hat thrown in the path of the oncoming machine; rapid acceleration; slow running in traffic – all this can be performed as naturally as playing ball.

John Ruskin's soul would have been delighted at this example of the artist-artisan; of the engineer who seeks to vent his artistic temperament in terms of mechanics, and who does so without violating any of the principles of modern efficiency; of the man who has happily combined an artistic home with production methods and who has succeeded in transmitting this joyous creative spirit to all those who labour with him.

Bugatti Coachwork

WHO BUILT THE BODY ON THE BEAUTIFUL ROYALE ROADSTER delivered in 1932 to Armand Esders? Consultation with Noel Domboy who was Technical Director at Molsheim before the war provided the answer and much data of historical importance.

Bugatti's building of bodywork, he writes, began in 1923 when he designed and built the 1923 A. C. de F. Tours tank – the famous tank which was later to be copied by Bugatti himself and many others.

Then came the beautiful 1924 G. P. de Lyon car and the classic body on the Grand Prix models. All subsequent single and two seat racing bodies were built at the works. By 1939, on the eve of war, the coachwork shops were well equipped with machine tools and equipment enabling them to make bodies for Type 57s, trimmed and finished in all respects.

This indeed had applied also to many bodies on Types 46, 46S, 49, 50, 55 and so on. The Esder Roadster was built at Molsheim in 1932. Domboy himself remembers clearly going over the works with Jean Bugatti at Easter that year, on the Saturday, and seeing the body in course of manufacture.

On the Type 57, Molsheim built
- the Galibier coach or saloon (4 door)
- the 2 door Ventoux coach
- the coupé Atalante on 57C and 57S
- the coupé Atlantic on 57S and 57SC
- the 4 door saloon on the 1939 57C

The racing tanks Type 57G which won at Le Mans in 1937 and 1939 were made in their entirety at the works, as well as the Model 64, the last creation of the pre-war period and still at the prototype stage when Jean Bugatti was killed in 1939.

The Gangloff firm at Colmar was another principal supplier of coachwork to Bugatti on several models (e.g. the Stelvio coupé) even after the war (on Types 101 and 101C). And as Mr. Domboy points out, from the beginning of Type 57 production, the works produced the greater part of the bodywork.

It was Jean Bugatti himself who was really responsible for this works coachwork from a period which probably dated from about 1930. In truth it is difficult to separate the role played by the two creators, Ettore Bugatti and his son Jean in the conception of these new models.

Taking over more and more the initiative, Jean Bugatti, as his father had done before him made his own imprint on each new design, and contributed himself to the continuing success of the marque.

The conception, the design and the practical realization in the factory fell to him entirely. He instructed the preparation from his own ideas of small scale models, using drawings produced by the draughtsmen allocated to him personally; then outline drawings were made and finally when a particular model was adopted for production, the draughtsmen made outline drawings for the factory itself.

The closed coachwork (coach, coupé, berline, etc.) had a framework in wood (mainly in ash) on to which the sheet metal was nailed or screwed.

For each new model, the wood framework was first of all drawn out in full scale on a large vertical drawing board, giving:
  – a vertical elevation
    a half view in plan
  – longitudinal sections of the main forms of the body profile.

It is to be noted that these layout drawings, fully detailed in all aspects were used by the joiners in the body shop to determine the body lines under the orders of the Chief of the Coachworks and Jean Bugatti himself. The joiners then built the wood frames with their complex profiles as required by the layout drawings, assembling them by rebates and glue, and attaching them to the chassis by appropriate metal work.

At the same time the sheetmetal shop produced the covering

419

sheet-work, the body sides, top, rear part, wings, bonnet (hood) and so on. These sheet parts were offered up to fit the wood-work, then welded to each other and attached as already indicated.

The coachwork joinery department was a section of the general woodwork shop, and had a considerable complement of wood working machines, as well as a large drying autoclave.

The sheet metal shop was fully equipped with all necessary machines for working sheet by the methods of contemporary sheet metal workers – shears, bending machines, presses, hammers, rivetters, welding machines and so on.

Naturally this sort of hand made coachwork had no relation to the modern production methods which produce the many hundreds or even thousands of bodies a day of the modern car.

The trimming shop which had many highly skilled workmen, completed the trimming and upholstery of the bodies as well as the seats; and then finally there was the paint shop.

The Guide*

ALTHOUGH A BUGATTI ENTHUSIAST OF SOME YEARS' STANDING, I AM A hopeless mechanic, but when there's a job of work to be done there's no one more willing than I am to tackle it in the right and proper way, and the Guide Book is my constant companion.

Now for the benefit of those who perhaps are less gifted than I am, I will show you exactly how to set about any little job which may require attention.

In order to make sure that everything is functioning as it should I suggest that each page of the Guide Book be studied, and by carefully comparing what it says with what you know, you can tell at once whether all those little interesting processes which go on all the time inside the car are doing their job.

First of all take the Guide Book in your left hand (you will need your right to turn over the pages) and firmly open the cover. The cover only says, *E. B. Bugatti* surrounded by pearls, and 3L300

* *Bugantics*, 6, 6, pp. 25-6, November 1937.

Type 57. This information is of so little use that you can now tear the cover off and throw it away.

The first page is completely blank on both sides, and I assume that this is intended to set your mind completely at rest in preparation for the task it is about to undertake.

We now come to page 1, and it is headed *Caractéristiques Générales.* Although, at first glance, this would appear to be something to do with Army manoeuvres you will find by referring to your dictionary that it merely sets out in order all those things that you can see for yourself by looking at the car.

Page 2 is far more important. It says *Précautions D'usage Courant.* It is a serious warning, but do not worry unduly. I am assuming that you have already used your car, and as this merely tells you all those things which are essential before you do, as you have, things must be all right otherwise it wouldn't, if you understand.

For instance – *placer le levier de changement de vitesse au point mort.* I mean you are bound to have known if you hadn't.

And again – *s'être assuré que le frein à main est serré et des niveaux d'eau du radiateur, d'huile du carter-moteur ainsi que de la provision de combustible,* etc. You simply couldn't have motored at all if you hadn't, especially the combustible – I like that word

Therefore both sides of this page have been dealt with and, as you know them by heart, you can tear them out and throw them away. It will save you time next time you refer to the Guide.

Page 3 has a pretty picture so you can keep this one, especially as it tells you what to do when you get back, *à la rentrée au garage.* This is far more important than going out, because *pour arrêter le moteur, retirer la clef de contact.*

If you fail in this important procedure little will be left of your 3L300 Type 57 when you go to the garage the next morning.

Before turning to page 4, note the heading at the foot of page 3, *Réglage du Moteur.* My dictionary tells me that this means 'Regulating the Motor', and the diagrams that follow are frightful and far beyond my limited compression – I mean comprehension. Also it tells me to *Demonter le couvercle de l'arbre à cames,* and I simply wouldn't dare, would you? Then I advise that you tear out this page and throw it away – it will only confuse you.

Page 5 is a continuation of page 4 only worse, but it goes on to tell you all about *Allumage.* This sounds very much like *Réglage;* in fact, most things in the Guide seem to end in 'age', and it is probably done to rhyme with garage.

Both pages 6 and 7 talk about *Réglage* again, it's awful the amount of this that seems necessary, and in any case I would never dare tamper with a *Carburateur*, especially a thing full of *pompes*. We now come to the *Réglage* (there it is again) *des Freins*. The first line says, however *le réglage des freins est correct*. Well, they must know best so don't worry, just pass on to page 9, *Graissage*.

I find this rather puzzling. In addition to keeping one eye on the speedometer to make sure that the 30 mph limit is not being exceeded, you must also keep this same eye on the mileage department. As you go along you must indulge in mental arithmetic and as soon as you reach 187·5 miles your quick calculation will tell you that it is equivalent to 300 kilometres, and you must jump down and *nettoyer le filtre du moteur* (*fig. 9*). My dictionary translates this as to clean, to cleanse, to scour, to sweep, to wipe, to pick. This apparently could mean 'Pick 9 figs from the moving strainer', but I don't believe this is really what they mean.

And again, as soon as you reach 312·5 miles you find this is 500 kilometres, and once more you must dismount, but horrors, you must now *Graisser les articulations de la bielle du direction, les axes des jumelles des ressorts AV et les pivots de fusée* (*seringue speciale*) *voir fig. 12.* If you are like me, you must again refer to the dictionary, and it tells me to 'Dirty the allegation of the Government Rod (or should it be Whip?) the semi-detached axle of the front lock, and the hinge of the intricate business (the peculiar squirt). Examine 12 figs'. Or have I got it wrong?

Well, anyway, you probably get the hang of things now. Personally, I've thrown the Guide away. I find Brixton easier.

ELGY

A Bugatti controversy*

BUGATTI'S CARS HAVE FREQUENTLY BEEN INVOLVED IN HEATED controversy, due no doubt to an unusual blend of qualities leading (certainly) to endearment and (sometimes) hysterical enthusiasm, and faults which irritate or leave cold the less sensitive (or is it sensible?) of car owners. An enchanting example, probably forgotten and certainly worth recording, is contained in the *Automotor Journal*, 25, 1920. (This journal was founded by Stanley Spooner in 1896 and ceased publication about 1932.)

---

* Originally published in the *Bulletin V.S.C.C.* No. 66, Spring 1960.

An excellent illustrated description of the 1920 models is given in the 8 July issue, this referring to the 4 cylinder models as Types 22 and 23 (the latter with a longer wheel-base), and shows the steering box separate from the engine bearer unlike the later models. The engine size in both models is 68 mm × 100 mm (most people consider that Type 23 is always 69 × 100).

The fun begins on 9 September when the contributor 'Omega', referring to the success of the car at the 1920 Le Mans race, was so bold as to suggest that 'sensible people know that a machine like the Bugatti is built primarily to race, although [he] was prepared to hear that a Bugatti can be a very pleasant little car for ordinary driving'. On 23 September 'Omega' had to defend himself with a whole column against numerous correspondents:

They tell me, with one accord, and almost in identical phrases, that the Bugatti is eminently a touring car. I receive their protests. I have never personally handled, nor even sat in, a car of this make. But turning up my *Auto* of 8 July last, I find that the 1920 standard model Bugatti of 12 hp nominal rating, with a cylinder-bore of 68 mm, has two inlet and two exhaust valves to each of its businesslike four cylinders, and enormously long pistons, with four rings apiece, and other signs of something more than 'touring' efficiency in the mind of the man responsible for the design.

Now it may well be that duplex valve-ing is something to which nearly all manufacturers may come in time, excepting those who go to the other extreme and do without valves (as generally so-called) altogether. But for the present I regard the mere duplication of valves as suggesting racing, or extreme, high, 'stunt' efficiency practice. This being so, I am not going to take back what I said. A machine like the Bugatti – I quote my exact words – is built primarily to race, although I am prepared to hear that a Bugatti can be a very pleasant little car for ordinary driving. My withers are unrung. I am prepared to be prepared, because my sagacious friend Lefrère, of Messrs Jarrott & Letts Ltd, tells me that if he sat me blindfolded in a Bugatti, in standard tune (which means one good for 70 to 80 mph on a straight stretch of level British road), and drove me along at from 35 to 40 miles per hour, I should never dream that I was on something which had twice the speed-potentiality tucked away under its bonnet.

This is all very well. I accept anything Lefrère tells me, about either cars or cider; and I am equally satisfied of the truth of the

423

statements made in this matter by other friends, so many of whom have written me more or less abusively.

In the same issue was a letter from a Lt-Colonel C. Dawson in defence of the car. He was almost certainly the previous owner of the famous Peter Hampton Type 13. 'I can assure Omega', he says, 'that the Bugatti is an extraordinarily pleasant little car to drive in an ordinary way, and will go so far as to say that we have nothing to touch it here'.

On 30 September 'Omega' contributed this interesting column:

It appears that this gentleman's own Bugatti is of fairly early date (about 1912, I gather), and was originally fitted with a saloon body. It was, in fact, essentially a touring car, although possessed of ginger and running-freedom notably in excess of those of most standard cars. Thus its owner is quite justified in saying that the Bugatti is just as suitable a car for everyday touring use as for stunts of the Le Mans circuit order.

Further than this, my friend (who is also Colonel Dawson's friend, and has personally satisfied himself of the magnificent running of the Colonel's eight-year-old car only this summer) tells me something about M. Bugatti which makes interesting reading. Directly the results of the voiturette race were published, he wrote M. Bugatti, asking him if he could have one of the cars used in the Grand Prix, to run at Brooklands.

And how did the constructor reply: 'You can, possibly, but why do you specify one of the racing cars, when every Bugatti of this year will give you practically the same performance? Please understand, my dear man, that I never did and never will build two sorts of cars – one for sale and the other for demonstrations. Any performance of one Bugatti is easily repeated with another Bugatti. We do not build "special" chassis. Some seem better than others, because no two articles made even by the most skilled artificers are ever exactly alike in performance. But we have always a minimum standard of efficiency, and it is perhaps because we allow to leave the factory nothing which will not come up to this minimum standard of efficiency that our factory remains comparatively small, and modest as to its production.

'I could build six times the number of cars if I were satisfied to let anything with a Bugatti name-plate go forth on to the road as a

Bugatti. But I am not. Our disposition, here, is that we will not allow to leave our gates any car which we are not perfectly satisfied will represent us with credit.

'Thus if you want a car for Brooklands you simply want a car – any car we ship you. It is idle of us even to try to "tune" it for you, there being such surprising differences in your atmosphere and ours, and your fuel and ours. Let me send you the next car I can spare, and do what you can with it. You will not be disappointed.'

Now this is a very free translation of M. Bugatti's remarks, but the 'freedom' is imported merely to make clear his exact meaning, in English English.

Is it not a magnificent working-principle? Is not that the spirit in which every constructor should regard his productions? It may well be that one Bugatti is enough for France, and that one similar product would, at present, be enough for England. But that is the spirit we want at work, on a car of the Bugatti type in this country.

'Omega' goes on to wonder if there is a market in Britain for a car of the Bugatti type, necessarily of rather high price; he remarks that Bugatti owners appear, one and all, deeply to resent a word of seeming depreciation (we still do!).

On 14 October a new contestant enters the battle in the shape of Mr G. P. H. de Freville, the designer of the Alvis car, and the sparks begin to fly; de Freville claims to have 'considerable experience of this car' and supports the views of Colonel Dawson as to its excellence. He was interested 'in "Omega's" remarks in regard to whether there is a Bugatti market in this country; this is a question which (he had) been trying to solve for a long time.' Well, well! So the Alvis sprang from Bugatti stimulus. 'Omega' in a footnote to the letter becomes petulant: 'with regard to the Alvis of which so many of us have heard so much, I will leave it to Mr de Freville the explanation of the reason that I never saw and tried his car, despite his making an appointment to do so'.

On 21 October Mr Lionel Martin, joining the fray, answers 'Omega' that he, in the Aston Martin, is trying to design a British Voiturette de luxe, having put the prototype on the road since Easter, 1915, and after 80,000 miles of development hopes shortly to put it on the market. 'While I have had in mind', he says, 'during the designing period the excellent and lively little

425

machine which bears (Bugatti's) name, I have also used as a standard the typically English Rolls-Royce and it is a blend of these two cars which I hope to produce'. Another one for the Patron! The correspondence continues in later weeks, mostly acrimonious and quibbling back and forth on what was or was not said, or meant, and then, on 18 November, the Editor really drops a brick in the editorial description of the Bugatti at the 1920 Olympia Show – detachable head and a 3-speed gearbox included! There are 'overhead valves in extravagant profusion', and he thinks the 710-90 tyres too large.

The next week 'Omega' replies to the Colonel: 'Anyhow, now that I have seen his pet at Olympia I think it more than ever remarkable that such a fly-weight should run at all. I agree with [the] technical writers that the engine looks "hot" but the rest of the chassis is not at all what I had expected. I hope that there is more in the Colonel's 1912 chassis, otherwise when one of these days I ram him with my 1921 Horstman, his mount will be sadly crumpled.'

The correspondence ends on 23 December with a further objecting letter from Colonel Dawson to which 'Omega' added a footnote:

I fear that I cannot follow the hon. and gallant member through his mazy intricacies. I can only pray for another war, to distract his attention, and offer my heartfelt sympathy to anybody who has ever sold him anything, or corresponded with him about anything. I have again read all through his letters, and found five more points on which I should like to question him, but forbear. His announcement that a veil must descend evidently means that he has been rash enough to go for a run on his dear old Bugatti, and must now go into dock for a spell. Only one protestation – I am not a 'critic'. I leave criticism to a brutal and licentious soldiery.

After which further comment is (temporarily) impossible!

The Sequel

A noticeable change however takes place in the following year (1922). In February 'Omega' begins to weaken:

I have been learning a little more about this very special voiturette

426

chassis. I have not yet tried it, but I have been privileged to look into the experience of a number of owners. And really to read and hear what they say about it, you would wonder that anything else had ever sold anywhere at anything but Ford price! I have seen pictures of it with two, three and four-seated bodywork, and fuel-consumption-records, and speed-stunts, and tyre-mileages, and bills for replacement-parts over five years (and 120,000 miles). Now I am sitting down awaiting with what patience I can muster the day when I can see if all that these good people say about the car is justified by the behaviour of this year's model.

We know perfectly well that a man who has decent luck with his first car swears by its manufacturers for the rest of his life, as a rule. But these Bugatti-enthusiasts are no novices, revelling in the first flush of possession, and overlooking little things which would annoy old stagers. In at least fifty per cent of cases they are people who bought Bugattis when they were using other, larger cars. They bought Bugattis to be able to flip-about speedily on errands which could be done by a two-seater; but during the doing of those jobs of work they wanted to enjoy the refinement of performance to which they were accustomed on much larger and more powerful cars. Well, they all seem to have one opinion, and that decidedly complimentary to M. Ettore Bugatti and Alsace, and – as I have hinted – if the coach-builders keep up to their promised date, by about the time these words are in print I should be in a position to join the gladsome, if still small, band of Bugattini, and raise my voice to swell their chorus of praise [3 February 1921].

A few weeks later (24 February) he has to defend himself against a correspondent who wonders why people buy Bugattis at high prices when similar performance can be obtained with the British light cars. 'Omega' retorts:

There are, however, buyers for all the Bugattis Messrs Chas. Jarrott and Letts, Ltd, are likely to get, this year or next, to be recruited from among people who would not look at a car of the type and class amply satisfying [the gentleman from Leicester]. These are people who are becoming small car users by stress of circumstances, or by conviction. They have given up, or are giving up, big fast cars. . . . There are many of those people, wanting high efficiency at low running-cost, that they will readily absorb all the chassis M. Bugatti can produce. The British sole concessionaires are advertising the 'Bug.', I understand. But M. Bugatti has never done so. He does not think it necessary to do so now. He sells chassis today as Antonio Stradivari

427

sold fiddles, in old Cremona; steadily, but only as he builds them (which means every one as fine as he knows how) and when he builds them (which means as soon as he can, they being as they are).

In the weeks that follow the signs of weakness continue as 'Omega' enjoys his Bugatti (a 16 valve 2 seater Type 22)! By 13 October 1921 he is fully indoctrinated:

The great delights of the Bugatti, as I find them, are its wonderful acceleration (accompanied by marvellous freedom from over-run), its suspension, its steering, and that wonderful bubbling song of the exhaust, be the cut-out opened ever so modestly. Fully open, the little beast sounds like the whole of Brooklands paddock gone mad. But only a hog would use it fully open within a mile of any houses, so we need not worry about that!

Oh! I forgot another charm – the marvellous ease and lightness and surety of the speed-changing mechanism. A finger suffices to engage any gear; two fingers suffice to shift the lever across the pretty little gate; and the merest pat of the clutch-pedal is all that is required. I double all my changes, up and down, from habit, and I don't intend to drop a good habit, because to do so would spoil me for other cars I have to drive, by way of making a living. But I have already discovered that one can get third-to-fourth or fourth-to-third changes cleanly and noiselessly without touching the clutch-pedal at all, and I can well believe that Bugatti experts, like Cushman, Blackstock, Major Lefrère and Colonel Dawson can go right through the four changes without declutching, as I am told.

L'Amende Honorable! Now to grovel! Suitably garbed in a white sheet, a halter round my neck, ashes on my head and contrition in my errant heart, I apologize to Colonel Dawson for having ever doubted any of the charming things he said about his Bugatti.

He was quite right. Before mine is run-in, I agree that it is a touring car, at will, though it is also a little terrestrial flying-machine, at will. But it can be driven, even in its first 1,000 miles, as smoothly and sweetly and economically as the woolliest, heaviest old hay-barge imaginable, if one will make full use of the gearbox (put there to be used) and watch one's spark-lever. It will dawdle along at 20 mph in the sedatest manner imaginable. . . .

Colonel Dawson was right, and I was wrong, and I regret all the nasty, petulant things I was provoked to write, when he was justly belabouring my imprudent head. Don't shoot, Colonel! I have already 'come down'!

A surprising, but happy ending to an interesting quarrel!

Colonel Sorel

(from the *Automotor Journal*, 4 March 1926)

Colonel W. L. Sorel has fine premises, a good and representative stock, and for adjustments, overhauls, repairs or tuning he has a staff recruited from Molsheim – a great point, this, because of late years there have been so many selfstyled 'Bugatti specialists' who were nothing of the sort. Any car which is inclined to be 'quick' creates its own 'specialists', at times with most direful consequences, because a fastish car which has been 'improved' by such people can in quite a few seasons be reduced to a sorry wreck, so many folk knowing so much more about Bugattis even than M. Ettore Bugatti himself.

Even as late as 1921, people stared with interest at every Bugatti they met. Today Bugatti-users are no longer embarrassed by this degree of interest on the part of other road-users, and there are almost as many lady owner-drivers as those of the other persuasion, simply because, although this car is so fast, it has latterly become just as easy to maintain as anything else of comparable performance. It has always, of course, been a very economical little machine to run. When I first had one it was rather prone to oil up if one ran the engine too slowly. To use fourth speed at less than 20 mph was not good for it, because it had been designed and built for faster work. I have changed four plugs in ten miles, on my first; but the lubrication system was very drastically redesigned in 1922, and since then people who have used really good and suitable plugs, like Bosch or KLG, have been quite free from the only (or at least the main) crab even of the earlier models.

It cannot too often be said that all 'quick' cars are much better when run as their designers intended them to be run than when fitted with all sorts of weird devices intended to improve upon nature. One has to be very clever indeed to show M. Ettore Bugatti how to get better than the best out of his own motorcars, and I would counsel anybody who has anything but a perfectly satisfactory Bugatti to get in touch at once with Colonel Sorel, in Brixton Road. Very little and inexpensive things will in some cases make very large differences in the behaviour of a car, but those little things are best done by somebody who really does know what he is doing. The village blacksmith, or his modern prototype, has great virtues, but unfortunately he does not know everything, and that is where he can slip up now and again, especially in playing with mechanism of the delicacy and beauty of that inside the little box on top of a Bugatti cylinder-block!

429

PART IV

BUGATTI CLUBS

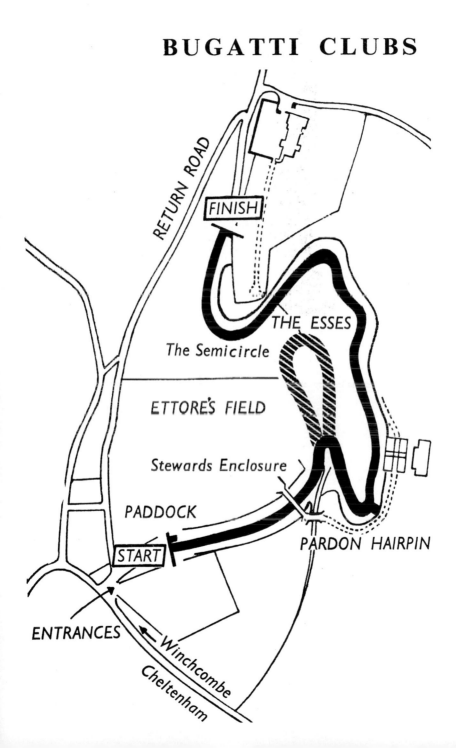

RETURN ROAD

FINISH

THE ESSES

The Semicircle

ETTORE'S FIELD

Stewards Enclosure

PADDOCK

START

PARDON HAIRPIN

ENTRANCES

Winchcombe

Cheltenham

337. *The B.O.C. was organizing hill-climbs long before Prescott was opened. Here is T.A.S.O. Mathieson on a G.P. in 1932. Note the road surface.*

338. *T.43, XV2783, about 1932.*

339. *J. Lemon Burton, 1931, in a magnificent burst of enthusiasm. The car is a T.37 but the mud wings are scarcely regulation.*

340. *Prescott has the atmosphere of a country garden rather than a race track. An impressive line up of Bugattis at a Rally.*

341. *Frank Wall in the very successful single seat Type 35B the very successful great verve and concentration.*

342. *Silverstone not Montlhéry.*

The Bugatti Owners' Club

IF THE BUGATTI OWNERS' CLUB CAN CLAIM TO HAVE STARTED IT all in 1929, others have followed in Holland, America and Germany – we even have one in France, two in fact now! These Clubs fan the flames of Bugatti's immortal glory, foster the enjoyment of the marque and generally provide a lot of pleasure to their many members.

Mr Eric Giles recounted the beginnings of the B.O.C. in the Silver Jubilee issue of *Bugantics*, 17, 1, February 1954:

The credit for the idea of forming a Bugatti Club in Britain belongs to one D. B. Madeley by name. He has another claim to fame because he is the only person we have ever known or heard of who owned a Crossley-Bugatti – the early Brescia model made in this country just after the 1914–18 war by the Crossley car people under licence from Bugatti.

I believe he started his ball rolling by writing to the motor press suggesting the formation of a Club for Bugatti enthusiasts and as a result of this, one evening way back in 1929, three people met over a glass of beer – two pipe smokers and one using a cigarette holder – and, as you know from the familiar picture at the beginning of every copy of Bugantics, out of the smoke of that meeting the Club was born. The three people? One pipe, of course, belonged to Madeley, the second belonged to Colonel Giles and the cigarette holder to T. Ambrose Varley.

At that time, probably as a result of Madeley's letter to the press, another little group, headed by the late Dr Ewan, got together with the same object in view. Colonel Giles attended one of these meetings to see whether the two groups could not amalgamate, but their ideas were so different from ours that it proved impossible and we immediately registered the name 'Bugatti Owners' Club Ltd' so as to prevent anyone else using the name Bugatti.

So the Club was formed and the first meeting was held at Colonel Giles' house in Regent's Park. Varley became the first Hon. Secretary, Madeley was made Hon. Treasurer and a Committee (which

434

we called a Council) was formed with Colonel Giles as Chairman.
Thus Madeley was No. 1 on the Club Register, Varley No. 2, Colonel Giles No. 3, I was No. 4, J. R. Crouch No. 5, J. Lemon Burton No. 6, K. W. Bear No. 7, H. J. Morris No. 8, followed by G. P. Powles, F. J. Fielding and J. D. Jevons.

Varley's tenure as Secretary was rather short-lived as he suddenly disappeared in rather curious circumstances and I remember rushing down to his house to retrieve the Club's books etc, before they also vanished. Bear then took over the Hon. Secretaryship and I became Trials Secretary until Bear relinquished his job and I took over as Hon. Secretary and Treasurer in January 1932.

Early in those days Earl Howe joined us and became our first President, followed by Malcolm Campbell as Vice-President, and not long after we received official recognition from Molsheim when Ettore himself gave us his blessing by joining the Club and becoming our first Patron.

This set-up remained in being for many years during which time the only changes were in certain members of the Council.

Finally I resigned as Secretary in 1946 and was elected Chairman in place of Colonel Giles who became Vice President, a position which I held until the A.G.M. of 1951, when I resigned from the Council and was elected President after Earl Howe had been made Patron.

After having served on the Competitions Committee for some time, and later on the Council, our present dynamic Chairman then really came into the picture and all present day members know full well how much he has done for the Club.

No history of the Club could possibly be complete without a reference to *Bugantics* and its various Editors because those who are lucky enough to have a complete set (and there are very few) have in their possession a complete record of the Club and its doings.

The first Editor was Madeley, who successfully launched the first issue in June 1931, and kept it going from strength to strength until J. S. Steele took over in August 1932.

Steele did a wonderful job and ran it right up to November 1935, when Colonel Giles took over, and kept it going so successfully until Peter Hampton relieved him of the burden in December 1948.

And now, with this Jubilee Number we very reluctantly say farewell to him as Editor after what has undoubtedly been the most successful period in the whole history of this famous little book.

Only those who have had anything to do with the preparation of *Bugantics* can have any conception of the terrific amount of work and thought which has been put into the production of this unique publication over the past 23 years.

435

In 1937 (in order to provide themselves with a hill-climb course) the Bugatti Owners' Club purchased the estate of Prescott House, which lies in the beautiful country close to Cleeve Hill. It is about five miles from Cheltenham, in Gloucestershire, and ninety miles from London. The house is a delightful one, built of Cotswold stone and owned, up to 1871, by the Earl of Ellenborough. In the grounds will be found the lovely wrought-iron gates put up in memory of the late Ettore Bugatti and his elder son, the late Jean Bugatti.

The original course was roughly 1,000 yards long with an average gradient of 1 in 20, cars attacking the hill singly and being timed electrically. The record for the original course stands to David Boshier-Jones in a Cooper at 41·00 sec. The present record on the longer course of 1,127 yards is held by Roy Lane in 43·07 sec. (September 1972). Approximately five meetings are held a year.

The American Bugatti Club

THE BACKGROUND TO THE FORMATION OF THIS CLUB IS BEST TOLD from the following extract from the Club Journal *Pur-Sang*, 1, 1, 1960:

In the late 1920s and early 1930s, there were approximately seven Bugattis in the Los Angeles area, and all of the owners more or less knew each other. Several picnics took place, and there was talk of forming a U.S. Bugatti Club, but, as usual, nothing came of it except informal meetings and unorganized tours to such places as Lake Arrowhead and Muroc Dry Lake. It was a pleasure then to be able to drive a Grand Prix model on the streets without full road equipment, and if the local policia took exception, well they were only equipped with Dodge 4's and underpowered Buicks (and no radios), so it was really great sport to make a run for it.

At this time Bugattis were also being raced on the East Coast by such long-time enthusiasts as George Rand, Dick Wharton and Walter Gerner, to name but a few. The racing activities of the marque at Indianapolis and Vanderbilt speedways during this period have largely been overlooked or forgotten. Later in the 1930s, Bugatti activity in this locality almost died out, and there appeared to be little interest in these cars; to such an extent that Grand Prix models and excellent Type 38s and 57s were offered for sale for a few hundred dollars, often with no takers. From 1940 to 1950, with World War II intervening, there was no interest at all in this area.

Within the last six years, a number of ardent enthusiasts began to import Bugattis in appreciable quantities and, owing to this movement, interest began to freshen. Occasionally a Bugatti would be shown at a Concourse, and, thanks to Dr Milton Roth, a Type 35C and Type 55 were shown at the Los Angeles Auto Show in 1955. This activity, plus the kind assistance of John Bond of *Road and Track* who has featured Bugattis several times in his publication, including Bob Day's and Al Crundall's Type 51As, John Caperton's Type 50, and Lucille Phillips' Type 49, has done much to stimulate interest in the marque.

On 15 October 1958 a local group of owners organized a picnic which took place in Arroyo Seco Park, in South Pasadena. This was attended by 17 Bugattis and their owners. A report and pictures of this gathering was published in the February 1959 issue of *Road and Track*. Although this event was a great success, the first picnic held at Fred Treat's estate was even more so, and we were now assured that we must form our own Club. After several informal gatherings we finally decided to 'give it a go' and on 10 February 1960 a meeting was held to select officers and set dues, and to finalize the name of the Club.

Bugatti Club Nederland

(Communicated by Mr W. M. Pieters 7 April 1961)

IT WAS BACK IN OCTOBER 1955 THAT, DURING A VETERAN CAR RALLY organized by the now famous Pionier Automobielen Club, five Bugatti owners met each other, virtually for the first time in their lives, each of them driving a well preserved specimen of 'le pur-sang de l'automobile'. The city of Utrecht was selected as rallying place and there, before the start of a joint drive through beautiful country towards the Zandvoort-race track as a finishing point, one had the opportunity of inspecting at leisure a Type 37A, a mighty looking Type 43, two Types 40 and another Type 43 carrosserie-roadster. In the evening of that memorable day of motoring, during dinner at Zandvoort, the five Bugatti owners* spontaneously decided to form their own club which is now well known as the Bugatti Club Nederland consisting of some 40 members and totalling 36 Bugatti cars.

The Dutch are notorious individualists and especially when driving their always new looking mass-production vehicles of any European or American make on the well maintained roads of their small country most of them behave as if alone in the world. Bearing this in mind the reader will readily appreciate the fact, that, long before there was any sign of the birth of a B.C.N., it was quite an event when two Dutchmen driving their 'pur-sangs' met each other by chance, each of them being convinced he was driving the one and only Bugatti in the country.

The B.C.N. brought all owners of Bugatti together and what a variety of individuals they turned out to be! A dentist, a musician, a salesman, a printer, an industrial designer, a medical student, a psychiatrist, an automobile engineer, a ship owner, an oil specialist, an importer of timber, a banker, a farmer; in short, really every conceivable profession seems to be represented in this Club. All these people had become at some stage in their lives ardent lovers of 'la marque', fascinated by the pecularities, effectiveness, simplicity and beauty of design, intent on experiencing over and over again this

---

* Founders: B. Laming, W. M. Pieters, van Ramshorst, G. F. M. F. Prick, R. Andersen.

automobile's extreme road worthiness, the strange feeling it gives one that it has a mysterious life and a will of its own, that with a driver's skill and quick reaction it will do the impossible and perform magnificently under any road and weather conditions. Add to these qualities the symphony of mechanical sound plus that very particular exhaust note and there one has a true picture of Ettore Bugatti's automobile which united all these different people in the B.C.N.

In 1958 the B.C.N. successfully organized the Grand Rally International Ermenonville – Le Mans which, amongst others, lead to the Bad Honnef Rally, so well organized by the German Bugatti Club in 1960.

Bugatti-Club Deutschland

THE GERMAN BUGATTI CLUB WAS FOUNDED BY KURT KIEFFER on the occasion of the *Grosser Preis von Deutschland* (Grand Prix of Germany) at the Nürburgring on 4 August 1956. Mr Kieffer was a Bugatti enthusiast of long standing (owner of a Type 35B from 1931 until 1937 and from then up to now of a T.49).

The Club consists at present of some twenty Bugatti owners, ten former Bugatti racing motorists, another twenty enthusiasts for the car and three owners from Luxembourg, over fifty in all. There is no subscription fee to the Club; its offices are at Am Reichenberg 17 in Bad Honnef (Rhein).

The aims of the *Bugatti-Club Deutschland* are the maintenance of the Bugatti tradition, the promotion of comradeship amongst the Bugatti drivers and mutual support in all Bugatti affairs as well as the care of the Bugattis still existing. Members are under the obligation not to trade with Bugattis. Louis Chiron and Maurice Trintignant are Honorary Members.

Since 1950 the '*Bugattisten*' have met every year on the Nürburgring during the *Grosser Preis von Deutschland*. In addition the *Bugatti-Club Deutschland* have organized, at Bad Honnef in 1960 and at Diez (Lahn) in 1962, international Bugatti meetings. These were well attended and made a lasting impression on everyone attending of the pleasure and good fellowship among owners of these vintage cars.

A Restoration Controversy

THE RICHARDSON RULES

IN 1959 THE BUGATTI OWNERS' CLUB JOURNAL *Bugantics* PUB-
lished an article by Lt Colonel Eri Richardson, a long-time
Bugatti owner and enthusiast. This article was entitled 'On Pur-
Sang' and dealt rather critically with the 'phoney' restoration of
Bugatti cars. This article caused something of a stir among
Bugattistes on both sides of the Atlantic; several hear! hear!'s (or
whatever the North American equivalent is) were heard, many
sighs of dismay, a few angry outbursts mainly from a few who
know that Richardson had 'sinned' himself (although now
repentant), and a few smiles from those who enjoy their Bugattis,
but don't take them as seriously as all that.

Few serious Bugattistes would quarrel with the bulk of the
Richardson Rules, although some feel he goes too far for the
normal owner with a finite purse. But the article is worth
reproducing:

ON PUR-SANG

by Eri Richardson

The sixteen years, 1945–61, since the cessation of World War II
have marked the transition of the name Bugatti from a fading
position in competition to a worldwide revered place in the history
of the racing and competition car. Hardly a month goes by without
the appearance of a pictorial article on this famous man and marque.

Roland Bugatti's reputed ejaculation upon the death of his father:
'Le Patron est mort, La Voiture est mort aussi!' appears more and
more prophetic as time passes and we fail to see the hoped for
Phoenix-like re-ascendancy of a new and great Bugatti car in the
tradition of le Patron. Pierre Marco's tenacious efforts in the 1950s
once again to produce a true Bugatti were doomed by lack of funds
and lack of any sincere dedication among the Bugatti heirs to the
perpetuation of the great name of their father.

The Colombo-designed Type 251 paid little homage to le Patron –

not even utilizing the traditional squared format of engine styling; in fact, so little did this car present itself in the Bugatti design pattern, that few if any Bugatti purists would care to exchange a well preserved Type 51 for a new model 251 at the factory door.

The typical Molsheim advertisement of the middle 1920s showed the closed racing horseshoe origin of the Bugatti radiator, the theme 'Le Pur-Sang des Automobiles' clearly publicizes Ettore Bugatti's dedicated purpose that his automobiles would have no peer in purity of design, fine craftsmanship, appearance and performance. This objective existed from the earliest years of the century but was most uncontestably established in the years 1925 through 1927 by the types then produced and the accomplishment of the historic 1,045 victories in the years 1925–26 alone. It has been said that this two-year total for Bugatti exceeds the combined wins of all the other great marques of the period.

Bugatti automobiles now appear to have passed from the period of competition to a time for preservation and restoration of even the most prosaic models. Factory catalogue original cars are virtually unobtainable, except for the 57 series; and few of these have escaped the ravages of time and the ego of past, and even present owners. One hundred per cent pure restorations are not being made either because owners and repairers lack the knowledge or because there has not, as yet, developed sufficient incentive in prices and prizes to foster PUR-SANG preservation.

The author of this article knows of only a bare handful of restored or catalogue original Bugatti cars of any type in America and few in Great Britain or Europe. Of dozens of Bugatti cars inspected not one would gain full marks and the recurrence of modifying brake and suspension systems; modernized wheel types and sizes; non-original fuel pumps, oil filters, electrical components; and excessive nickel and chrome plated parts and garish rotary polishing on the wrong parts is most disheartening to see in that it detracts from the conservative elegance and collector's value of Le Patron's masterpieces.

In the post-war years there have appeared a rash of articles and illustrations on Ettore Bugatti and his 'fabulous' creations. Unfortunately due to ignorance, *Concours d'Elegance* judges are making awards to new paint and chrome plating on cars desecrated with all manner of non-original engine, chassis and coachwork modifications, including non-period instruments and other accessories not even French in origin. A new line of imitation trophies should be established for the owners of these false examples of le Patron's works.

The genius of Ettore Bugatti as a painter in metals merits and receives increasing acclaim. Here was one stocky and sometimes cocky little master of the metallic arts who, well into the 1930s, matched his unique creations against the finest cars fielded by dictator subsidized factories operating with unlimited funds and engineering talent to develop design concepts on which they are still capitalizing today.

Only a hardy five or six Bugatti owners, world-wide, still continue to compete with various model Bugatti cars. These keen enthusiasts are found primarily within our own Club at Prescott, and in the American Bugatti Club organized in 1959–60. Most Bugattis are now seen as enthusiast-driven Road and Exhibition cars. The great days are long past and the great names even within the B.O.C. are now present only as greying and honoured patrons and sponsors, primarily concerned with steam trains, sedentary hobbies and nostalgia.

At this period, it appears essential, in order to preserve one or two examples of each Bugatti type that a small group of critical and dedicated purists such as we have in Sweden must band together within the B.O.C. and devote themselves to seeking out, recording transfers of possession and fostering the preservation and restoration to catalogue original of the few remaining Bugatti automobiles.

The author has owned various Bugatti types over a period of nearly thirty years and maintains a constantly growing extensive file of articles, clippings, photos, and factory published data on all the Bugatti types; and yet in reviewing all of this one finds an astonishing scarcity of examples of Pur-Sang Bugattis. Almost all engines or chassis carry some brazen oddity of equipment or modification expressing a prior or present owner's desire to out-engineer le Patron. In an era when Bugatti cars of all types are ascending in value as collector's items such mustachios on the Mona Lisa are deeply regrettable.

British and Continental magazines have been slow to publicize well preserved or restored Bugatti cars, possibly because they are nearly non-existent. American magazines have gone overboard with publicity – and not always of the best examples. The coloured wrapper of a leading book on sports cars pictured a post-war assembled model. A much publicized Type 59 has several primary components which are non-Bugatti in origin. One of the most publicized Royales is carburetted with American equipment and has other extensive non-Bugatti 'improvements' (?). Of four Bugatti cars used as magazine cover illustrations in the past two years, not one is factory catalogue original in all respects. Current owners are not even aware in most cases that their Bugattis are no longer PUR-SANG automobiles in the strictest sense.

444

The purpose of this article is to propose a set of rules for the restoration and preservation of all Bugatti types. The author has himself passed through the experience of modifying his early Bugatti cars; but is now dedicated to preserving or assisting others to restore and preserve the works of le Patron to catalogue original.

To further the above objectives we submit the following notes for the true Bugatti purist:

CRITERIA FOR PRESERVATION OR RESTORATION OF CATALOGUE ORIGINAL BUGATTIS

1. Remove all chassis and engine components (proprietary and personal) which were not factory installed on this or a related model Bugatti in the original period of manufacture. This means an item by item validation particularly of such items as lights, horns, fuel and oil pumps and filters, magnetos, coils, distributors; and all fittings, nuts, bolts, clamps etc. It obviously excludes acceptance of modifications to major components such as manifolds, brake assemblies, etc. etc.

2. Obtain 100 per cent original components as installed at Molsheim originally. The factory itself cannot be relied on always to furnish parts identical to the catalogue original. In the matter of perishable components like coils and fuel pumps which cannot be rebuilt to new – it is considered desirable, at least, to fit a similar type by the same maker as in the case of Bosch and Scintilla equipment. If new original parts are not obtainable then it is necessary to haunt such stockists as . . . and other known dealers in Bugatti used spares. There are still a few partial Bugattis being broken down for parts sufficient to fill most needs. Alternative measure is expertly to repair worn used parts to original. This includes casting and forging new stock and machining components identical to original. Using this procedure to *modify* le Patron's designs has been acceptable for competition cars, but should count points off in any PUR-SANG competition. *Exact* replica parts are considered essential including use of the same or similar materials – bronze, steel, aluminium, leather etc.

3. Restore from the frame out. When possible, sand down the frame and determine the original factory finish in type and colour. This is generally grey primer except in a few show models in which the frames were finished in Bugatti blue or red. Frames were not nickel or chrome plated so far as can be determined. Other painted components such as friction dampers and brake backing plates should be finished as original. Polished brake drums and axles and steering components show up much more beautifully in contrast to painted parts. An all polished or plated car is about as drab as a woman without make-up.

4. Metal components originally in natural (unplated) finish should be similarly restored. Bronze, copper and aluminium parts must never be nickelled or chromed. Polish them and cover with light oil or if too lazy to polish frequently, then polish dry and spray coat with clear lacquer as used for exterior hardware, or chrome protection on modern cars. Never use aluminium paint anywhere. This applies particularly to engine parts and especially to the Bugatti aluminium wheels where coats of paint are dangerous since they cover incipient cracks which should be noted and repaired without delay. Bugatti only applied rotary polishing to water jacket covers, firewalls, footwell ends and some G.P. instrument panels. All cam-cases and crankcases were done with diagonal scraper strokes and should be lightly polished or restored to original finish. [This is not correct – see later.] A fully rotary-turned engine no longer looks like le Patron's workmanship and a considerable element of the conservative elegance is sacrificed for a Hollywood garishness.

5. The German silver (white bronze) radiator casing of all earlier models should never be plated. If found to be plated it should be deplated and

445

RESTORATION
at its finest

343 and 344. *B. Lin-
blad's T.35B in Sweden.
The cambox and dash
finishes are correct. The
Tacho belt, originally
leather, can conveniently
be a modern grinding
machine belt.*

(photos: Olle Rosenquist)

345. *The temperature gauges are a modern fitment; inevitably an unobtainable air gauge has had to be replaced by an oil gauge.*

346. *Coachwork in pristine condition; Mr R. Campbell's 57806C.*

polished. As a special symbol of the marque Bugatti the radiator should be finished as original with a light coating of wax or clear lacquer. A plated German silver radiator should be a ban to a concours award anywhere but in Southern California where flamboyancy is normal to the local psychosis.

6. The front axle beam and the rear axle housing were usually left in polished and unplated form on the G.P. cars, to facilitate inspection and detection of incipient cracks. Some sports and Type 57 models had nickel plated front axle beams and steering linkage and in the 1930s chrome was used discriminately; but painted surfaces were always retained even on the Paris Show models to set off the beauty of the finely machined parts. Finishes in this tradition are the only acceptable ones for a PUR-SANG exhibition Bugatti.

The current trend on the part of some Bugatti owners to 'gild the lily' is resulting in the destruction of the conservative and distinctive elegance of le Patron's original creations. In the preparation of a Bugatti for Concours d'Elegance competition the appearance of ostentatious brilliance should result in points off rather than cups won. Chrome plating of radiators on G.P. models and on brake backing plates, frame members and other parts not originally plated only serve to cheapen the artistic beauty of Ettore Bugatti's masterpieces in metal.

7. Steel parts on Bugatti cars present a preservation problem. For 100 per cent originality they should be polished and oiled or waxed. It may be worth a few points off to give an unpolished, rust-inhibiting cadmium plating to such items as nuts, bolts, pins, clamps, levers etc., and a cadmium undercoat to other steel components which are to be painted. Plating of stressed parts is dangerous as it nearly always has an embrittling effect – inducing failure under stress.

This writer has enjoyed nearly thirty years of Bugatti ownership and thousands of hours spent searching out various models, replacement parts and technical data; and many added hours of patient and sometimes costly work, much of it with his own hands and hand tools. In recent years it has been noted that any well maintained original Bugatti of any type increases in value constantly. Bugatti cars may still be found in restorable order for £200 or so in remote parts of France and Germany and for twice that in the U.K. and the U.S.; but show me if you can a perfect and original car in sound running order for less than £500 un-restored. Any concours condition Bugatti is worth at least £1,000 (plus freight and customs, if in America) – and they are unobtainable. With a thorough restoration costing a minimum of £500 and usually two or three times that amount, the value is there.

The controversy was continued in the American journal *Road and Track*. The following addendum to the article is based on a letter to that journal in the May 1960 issue:

Since my article in *Bugantics*, 'Winter, 1958' has been frequently misinterpreted and hotly contested in extensive and out-of-context quotations, I assume you will not be too amazed to receive a few comments in further defence of the preservation of Bugatti automobiles; in fact – a cry for mercy for all classic, sports and racing vehicles which, while unable to cope with current competition machinery, are in nearly all respects more superbly constructed as to machine and hand finish, and as well engineered for their day, as cars in current production.

The point of view of those who defend modification of classic cars typifies to me, the post hot-rodder's misguided attitude that it is perfectly acceptable to mutilate a classic vehicle in the name of improved performance – or for personal amusement. Turned loose in a fine arts gallery, this delinquent would, as a small boy, have carved his initials into classic fine arts.

Bugatti cars have attained an apparently merited legendary interest and respect, as attested by their frequent presentation as 'cover' cars and the subject of articles in *Road and Track*, the *Autocar*, *Motor Sport*, and other enthusiast periodicals. Most of these cars have not been written of or photographed to emphasize their deviations from the original nor the improved performance resulting from some owner's showing engineering capabilities superior to le Patron. By hindsight any average engineer may out-design Bugatti today. In the mid-1920s, and even the 1930s, this was not apparently so glibly spoken of, nor accomplished by even such great combines as Mercedes-Benz, Alfa Romeo or Bentley. Bugatti cars won two Le Mans races in the late 1930s and le Patron's machines held many world records as late as 1950. A stock Type 57 Bugatti, unblown, exceeded 132 miles per hour well over ten years before Jaguar cars merchandised a name for themselves by running 10 miles per hour slower at Jabbeke. A 3 litre G.P. Bugatti was running the straightway at Cork in 1938 at 146 mph – a rather handsome speed even today.

I would like to mention the following clarifications:

(a) It is possible to 'obtain 100 per cent original' Bugatti components in many cases from the factory at Molsheim. They even have parts for the Type 13 (1910)! The stock of certain critical parts is exhausted and no longer produced but *exact* replicas can be cast and/or machined. It is particularly hard to see why so many Bugatti owners still insist on lowering the value of their cars by fitting bastard components.

(b) As to excessive chrome plating of classic cars (originally polished natural metal or nickel plate) that is the owner's prerogative, of course. He can also light his cigarettes with shiny new dollar bills or £1 notes, if his desire to attract a certain cheap attention exceeds his good judgment. A great many classic-car owners consider that any one of these vintage machines of any make, in perfect original condition, is outstanding enough not to require further embellishment by sparkling adornments – it is all a matter of taste and point of view.

449

The preservation or restoration of any classic item, in machinery or other arts, is not to be expected as any mass movement. My appeal continues to be to those few who are willing to practise sufficient discipline of their personal ego to retain a very few Bugatti cars as pure examples of just one man's genius – that of Ettore Bugatti!

Author's comments

The reader may make what he will of the proposed rules, but the Author offers the following comments for what they are worth, and from the point of view of an enthusiast doing most of his own work:

1. Quality of workmanship was a tradition at Molsheim; doing the job properly should be the main objective of all restoration. The Molsheim mechanic was trained to work with clean tools and a clear bench and to do the job right.

2. It is more fun having an original car than a bastardized, hotted-up car. Bugattis are (at last) outclassed by modern vehicles and it is not worth trying to squeeze the last ounce of performance from the car at the risk of very expensive noises. But it is hardly worth having a car if you don't drive it.

3. Molsheim stock of parts, although surprisingly good, is rapidly dwindling*. So it is inevitable that substitute parts are used, or even that a T.46 engine is put in a T.50 chassis and so on.

4. Many keen owners could not afford to purchase new Molsheim or original parts, let alone have new ones made or cast – G.P. wheels for example.

5. In the case of electrical equipment, unless you are prepared to go to France and search car breakers' yards, Marchal equipment is unobtainable; original Bugatti instruments, pressure gauges and clocks are rarer than gold today.

6. Modifications to improve road safety are both necessary and desirable whatever Molsheim may have produced, and this unfortunately may involve hydraulic brake conversion, rebuilt

* Correct in 1968, but now virtually non-existent.

wheels, and so on, on some models poorly equipped. It is generally possible to find new equipment of this type in old fashioned patterns, for example, lamps etc., or which alter the basic chassis as little as possible, as in the case of brakes.

7. As to finish: Bugatti cars of the Brescia or earlier types left the factory with the engines painted and comparatively poorly finished. The correct polish standard on T.30 and later cars, as produced at Molsheim, was mottling or fine hand scraping on the *visible* parts of the dash, plain polishing on manifolds and such things as blower drive casings and blowers, an as-cast finish on parts not showing (e.g. lower crankcase, gearbox etc.) and wavy scraper finish as on a lathe bed on camboxes and visible parts of the crankcase. Mottling on camboxes is definitely wrong. G.P. wheels were plain polished. All circular axles on early cars were polished and oiled, on later cars being nickel plated.

8. The Author feels that modern nickel plate, possibly chrome, is permissible on axles and back plates, but not on the radiator cowling, mainly to facilitate keeping the parts clean. He would stove-enamel chassis frames, propellor shafts and rear axle housings and tubes to prevent corrosion, and believes in cadmium plating all steel parts, certainly all small ones including studs and nuts, again to prevent corrosion and to lengthen the restored life of the car – certainly not Molsheim practice.

9. To summarize: a good restoration should be such that the car lasts a very long time – and protection against corrosion is a prime consideration.

Tailpiece 1

And I personally feel that Bugatti, in all respects, deserves to have a car occasionally, as a tribute, completely gone through with chrome, bare polished metal, and made into a complete showpiece, such as X has done. This was certainly done in deference to the car, and not with the thought that it was original, unoriginal or was going to collect trophies for the owner, or that it was a better car than anyone else's. And least of all, I can see nothing garish or so-called Hollywood about it, perhaps a little showy, but doesn't the car deserve it? It's really impossible for the car to be the same as it left the factory, so why not let the owner, as an individual, use as much initiative as he can muster to make a showpiece of his car. A polished, perfect body shows more appreciation to me than the correct shade of colour.

(K, 13 March 1961)

Tailpiece 2

If I were to have a last line or two, I would say that much has been read into my remarks which is not there. At no time did I say a Bugatti should not be used; I categorically stated it should not be abused by overstressing it to compete with more modern and less fatigued machinery. I did not forbid *exact* replica parts. I do decry modified parts.

PUR-SANG needs no defence. Either a thing is a thoroughbred or it is not – and in a mechanical device the degree of impurity is quite simply measurable. I merely propose that this degree be measured. After that I stand by my concluding article in which I stated that the preservation of PUR-SANG in anything is no mass movement. When you can call my attention to a virgin who is a little bit pregnant – with one notable exception – I may possibly agree with you that all your little 'minor mods' are good clean fun for the boys.

(Eri Richardson, 22 May 1961)

347. *Bugatti made his own bench vices, with hardened steel jaws and sometimes a flat anvil as shown—today a prized possession of the keen mechanic.*

348. *He also produced his own oils in his own 2-litre cans, both mineral and castor based. Some cans bore an illustration of a thoroughbred horse.*

LEADING PARTICULARS OF BUGATTI CARS

(For fuller data and engine adjustments see Data Sheets in the Bugatti Register published by the Bugatti Owners' Club of London.)

Type	Category	No. of Cylinders	Bore × Stroke mm	cc	Valves per Cylinder	Supercharger	Clutch	Forward Gears	Typical Axle Ratio	Wheelbase m	Track m	Original Tyres	Years Made	Remarks
13	Touring	4	65 × 100 66 × 100	1,327 1,368	2	No	Wet	4	14/48	2·0	1·15	650 × 65	1910–14	
13	Racing	4	68 × 100 69 × 100	1,453 1,496	4	No	Wet	4	14/45	2·0	1·15	710 × 90	1919–26	Brescia
15	Touring	4	65 × 100	1,327	2	No	Wet	4	14/48	2·4	1·15	700 × 85	1910–13	
17	Touring	4	65 × 100	1,327	2	No	Wet	4	12/50	2·55	1·15	710 × 90	1910–13	
22	Touring	4	65 × 100 66 × 100	1,327 1,368	2	No	Wet	4	14/48	2·4	1·15	700 × 85	1913–14	
22	Touring	4	68 × 100 69 × 100	1,453 1,496	4	No	Wet	4	14/45	2·4	1·15	710 × 90	1919–26	
23	Touring	4	65 × 100 66 × 100	1,327 1,368	2	No	Wet	4	13/45	2·55	1·15	710 × 90	1913–14	Modified Brescia
23	Touring	4	68 × 100 69 × 100	1,453 1,496	4	No	Wet	4	13/45	2·55	1·15	710 × 90	1919–26	Modified Brescia
Garros	Racing	4	100 × 160	5,027	3	No	Wet	4	Chain	2·55	1·25	880 × 120	1912–14	
30	Touring	8	60 × 88	1,991	3	No	Wet	4	12/50	2·85	1·2	765 × 105	1922–26	
35	G.P.	8	60 × 88	1,991	3	No	Wet	4	14/54	2·4	1·2	710 × 90	1924–30	Roller bearings
35A	Sport	8	60 × 88	1,991	3	No	Wet	4	13/54	2·4	1·2	710 × 90	1926–30	Plain bearings
35B	G.P.	8	60 × 100	2,262	3	Yes	Wet	4	14/54	2·4	1·2	28 × 4·95	1927–30	Roller bearings
35C	G.P.	8	60 × 88	1,991	3	Yes	Wet	4	14/54	2·4	1·2	28 × 4·95	1927–30	Roller bearings
35T	G.P.	8	60 × 100	2,262	3	No	Wet	4	14/54	2·4	1·2	28 × 4·95	1927–30	Roller bearings
37	Sport	4	69 × 100	1,496	3	No	Wet	4	14/54	2·4	1·2	27 × 4·40	1926–30	
37A	G.P.	4	69 × 100	1,496	3	Yes	Wet	4	14/54	2·4	1·2	27 × 4·40	1927–30	
38	Touring	8	60 × 88	1,991	3	No	Wet	4	12/56	3·12	1·25	28 × 4·95	1926–7	
38A	Sport	8	60 × 88	1,991	3	Yes	Wet	4	12/56	3·12	1·25	28 × 4·95	1927	

39	G.P.	8	60 × 66	1,493	3	No	Wet	4	13/54	2·4	1·2	28 × 4·95	1926–9	Roller bearings
39A	G.P.	8	60 × 66	1,493	3	Yes	Wet	4	13/54	2·4	1·2	28 × 4·95	1926–9	Roller bearings
40	Touring	4	69 × 100	1,496	3	No	Wet	4	12/56	2·56/2·71	1·2	27 × 4·40	1926–30	
40A	Touring	4	72 × 100	1,627	3	No	Wet	3	12/56	2·71	1·2	27 × 4·40	1930	
41	Touring	8	122 × 130	12,763	3	No	Wet	4	15/54	4·3	1·6	6·75 × 36	1929–33	Royale
43/43A	Gr. Sport	8	60 × 100	2,262	3	Yes	Wet	4	13/54	2·97	1·25	28 × 4·95	1927–31	Roller bearings
44	Touring	8	69 × 100	2,991	3	No	Wet	3	12/50	3·12	1·25	28 × 4·75	1927–30	
45	G.P.	16	60 × 84	3,801	3	Yes	Wet	3	15/42	2·6	1·4	32 × 6	1929–30	Roller bearings
46	Touring	8	81 × 130	5,359	3	No	Wet	4	12/47	3·5	1·4	32 × 6	1929–36	
46S	Touring	8	81 × 130	5,359	3	Yes	Wet	3	12/47	3·5	1·25	28 × 4·75	1931–36	
47	Gr. Sport	16	60 × 66	2,986	3	Yes	Wet	4	13/54	2·75	1·25	28 × 5·25	1929–30	Roller bearings
49	Touring	8	72 × 100	3,257	3	No	Dry	3	12/50	3·12/3·22	1·4	6·50 × 20	1930–34	
50	Sport	8	85 × 107	4,972	2	Yes	Dry	3	14/54	3·1/3·5	1·2	28 × 5	1930–34	
51	G.P.	8	63 × 100	2,262	2	Yes	Wet	4	13/54	2·4	1·2	28 × 5	1931–5	Roller bearings
51A	G.P.	8	63 × 66	1,493	2	Yes	Wet	4	14/54	2·4	1·2	28 × 5	1931–5	Roller bearings
51C	G.P.	8	60 × 88	1,991	2	Yes	Wet	4	13/54	2·4	1·25	28 × 5	1931–5	Roller bearings
53	G.P.	8	86 × 107	4,972	2	Yes	Dry	3	14/42	2·6	1·25	29 × 5	1932	F.W.D.
54	G.P.	8	86 × 107	4,972	2	Yes	Dry	4	13/45	2·75	1·35	28 × 4·75	1931–4	
55	Super Sport	8	60 × 100	2,262	2	No	Dry	4	13/54	2·75	1·25	28 × 4·75	1932–5	Roller bearings
57	Touring	8	72 × 100	3,257	2	Yes	Dry	4	11/46	3·3	1·35	5·50 × 18	1934–40	
57C	Touring	8	72 × 100	3,257	2	No	Dry	4	11/46	3·3	1·35	5·50 × 18F	1937–40	
57S	Touring	8	72 × 100	3,257	2	Yes	Dry	4	11/46	2·98	1·35	6·00 × 18R	1936–8	
57SC	Touring	8	72 × 100	3,257	2	Yes	Dry	4	11/46	2·98	1·35	5·50 × 18F / 6·00 × 18R	1937–8	
57S45	Racing	8	84 × 107	4,743	2	Yes	Dry	4		2·98	1·35	5·50 × 19F / 6·50 × 19R	1936–8	
59	G.P.	8	72 × 100	3,257	2	Yes	Dry	4		2·6	1·25	5·50 × 19	1934–6	Double reduction
64	Touring	8	84 × 100	4,432	2	No	Dry	4		3·3	1·35		1940	
68	Touring	4	48·5 × 50	369	4	Yes							1942	
73A	Sport	4	76 × 82	1,488	3	Yes				2·6	1·26	165 × 400	1947	
73C	G.P.	4	76 × 82	1,488		No				2·4	1·2		1947	
101	Touring	8	72 × 100	3,257	2	Yes	Dry	4	11/46	3·3	1·35	6·00 × 17	1951	
101C	Touring	8	72 × 100	3,257	2	Yes	Dry	4	11/46	3·3	1·35	6·00 × 17	1951	

Type Number List

Index

461

462

463